# THE AI-ENABLED LAW FIRM

LEE DITTMAR
CAROLE STERN SWITZER



AMERICAN BAR ASSOCIATION
Solo, Small Firm and
General Practice Division

**Cover design by Mary Anne Kulchawik/ABA Design**



Printed in the United States of America.

30 29 28 27 26 5 4 3 2 1

978-1-63905-716-0

**Library of Congress Cataloging-in-Publication Data is available upon request.**

Discounts are available for books ordered in bulk. Special consideration is given to state bars, CLE programs, and other bar-related organizations. Inquire at Book Publishing, ABA Publishing, American Bar Association, 321 N. Clark Street, Chicago, Illinois 60654-7598.

www.shopABA.org

# Contents

# About the Authors

**Lee Dittmar** is a forward-thinking leader whose work in artificial intelligence lies at the intersection of governance, data integrity, and business transformation. He is co-founder and president of Infinity Data AI, which is focused on *engineering the intelligent data future* and pioneering solutions to improve the accuracy, scalability, and trustworthiness of AI systems. Lee is also an A360 Fellow and a Limited Partner at Untapped Ventures.

Lee's extensive experience working with law firms, general counsel, and regulators as an expert witness, litigation-management consultant, management auditor, and compliance advisor was inspirational and valuable in his work on *The AI-Enabled Law Firm*. An OCEG Fellow, former global leader at one of the Big Four firms, speaker, and author, Lee helped shape the foundational concepts of GRC and was recognized by the *National Law Journal* as one of the Top 50 "Governance, Risk and Compliance Trailblazers and Pioneers." He was named among the Top 25 Consultants in the world by *Consulting Magazine* and one of the 100 Most Influential People in Finance for three consecutive years by *Treasury & Risk Management Magazine*. What drives Lee is his ability to see around corners—anticipating how emerging technologies will reshape business landscapes. His global perspective, built on experience spanning six continents and organizations from startups to the world's largest enterprises, informs his uncanny talent for distilling complex technological concepts into strategic frameworks that executives and boards can confidently act upon.

Lee has spoken and written extensively about AI governance, AI's risk management implications, and the challenges around enterprise data being AI-ready. Lee believes we stand at a historic inflection point where artificial intelligence will reshape every domain of human endeavor—law, business, governance, education, and every aspect of daily life. To him, AI represents more than technological disruption; it marks a new social contract between intelligence, data, and human judgment. He calls on today's leaders—and here, especially the legal profession—to pioneer this frontier: to build the frameworks of trust, accountability, and fairness that will determine how AI shapes the rule of law itself. His mission is to help leaders harness AI responsibly, transforming not only how organizations operate but also how societies sustain trust in an intelligent age.

**Carole Stern Switzer** brings together two powerful streams of expertise: 20 years as a nationally recognized environmental lawyer followed by two decades as a pioneering force in integrated GRC. As co-founder of the nonprofit thinktank OCEG, she was an integral contributor to creation of the GRC Capability Model framework that transformed how organizations approach governance, risk management, and compliance worldwide. Her groundbreaking work has become the global standard, adopted by professionals, academics, and regulators worldwide. She is the author of *Mastering GRC: A Lawyer's Guide to Success in Governance, Risk and Compliance*, published by the ABA in 2025.

Prior to co-founding OCEG, Carole had a 20-year legal career, during which she was a partner in the Washington, DC, offices of several national and global law firms, where she had a widely recognized environmental law practice. During this time, she was an active member of the ABA, serving on the Council of the (now named) Environment, Energy, and Resources Section, chairing the Solid and Hazardous Waste Committee, and serving a three-year term on the ABA Standing Committee on Environmental Law. She also was recognized in the Martindale-Hubbell Bar Register of Preeminent Women Lawyers.

In 2023, Carole began writing for OCEG on the topic of AI governance and, together with Lee Dittmar, authored *The Essential Guide to AI Governance*, an e-book that has been used by thousands of OCEG members to oversee their organizations' AI use with effective consideration of governance, risk management, and compliance. Her combined background in large law firm practice, GRC, and AI governance lends a solid foundation to the guidance provided by this book.

Whether speaking on global stages, publishing books and appearing in leading business magazines, or developing comprehensive training programs, Switzer consistently demonstrates why her unique blend of legal acumen and GRC innovation makes her an authoritative voice for organizations navigating today's complex risk landscape.

# Prologue: A Day in the Life of a Lawyer in 2035

**Note:** While this imagined scenario may seem far-fetched to some, others will see it as a plausible example of a lawyer's future life using AI. Let it serve as the starting point for thinking about what the future may look like for you.

**6:30 AM** Emily wakes up as her Artificial General Intelligence (AGI) legal assistant, Bailey, delivers a morning briefing. "Good morning. I've detected two smart contract anomalies in the Quantum Dynamics portfolio that self-corrected overnight. Their regulatory compliance system aligned with the new Asian trade parameters without disruption." Emily reviews the autonomous enforcement actions through her neural interface while having breakfast. Unlike lawyers of the past, she doesn't need to draft amendments or advise on compliance—the AGI has already resolved these issues.

**8:00 AM** At her home office, Emily focuses on her primary role as a legal technologist. She reviews an alert from the firm's AI auditing system flagging an ethical boundary case in a client's self-executing contract network. "The dynamic evolution protocol is attempting to optimize beyond established parameters," she notes, and implements a temporary constraint. Ten years ago, this would have involved days of research and multiple attorney reviews; now it's a 30-minute task for a specialized legal technologist.

**9:30 AM** Emily joins a virtual dispute resolution forum where her firm's AGI litigation model is representing a client in a routine commercial dispute. No human attorneys present arguments—instead, Emily monitors the proceedings as a supervisor, ready to intervene only if the AI encounters a novel legal question. The opposing party's AGI legal representative presents counterarguments based on predictive modeling. Emily observes as the AGI judge—handling one of thousands of similar cases simultaneously—renders a preliminary judgment after just 15 minutes of proceedings.

**11:00 AM** A notification alerts Emily that the AGI judge has flagged an unusual aspect of the case requiring human oversight. Emily shifts her attention to this complex issue—a question about the authentication of AI-generated evidence that hasn't been fully addressed in precedent. Drawing on her expertise in digital verification protocols, she provides guidance to the firm's AGI, which incorporates her input into its advocacy strategy. This human–AI collaboration represents the new division of labor in legal practice.

**12:30 PM** During lunch, Emily meets with the CEO of a multinational client to discuss the legal AI arms race affecting their industry. "Your competitors have deployed aggressive loophole-finding systems," she explains. "We need to upgrade your compliance AGI to counter these tactics." Rather than discussing specific contract terms or litigation strategy, Emily focuses on the algorithmic safeguards that protect the client's business interests in an environment where legal battles happen at machine speed.

**2:00 PM** Back at her workstation, Emily dedicates time to her role as an AI auditor. She reviews how the firm's regulatory interpretation algorithms are functioning within the global machine-readable legal framework. She identifies a potential bias in how the system is interpreting a new set of cross-border regulations and works with her technical team to recalibrate the model. This work represents the new core of legal practice—ensuring that automated systems properly understand and apply the law.

**4:00 PM** Emily mentors a mid-career attorney who recently transitioned from traditional litigation to legal technology. "Your experience with human persuasion is valuable," she explains, "but we need to translate that into algorithmic parameters for our advocacy AGI." She demonstrates how the firm's system develops competing legal narratives and tests them against simulated judicial models before deployment in actual cases. This knowledge transfer is crucial as the profession continues its transformation.

**5:30 PM** Before ending her day, Emily reviews analytics from the firm's automated pro bono platform, which provides AI legal assistance to thousands of individuals simultaneously. The system has eliminated many access-to-justice barriers by handling routine legal matters without human intervention. Emily's oversight role ensures these systems remain fair and unbiased—fulfilling the profession's ethical obligations in new ways.

**7:00 PM** At home, Emily receives notification about a landmark ruling in a case involving competing AGI systems. She spends a few minutes authorizing an update to her firm's advocacy models to incorporate this new precedent overnight. As she logs off, she reflects on how her role has evolved from practicing law to guiding the systems that now practice law—a transformation that has reshaped the entire legal profession.

# How to Use This Book

While you could read this book from cover to cover, we've designed it to serve as both a strategic guide and a practical reference for legal organizations implementing AI. Understanding how to navigate its different components will help you get maximum value from its content.

## ORGANIZATION AND FLOW

The book presents a structured progression from examining AI's impact on legal practice through specific implementation guidelines to future considerations. Each chapter also functions as a standalone guide to its topic. Chapters 1–3 provide essential context about AI in legal practice. Chapters 4–8 focus on core implementation elements like knowledge management, ethics, and technology selection. Chapters 9–14 address specific operational aspects such as training, governance, project management, and international issues. Chapters 15–16 look toward future considerations and building sustainable capabilities.

## KEY COMPONENTS

Throughout the book, you'll find several recurring elements designed to support practical implementation:

- **Examples:** Various scenarios demonstrate how organizations might address specific challenges. While hypothetical, these examples reflect actual experiences and lessons learned.
- **Frameworks:** Practical frameworks help you structure your approach to different aspects of AI implementation. These are designed to be adapted to your organization's specific needs.

- **Action items:** Many chapters end with prioritized actions you can take to implement the chapter's guidance. These aren't just checklists; they're structured approaches to addressing each aspect of AI implementation. A more detailed action plan to help you bring AI into your law firm or legal department is available.

## APPENDICES AND ADDITIONAL RESOURCES

We have included three appendices to this book that you may find useful. Appendix A presents ten essential recommendations for law firms preparing for the AI era, and Appendix B does the same for legal departments. Appendix C offers a list of 25 essential questions to use in discussions as you plan your AI strategy and implementation.

## DIFFERENT READING APPROACHES

Depending on your role and your organization's needs, you might approach this book in different ways:

- **For organizations just starting with AI:** Begin with Chapters 1–3 to understand the landscape, then move through the implementation chapters sequentially, using the action items to build your approach step by step.
- **For organizations already using AI:** Focus on specific chapters that address your current challenges. Use the frameworks and action items to assess and improve your existing approaches.
- **For legal technology leaders:** Pay particular attention to Chapters 4–8 on implementation and technical considerations.
- **For managing partners and general counsels:** Focus initially on Chapters 1–3 for strategic context, then Chapters 15–16 for future considerations. Review other chapters as needed to understand specific aspects of implementation.
- **Using with your team:** Many sections of this book will be most valuable when used in a team context. Consider:
    - Using the action items as meeting agendas or project planning tools.
    - Sharing relevant chapters with team members responsible for specific aspects of implementation.
    - Using the frameworks to structure team discussions and decision-making.

## STAYING CURRENT

Given the rapid evolution of AI technology, we've focused on sustainable approaches rather than specific tools. The frameworks and principles presented should remain valuable even as specific technologies change. Consider revisiting Chapters 15–16 periodically to align your organization's approach with emerging developments.

Whatever your current situation, we recommend reading the following section, Establishing the Context, to ensure you have appropriate understanding of influencing factors for the specific guidance that follows. Then, use the table of contents to identify the chapters most relevant to your immediate needs. Remember, successful AI adoption isn't a one-time project but an ongoing journey. Use this book as a continuing reference, returning to relevant sections as your organization's needs evolve and new challenges arise.

Planning for the effective integration and management of AI within a global law firm or corporate legal department represents a significant commitment—one that will undoubtedly consume substantial time, resources, and ongoing attention from leadership. This investment may initially appear as an unwelcome expansion of non-billable overhead, leading some to question its value proposition against traditional legal service delivery models. However, this planning process is not merely advisable but essential in a legal landscape where technological adaptation has become a competitive necessity rather than a discretionary advantage.

The considered implementation of AI governance frameworks, training programs, and ethical guidelines serves multiple critical functions: It mitigates potentially severe regulatory, liability, and reputational risks that could arise from unstructured AI adoption; it creates the foundation for more efficient legal operations that will ultimately enhance client value; and it positions the organization to thrive amid unprecedented technological disruption that is already transforming client expectations, competitor capabilities, and the fundamental economics of legal practice. What may seem like an administrative burden today represents the scaffolding upon which tomorrow's successful legal enterprises will be built.

# Establishing the Context: AI and the Legal Profession in 2025 and Beyond

Picture this scenario: You're a law firm managing partner, general counsel, or legal department director facing increasing pressure to "implement AI" in your organization. Your clients are asking about it. Your competitors are advertising their AI capabilities. Your younger lawyers are experimenting with various AI tools, sometimes without formal approval. Meanwhile, you're trying to separate genuine opportunities from marketing hype while ensuring your organization maintains appropriate professional standards and risk management.

You are struggling to overcome skepticism about the use of generative AI, which is raised each time there is a new judicial decision or article published highlighting the propensity for "hallucinations" by AI, even while realizing that this is more reflective of the need for strong policies and training about such use than it is a reason to avoid the use entirely.[1]

If this situation sounds familiar, you're not alone. According to surveys by Wolters-Kluwer, Thomson Reuters, the American Bar Association, and others, the legal industry is rapidly adopting AI and views it as critical for future success, but significant challenges remain in developing and executing clear implementation strategies. The gap between recognizing AI's importance and knowing how to adopt it effectively creates significant risks for legal organizations.

[1] A key example is found in the Order to Show Cause, Coomer v. Lindell, No. 1:22-cv-01129-NYW-SBP (D. Colo. Apr. 23, 2025), where the court found about 30 false quotes, misrepresentations of principles of law, and citations of cases that don't exist (clearly generated by AI) in a brief filed by the Lindell attorneys.

The future isn't waiting politely in line—it's already barging through the door. Throughout this book we talk about changes coming to the legal business by 2030 like it's some distant sci-fi horizon, but it's barely a presidential term away. Think about 2020—feels like yesterday, right? That's how quickly 2030 will be in our rearview mirror. While partners are still debating whether to green-light basic AI tools, the entire technological landscape is shifting under their feet. By the time the industry's cautious players finally approve that "innovative" pilot program they've been considering since 2023, their competitors will have completely reinvented how legal work happens. The law firms still asking "should we?" while others are deep into "how can we do more?" won't just be playing catch-up—they'll be struggling to recognize the game that's now being played. This isn't about gradual change anymore; it's about keeping your footing during an avalanche.

This book aims to help you make that journey with few missteps. Rather than focusing solely on AI technology, we'll examine the broader challenge of building AI-enabled legal organizations that enhance rather than compromise professional standards. We'll explore not just what AI tools can do but also how to implement them effectively while maintaining appropriate oversight and risk management.

Before we get tactical, though, let's first step back and think about the bigger picture and these important questions:

- How is AI changing the legal profession?
- How might it change the overall legal landscape and ecosystem?
- What might be coming that we haven't even conceived of yet?

## WHAT'S COMING NEXT

In February 2025, as we began work on this book, we posed these questions to a large language model (LLM). Our prompt recognized that many experts have predicted AGI could surpass human cognitive abilities, becoming a reality in three to five years. This is far beyond what generative AI can do today.

We directed the LLM to provide outcomes we could see within five years, that is, by 2030. The response suggested that AI could fundamentally disrupt how we design and manage legal agreements, dispute resolution, and litigation within the next five years. The proposed outcomes could go well beyond incremental improvements in legal operations and envision a restructured legal ecosystem subject to constitutional and legal process requirements being addressed.

Note: We aren't suggesting that an LLM's predictions of AI's impact are certain, but rather that potential scenarios like these are worth considering as you think about your own AI-enabled future.

Here's what the LLM predicted:

## Outcome 1: Smart Contracts and AI-Driven Enforcement Replace Traditional Legal Agreements

- **Contracts become self-enforcing:** AGI-enabled smart contracts, built on blockchain or similar immutable ledgers, eliminate the need for traditional enforcement mechanisms. These contracts autonomously verify performance conditions, execute obligations, and release payments without human intervention.
- **Automated real-time compliance:** AGI monitors business transactions, regulatory filings, and contractual obligations in real time. It flags risks and takes corrective action before disputes arise, potentially making breach-of-contract litigation obsolete.
- **Dynamic contract evolution:** Contracts are no longer static. They evolve dynamically based on real-time data, industry standards, and updated regulations, reducing the need for legal renegotiations and amendments.

### Implications for the Legal Profession

- **Transactional lawyers shift roles:** Instead of drafting and negotiating contracts, they oversee AI-driven contract frameworks and compliance automation.
- **In-house legal teams become risk mitigators:** Legal teams act as AI auditors rather than dispute handlers.
- **Judicial intervention in contract disputes diminishes:** Courts rarely intervene in business disputes since contract enforcement is automated.

## Outcome 2: AI-Powered Dispute Resolution Makes Traditional Litigation Obsolete

- **AGI courts handle routine disputes:** AI judges, leveraging vast legal datasets, issue real-time rulings on contractual, administrative, and minor criminal cases with near-perfect consistency and fairness.

- **Parties opt for AI mediation:** Corporations, individuals, and even governments use AI-powered mediation instead of traditional litigation, as AGI-based dispute resolution systems provide faster, more transparent, and data-driven outcomes.
- **Virtualized legal processes:** AI-driven arbitration hearings and trials take place in digital environments, with parties interacting via AI-generated legal avatars and case arguments generated through predictive modeling.

## Implications for the Legal Profession

- **Traditional courts handle only high-stakes disputes:** Human judges focus on novel legal issues, constitutional questions, and cases with significant ethical implications.
- **Litigators become legal technologists:** Instead of appearing in court, trial lawyers train and refine AGI-based litigation models to optimize case outcomes.
- **Regulatory bodies act as AI ethicists:** Instead of drafting new regulations reactively, legal experts focus on training and refining AI models to ensure fairness, accountability, and transparency.

## Outcome 3: AGI Redefines the Concept of Legal Representation

- **AI becomes every individual's legal assistant:** Every person has access to an AGI-powered legal agent capable of providing real-time legal advice, document drafting, and advocacy services.
- **AI lawyers replace human attorneys in routine matters:** Low-value legal services (wills, contracts, lease negotiations, employment disputes) become fully automated, reducing the need for entry-level attorneys.
- **Judicial decision-making becomes predictive:** AGI, trained on centuries of case law, predicts outcomes with such high accuracy that most cases are settled without formal litigation.

## Implications for the Legal Profession

- **Massive workforce restructuring:** The need for junior associates and paralegals declines dramatically, forcing law firms to rethink their business models.

- **Public access to justice expands:** High-quality legal services become universally available at near-zero cost, reducing economic barriers to justice.
- **Bar associations redefine ethical obligations:** New ethical standards emerge regarding AI-driven representation, legal liability, and accountability.

## Outcome 4: Governments and Legal Systems Redesign Themselves for AGI

- **Regulation becomes AI-native:** Laws are no longer text-based but encoded in machine-readable formats, allowing AGI to autonomously interpret and enforce them.
- **AI judges and legislators propose laws:** AGI-driven legislative engines draft new policies and regulations based on real-time societal trends, reducing legislative lag.
- **Global harmonization of legal systems:** AGI enables cross-border legal harmonization by standardizing regulatory frameworks, eliminating jurisdictional inconsistencies.

## Implications for the Legal Profession

- **Legal experts focus on AI auditing:** Instead of advising clients, lawyers work as ethical AI auditors ensuring that legal decision-making remains fair and unbiased.
- **National legal distinctions blur:** Legal systems become more interoperable, reducing the relevance of localized laws and increasing global consistency.
- **Government regulators rely on AGI enforcement:** Legal compliance shifts from human interpretation to algorithmic rule enforcement, making traditional compliance departments redundant.

## Outcome 5: The Emergence of a Legal AI "Arms Race"

- **AI-supported advocacy becomes the norm:** Legal battles become contests between competing AGI systems, each crafting persuasive arguments based on real-time data analysis.

- **Deepfake litigation and AI-generated evidence:** AGI-generated evidence (contracts, recordings, forensic data) raises unprecedented questions about authenticity, requiring new verification mechanisms.
- **Cyber-lawfare increases:** AI-driven regulatory compliance systems battle against AI-driven legal loophole exploiters, creating a continuous legal arms race.

### Implications for the Legal Profession

- **Litigation strategy becomes AI-driven:** Lawyers focus on training AI models for legal advocacy, with AI drafting motions and predicting opposing counsel's arguments.
- **New legal specialties emerge:** Experts in AI evidence authentication, digital identity verification, and algorithmic bias litigation become essential.
- **AI creates and defends against legal risks:** Legal teams shift focus from procedural law to managing algorithmic risk and AI-driven legal manipulation.

---

Altogether, these scenarios paint a picture of **big fast change**. Even if only some of them play out, it means more change in the next five years than the legal profession has experienced in the past century or even longer.

## PREPARING FOR CHANGE

The legal profession stands at a precipice, where AI may not just augment but **fundamentally redefine** legal practice, regulatory enforcement, and judicial decision-making. Law firms, in-house legal departments, and government regulators must prepare for:

- **AI-augmented legal strategy:** Moving beyond traditional legal arguments and embracing AI-driven advocacy.
- **New professional roles:** Becoming AI auditors, legal data scientists, and ethical advisors.
- **Regulatory disruption:** Advocating for fair AI governance while ensuring AI systems do not entrench biases.
- **Shift in client expectations:** Delivering legal services through AGI-powered platforms, rather than traditional billable-hour models.

## EMBRACING CONTINUOUS CHANGE

The legal profession must acknowledge a fundamental truth: We are building the airplane while flying it. The pace of AI advancement means that waiting for stability before adopting its use is a recipe for irrelevance. Consider:

- Judicial systems are already adapting to AI-generated filings and research.
- Regulatory frameworks for AI in legal practice are emerging and evolving.
- Client expectations about AI use are shifting rapidly.
- The capabilities of legal AI tools are expanding exponentially.

Law firms that thrive in this environment will be those that develop institutional muscle memory for change itself. This means:

- Building technical systems with flexibility and changeability as core design principles.
- Developing knowledge management approaches that can rapidly incorporate new information.
- Creating governance structures that can quickly evaluate and implement emerging capabilities.
- Fostering professional identities that embrace adaptation rather than resist it.

## THE TIME IS NOW

The legal system's transformation is imminent. Whether law firms and professionals lead this revolution or are disrupted by it depends on how well and how quickly they adapt. The impacts and consequences will not just change how lawyers work—they will redefine what law itself means in an AI-driven society.

So, what should lawyers do now? Consider the complexity of the challenge. You need to:

- Evaluate and select appropriate AI use cases to begin your AI journey.
- Select AI tools from a confusing and ever-expanding marketplace.
- Develop governance frameworks that ensure responsible AI use.
- Create training programs that build necessary skills.
- Establish risk management approaches that address novel challenges.
- Maintain client confidence while evolving service delivery.
- Ensure compliance with evolving regulatory requirements.
- Build organizational cultures that support innovation while maintaining professional standards.

You also need to do all this while maintaining efficient operations and high-quality legal service. This isn't just about implementing technology—it's about transforming how legal work gets done while preserving the core values that define successful legal practice.

A quick note: After reading this book, you may think that you and others on your legal team will be spending all of your time selecting, implementing, training, monitoring, and updating AI systems and will have little time left to actually practice law and serve clients. This concern is understandable but misplaced. In practice, AI integration in law firms follows the same pattern as other technology adoptions—dedicated IT and knowledge management teams handle the technical implementation while individual lawyers simply learn to use new tools that enhance their existing work. Just as lawyers today don't spend their days managing email servers or legal databases, they won't be consumed with AI administration. Modern AI tools are increasingly designed to work seamlessly within familiar workflows, and the most successful implementations actually reduce time spent on routine tasks, allowing lawyers to focus more on substantive legal work and client service.

Each chapter of this book addresses a crucial aspect of the AI transformation, providing practical guidance based on real-world experience and current best practices. Rather than theoretical discussions, we focus on actionable approaches you can implement in your organization. We include specific examples, practical frameworks, and detailed action items to help you move from concept to implementation.

Most importantly, this book recognizes that AI adoption in legal practice isn't just about adding new technologies or improving the efficiency of certain processes. It is not a one-time project but an ongoing journey. The technology continues to evolve rapidly, and organizations need approaches that adapt to changing capabilities and requirements. We focus on building sustainable capabilities that will serve your organization as AI in legal practice continues to evolve.

The future of legal practice belongs to organizations that can effectively leverage AI while maintaining the highest professional standards. This book will help you build such an organization, creating a sustainable competitive advantage while preserving the core values that define successful legal practice.

Let's begin this journey of transformation.

# CHAPTER 1

# The AI Revolution in Legal Services

## INTRODUCTION

*The AI revolution in legal practice isn't something that will happen in the distant or even near future—it's unfolding now, reshaping how legal services are delivered and creating both opportunities and challenges for legal professionals.*

The AI revolution in legal practice isn't coming—it's here. And if you're leading a law firm or legal department, you're facing decisions that will shape your organization's future in profound ways. The question isn't *whether* to engage with AI but *how* to do so responsibly and effectively while maintaining the highest standards of professional service.

The practice of law is undergoing its most significant transformation since the digital revolution first brought computers to law offices decades ago. Artificial intelligence has arrived in legal practice not as a futuristic concept, but as a present reality that is already reshaping how legal work is performed, delivered, and valued. For legal leaders navigating this transformation, understanding AI's capabilities, limitations, and strategic implications isn't merely an academic exercise—it's a professional necessity.

This chapter provides a clear-eyed examination of AI's current and emerging role in legal practice, cutting through the hyperbole to deliver practical insights for law firm and legal department leaders. We'll distinguish between what AI can actually do today versus aspirational claims, explore how leading organizations are implementing these technologies, and examine the competitive implications of adoption versus hesitation.

The stakes are high. Organizations that successfully integrate AI stand to gain significant advantages in efficiency, quality, and competitiveness. Those that fail to adapt risk falling behind more technologically advanced competitors. But thoughtful implementation requires more than just purchasing new software—it demands strategic vision, careful governance, and a nuanced understanding of how these technologies complement rather than replace human legal expertise.

As you read this chapter, you'll gain practical insights on:

- The current capabilities and limitations of AI in legal practice.
- The trajectory of AI development and its implications for legal service delivery.
- Common misconceptions that can derail effective AI implementation.
- How leading legal organizations are using AI to enhance their services today.
- The key technologies driving legal AI innovation, from large language models to expert systems.
- Why AI adoption has become a competitive necessity rather than merely an option.

The AI revolution in legal practice isn't something that will happen in the distant or even near future—it's unfolding now, reshaping how legal services are delivered and creating both opportunities and challenges for legal professionals. This chapter aims to equip you with the knowledge to navigate this transformation successfully.

## DISTINGUISHING HYPE FROM REALITY

The legal industry is flooded with AI hype—headlines proclaiming the rise of robot lawyers and AI judges, along with vendor claims that their tools will transform legal practice overnight. The reality is both more measured in the short term and more profound in the long term.

### What AI Can Do Today

AI is already reshaping legal work by:

- Processing and analyzing vast volumes of documents—reducing review time for contracts, discovery, and regulatory compliance.
- Identifying patterns and anomalies—spotting risks in contracts, inconsistencies in case law, or trends in judicial rulings.

- Automating routine tasks—from document classification to legal research and summarization.
- Enhancing research and decision support—generating insights from large legal datasets.
- Powering predictive analytics—helping forecast case outcomes based on historical rulings.

However, as of this writing, these capabilities have important limitations:

- AI systems require human oversight—they can make mistakes, particularly with novel or ambiguous legal issues.
- Current models lack deep legal reasoning—they identify patterns in text but do not "understand" law as a lawyer does.
- AI does not replace professional judgment—it aids decision-making but does not assume ethical or strategic responsibility.
- AI models can embed biases from their training data, making fairness and transparency critical concerns.

## The AI Trajectory

While today's AI tools are best viewed as enhancements rather than replacements, it would be a mistake to assume that future AI won't take on increasingly complex legal functions. What seems like hype today is becoming reality:

- Legal document automation is evolving toward intelligent contract generation.
- Predictive legal analytics is getting closer to real-time risk assessment.
- AI-driven dispute resolution systems are already being piloted in some jurisdictions.
- Hybrid AI–human workflows will redefine legal service delivery in ways we are just beginning to explore.

Rather than focusing solely on what AI can't do today, legal professionals should prepare for a future where AI capabilities will continuously expand. The real challenge is not whether AI will be useful in legal practice—it already is—but how legal professionals will adapt, govern, and leverage these tools responsibly over time.

AI should not be seen as a replacement for legal expertise but as a force multiplier that enhances legal professionals' abilities. Just as digital research tools reshaped legal practice over the last few decades, AI will progressively alter how legal work is done, who does it, and what skills will be most valuable. The firms and professionals who learn to integrate AI effectively, stay ahead of its advancements, and apply governance wisely will gain a significant advantage in the years ahead.

### The Hidden Foundation: Why So Many AI Initiatives Fail

While the legal profession focuses intensely on AI's capabilities and applications, many organizations overlook the fundamental prerequisite for AI success: data readiness. It's widely documented that most enterprise AI initiatives haven't yet delivered material business value. Many commentors claim that **enterprise AI initiatives fail** not because of algorithmic limitations, but often due to unprepared data infrastructure.

Legal organizations face a particularly acute version of this challenge. Legal knowledge exists in fragmented silos across document management systems, email archives, practice databases, and individual practitioner expertise. This information lacks the semantic relationships, consistent metadata, and contextual frameworks that enable AI systems to generate reliable insights.

Consider a typical scenario: A law firm implements an AI-powered contract analysis system, expecting immediate efficiency gains. Instead, they discover that contracts use inconsistent terminology across practice groups, lack standardized metadata, and exist in dozens of different formats across multiple systems. The AI system, trained on well-structured data, struggles with this reality and produces unreliable results. The firm concludes that "AI isn't ready for legal practice" when the actual problem is that their data isn't ready for AI.

This data readiness gap represents both a significant risk and a competitive opportunity. Organizations that address data preparation proactively will gain sustainable advantages, while those that treat it as an afterthought will struggle with AI implementations regardless of which technologies they select.

## COMMON MISCONCEPTIONS

As AI continues to evolve, misconceptions about its role persist. Addressing these head-on is crucial for legal professionals looking to adopt AI strategically rather than reactively.

### The Robot Lawyer Myth

Despite bold headlines, AI will not completely replace lawyers, but it will change how lawyers work. Just as legal research tools and word processors reshaped document drafting, AI will automate repetitive tasks, enhance analysis, and support decision-making. The legal profession may not be replaced, but it will be redefined by those who learn to integrate AI effectively.

### The Illusion of Perfect Accuracy

AI systems can and do make mistakes, sometimes presenting incorrect information with unwarranted confidence. While their accuracy and proficiency will improve, we are a long way from AI being a substitute for legal expertise, reasoning, and judgment. But improved efficiency, consistency, and risk awareness are being delivered now, all of which improve legal service when used with appropriate quality control and attorney oversight.

### The Myth of Plug-and-Play AI

AI adoption is not as simple as flipping a switch. Success requires careful integration, ongoing training, and change management. Law firms and legal departments must ensure that AI aligns with their specific needs, workflows, and ethical obligations. Any vendor claiming an effortless implementation is overselling their product—responsible AI use demands continuous refinement and governance.

## THE CURRENT STATE OF AI IN LEGAL PRACTICE

Let's start with some statistics from Thomson Reuters, Future of Professionals Report, published in July 2024.[1] This report surveyed 2,200 professionals and C-level corporate executives from over 50 countries.

- By 2024, seventy-seven percent of respondents believed AI would have a high or transformational impact on their work within the next five years. That is an increase of 10 percentage points over the 2023 survey responses.
- Seventy-eight percent of legal professionals surveyed viewed AI as a force for good in their profession.
- Half of law firm respondents cited exploring and implementing AI as their highest priority. They also believe AI could help address other priorities, such as increased customer satisfaction and operational efficiency.

[1] Thomson Reuters, Future of Professionals Report (July 2024), https://www.thomsonreuters.com/content/dam/ewp-m/documents/thomsonreuters/en/pdf/reports/future-of-professionals-report-2024.pdf.

## Reality on the Ground

If you walk through most major law firms or legal departments today, you'll find AI already at work, though you might not recognize it as such. That contract review system your associates use? AI. The enhanced legal research platform your litigators rely on? AI. The system flagging potential conflicts or compliance issues? Also AI.

The adoption pattern typically looks like this: Organizations start with well-defined, repetitive tasks where AI's benefits are clear and risks are manageable. Think document review or basic legal research. As they build confidence and expertise, they expand into more sophisticated applications that augment professional judgment and insight.

But here's what's interesting—and potentially concerning if you're not keeping pace: The gap between organizations that have embraced AI and those still waiting is widening rapidly. Early adopters are seeing compound benefits: Their AI systems are getting smarter, their processes more efficient, and their competitive advantage more pronounced.

## What's Working Now

Let's look at where AI is delivering real value in legal practice today.

*Document review and analysis* have been transformed. Remember the days of armies of junior associates reviewing documents late into the night? While human review hasn't disappeared, and probably won't, AI systems now handle the first pass of document collections for discovery, due diligence, and contract review. These aren't just glorified search engines—they understand context, identify patterns, and learn from corrections. AI can cut document review time by as much as 70%, enabling lawyers to spend more time on strategic analysis and planning.[2]

*Legal research* has evolved from simple keyword searches to sophisticated analysis of legal authority. Modern AI platforms understand legal concepts and can find relevant precedents even when they use different languages. They're also getting remarkably good at predicting how specific judges might rule on

---

[2] *From Weeks to Days: How AI Halved Our Document Review Time*, ICG (Nov. 13, 2024), https://icg.co/ai-document-review-time-savings.

particular issues. Think of them as combining the institutional knowledge of a senior partner with the comprehensive recall of a database.

*Contract management* now spans the entire life cycle from drafting through ongoing obligation tracking. AI tools can flag nonstandard terms, identify potential risks, and monitor compliance across thousands of contracts simultaneously. By implementing AI contract analysis tools, contract review time can be cut substantially while catching more potential issues.

*Predictive analytics* is perhaps the most transformative development. By analyzing historical case data, these tools can predict likely outcomes, estimate timelines and costs, and inform litigation strategy. While they don't replace professional judgment, they provide data-driven insights that were simply impossible to see before.

## KEY AI TECHNOLOGIES IN LEGAL WORK

You don't need to become a computer scientist to lead your organization's AI initiatives, but you do need to understand the key technologies driving this revolution. Think of this as similar to understanding enough about baking basics to be able to produce a great bread or cake without being a food scientist who understands the underlying chemistry in baking.

Artificial intelligence is transforming the operations of law firms, in-house counsel, courts, and regulatory bodies. Following is a breakdown of key AI technologies and how they are applied in legal contexts.

### The Challenge of Large Language Models

By the time you read this, you've almost certainly interacted with a large language model (LLM). This technology is making headlines for good reason—they're genuinely transformative for legal practice. Think of them as incredibly sophisticated pattern recognition and generation systems that can understand and produce humanlike text with remarkable fluency.

In legal settings, they draft documents, summarize research, analyze contracts, and generate responses to routine legal queries with unprecedented speed and accuracy. Leading firms use LLMs to accelerate the creation of initial drafts for agreements, memos, and briefs, allowing attorneys to focus on higher-value analysis and strategy. They're also revolutionizing legal research by synthesizing information across thousands of cases and statutes, identifying relevant precedents, and summarizing key findings in seconds rather than hours. Client communication has similarly transformed, with LLMs enabling rapid responses to routine inquiries while maintaining consistent quality across practice groups.

Despite these impressive capabilities, LLMs present several significant challenges that legal organizations must address through careful governance and implementation. First, while remarkably powerful, they are not infallible. LLMs generate drafts, summarize research, and extract contract provisions with impressive speed and fluency, but they have also produced errors and fabricated information with unwarranted confidence. Unlike a trained associate, an LLM does not "know" the law and does not exercise judgment as a human. It predicts text based on statistical patterns. This means it can generate inaccurate or nonexistent citations, commonly referred to as hallucinations.

At this stage of AI development, human review is essential for all AI-assisted legal work. That said, the underlying models and quality control mechanisms—such as retrieval-augmented generation (RAG), fine-tuning, and AI validation tools—are continuously improving. Firms should stay informed on these advancements to ensure safe and effective AI integration into legal workflows.

The use of public LLMs also raises significant confidentiality and privilege concerns. When interacting with a public LLM, users may be sharing information with a third party, which could implicate client confidentiality obligations and, in some cases, attorney–client privilege or work product protections. The extent of these risks depends on the provider's data policies, including whether user inputs are stored, logged, or used for model retraining.

To mitigate these concerns, many law firms are adopting private, legal-specific LLMs. In addition to enhanced confidentiality and control, private systems allow firms to refine models using proprietary datasets, such as past work product and frequently used legal sources. However, firms still must ensure compliance with ethical and regulatory considerations, including data minimization, model governance, and safeguards against embedding privileged or confidential client information in ways that could inadvertently expose it.

Generative AI and LLMs are improving at an unprecedented rate. What they can do today far exceeds what was possible a year ago, and next year's capabilities surely will surprise us again. This rapid evolution means that legal organizations must develop flexible governance frameworks that can adapt to emerging capabilities and risks without requiring constant revision. The firms that gain the most advantage from LLMs will almost certainly be those that treat AI governance as an ongoing strategic priority rather than a one-time implementation project.

## Machine – Assisted Document Analysis: Opportunities and Risks

AI is already changing how legal teams handle documents. Machine-assisted document analysis is delivering practical value for legal professionals today. These systems transform document-intensive processes by analyzing thousands of contracts, case files, or regulatory documents in hours or minutes, surfacing key provisions, obligations, and risks that might otherwise take weeks to find.

These tools highlight inconsistencies, missing clauses, and unusual language that might escape human review, providing early risk detection for transactions and litigation. They identify relevant clauses, categorizes documents, and generates structured summaries that support due diligence and compliance activities across practice areas. By minimizing manual review effort, AI tools standardize analysis across cases or transactions, simultaneously improving consistency while lowering costs—a rare combination in legal technology investments.

However, successful adoption depends not just on selecting the right tools but on proper implementation and oversight. Think of these systems as highly capable junior associates: they need clear instructions, good examples, ongoing quality checks, and defined decision boundaries to perform effectively. Because they learn from past documents and patterns, accuracy and defensibility still rest with lawyers and must be easy to verify.

Bias and fairness concerns require particular attention, because systems can reflect or amplify biases present in historical documents or precedents. Without careful design and monitoring, AI tools may perpetuate problematic patterns in legal analysis or document categorization. Explainability presents another challenge—legal professionals must be able to justify AI-assisted findings, especially in regulatory reviews or litigation. Yet many powerful methods can be opaque and resist straightforward explanation.

Integration into existing workflows presents practical hurdles beyond the technology itself. Effective deployment requires workflow adaptation, human oversight, and quality assurance mechanisms to ensure AI recommendations are trustworthy and actionable. Many promising implementations falter not because of technological limitations but because of insufficient attention to process integration and attorney adoption.

Regulatory expectations are also rising as jurisdictions worldwide introduce AI-specific regulations that emphasize transparency, accountability, and risk management for AI-powered legal tools. Legal organizations must track these evolving requirements while implementing appropriate governance structures for their AI applications (for example, keeping an audit trail of what the system reviewed and what the lawyer approved).

Machine-assisted document analysis is not a replacement for human judgment but an augmentation tool. Organizations that invest in clear instructions, sensible oversight, and basic governance will achieve a substantial competitive edge by harnessing AI's speed and efficiency while ensuring defensibility and trust in its results.

## *Natural Language Processing: A Game Changer in Legal Practice*

Natural language processing (NLP) powers AI-driven legal research, contract analysis, and case law interpretation, enabling systems to process and interpret human language at scale. What makes NLP particularly valuable for legal professionals is its ability to identify patterns, relationships, and semantic similarities within complex legal texts.

Modern NLP applications recognize when different phrases convey the same legal meaning, enhancing contract review and statutory interpretation by finding provisions across varied linguistic formulations. These systems flag contradictory clauses within contracts, pinpoint ambiguous language, and detect missing obligations, providing an automated first-line quality review for transaction documents.

NLP excels at extracting structured data from unstructured legal documents by parsing court rulings, contracts, and compliance documents to pull key provisions for analysis. When trained on multi-jurisdictional datasets, these models help firms navigate differences in legal terminology across borders, though human validation remains critical.

In litigation settings, NLP identifies key statements, sentiment shifts, and patterns in witness testimony, improving strategic preparation. Advanced models even support cross-linguistic legal research by aligning legal concepts across languages, reducing reliance on manual translations while still requiring expert oversight for jurisdictional nuances.

While NLP has transformed legal workflows, it does not "understand" law in the same way a lawyer does—it detects patterns and makes statistical inferences. This fundamental limitation creates several challenges that legal professionals must address through proper governance and quality control. Context sensitivity presents a primary concern, as legal meaning often depends on precedent, statutory interpretation, and intent—factors that NLP alone cannot fully assess. Contractual provisions and testimony must be interpreted within their full context, not merely as isolated text, requiring human oversight to validate NLP-derived insights.

Ambiguity remains an ongoing challenge, as NLP models may misinterpret vague contract language or infer incorrect intent from testimony. Legal language is inherently nuanced, and while NLP excels at identifying patterns, it struggles with the kind of contextual interpretation that attorneys develop through years of practice. This is particularly evident when analyzing complex clauses with multiple qualifications or exceptions—areas where experienced attorneys naturally excel.

Bias and accuracy risks require vigilant monitoring, as NLP models are only as reliable as their training data. They can reflect and potentially amplify biases in legal precedent or statutory interpretations unless specifically designed to identify and mitigate such patterns. Organizations implementing NLP must establish quality control processes to validate outputs and ensure fair application across different contexts.

Explainability has become increasingly important as regulators scrutinize AI use in legal settings. Firms must ensure transparency, auditability, and defensibility of NLP-driven insights, particularly when these inform material legal conclusions or strategic decisions. The growing regulatory focus on AI governance means legal organizations must document how NLP systems inform their work product and decision-making processes.

NLP is a powerful enabler of legal efficiency, but its output must be reviewed, validated, and contextualized by experienced legal professionals. Firms that integrate NLP effectively while maintaining strong human oversight will be well-positioned to harness its benefits without sacrificing accuracy or legal integrity.

## Expert Systems and Decision Automation: Adding Consistency

Expert systems encode legal expertise through rule-based logic and decision trees, applying explicit rules rather than statistical patterns. These are not merely theoretical applications—many are already deployed in legal practice today.

Leading law firms and corporate legal departments use these systems to transform routine but complex workflows into guided processes with consistent outcomes. Several major law firms have implemented automated contract playbooks that encode firm-specific negotiation positions and flag high-risk provisions based on established client risk profiles. In the financial services and healthcare sectors, compliance teams use rules-based applications that continuously scan business activities against codified regulations, automatically escalating potential issues when specific risk thresholds are met.

Client-facing, legal self-service tools have become increasingly common, with large law firms and legal tech companies offering guided solutions for routine matters like employment policies or privacy compliance. Document assembly systems that adapt to jurisdictional variations and transaction-specific parameters are among the most mature applications (e.g., Thomson Reuters Contract Express and HotDocs).

The value of these systems lies in their transparency and governance advantages. Unlike the "black box" nature of many AI technologies, expert systems follow explicit rules that can be audited, validated, and explained to regulators or clients—a critical consideration in regulated legal environments. They also excel at preserving institutional knowledge by encoding the expertise of senior attorneys, creating scalable access to specialized legal reasoning that would otherwise remain tacit.

However, implementing expert systems requires careful consideration of several challenges. The knowledge acquisition process—extracting and formalizing legal expertise—demands significant investment in interviewing subject matter experts and translating their knowledge into structured rules. Once built, these systems require ongoing maintenance as laws, regulations, and organizational policies evolve. Without regular updates, their utility quickly deteriorates, potentially creating compliance risks.

Decision boundaries also present governance challenges. Legal organizations must establish clear accountability for determinations made or recommended by expert systems, with appropriate human oversight and escalation paths for edge cases. The rigidity that makes these systems reliable for routine matters can become a liability when facing novel scenarios, requiring careful scoping of their application domains.

Expert systems deliver the most value when focused on well-defined, rule-driven legal processes with clear decision criteria. While they lack the flexibility of generative AI for handling novel situations, they provide reliability and consistency that complement other AI approaches in a comprehensive legal technology strategy.

## Computer Vision and Document Intelligence: Making Data Searchable

Computer vision technologies address the visual and physical dimensions of legal practice that text-based AI cannot handle. These systems transform how legal professionals interact with documents and evidence by bridging the gap between physical artifacts and digital workflows.

Advanced OCR capabilities convert handwritten notes, legacy documents, and scanned files into searchable data while preserving critical formatting and spatial relationships. In forensic settings, computer vision can detect document tampering and forgeries by analyzing pixel-level inconsistencies, signature anomalies, and printing patterns with precision that exceeds human capabilities. While these tools exist, today their reliability and admissibility in legal proceedings remain debated among experts.

Litigation teams use these technologies to process visual evidence by automatically identifying objects, people, and activities in photographs and videos, tracking movement patterns, and extracting metadata relevant to case strategy. The latest systems can even analyze mixed visual and textual elements in contracts, identifying problematic redlines or discrepancies between diagrams and accompanying text.

Despite their value, computer vision technologies introduce distinct risks in legal settings. Privacy concerns are paramount when processing visual materials, particularly in sensitive cases involving personal injury, medical evidence, or surveillance footage. Legal teams must establish clear protocols for handling such materials and ensure all processing respects applicable privacy regulations. The risk of misinterpretation also requires attention; while these systems excel at pattern recognition, they may misinterpret ambiguous visual elements or miss contextual nuances that would be obvious to human reviewers.

Quality assurance presents another challenge, as errors in document processing or forensic analysis could have significant legal consequences. Organizations must implement validation workflows to verify the accuracy of computer vision outputs, particularly for evidential materials. Integration with existing document management systems is also essential, as fragmented workflows can create chain of custody risks and reduce adoption.

Security considerations extend beyond standard data protection measures, as visual data often contains sensitive information that may not be immediately apparent. Firms must implement appropriate controls for all processed images and videos, with particular attention to metadata that might reveal privileged information.

As legal practice continues to embrace digital transformation, computer vision will become increasingly important, particularly for litigation-focused practices and organizations handling large volumes of physical documentation. Those that address these implementation challenges thoughtfully will gain significant advantages in evidence handling, document processing, and forensic analysis.

## AGENTIC AI: FROM ASSISTANTS TO DOERS

**What it is.**

Agentic AI doesn't just answer questions; it **pursues a goal**. It plans a few steps, uses your firm's systems, checks its own progress, and asks a human when needed. Think of it as a **junior team member for digital chores**—capable, tireless, and fast, but still working under supervision.

**Where it fits now (no science fiction required).**

- **Contracts, end-to-end.** Intake a draft, compare it to the playbook, prepare a redline and issue list, route true exceptions to the right lawyer, and file the final in the document management or contract lifecycle management system—with a tidy summary of what changed and why it matters.
- **Regulatory and policy tracking.** Watch defined sources, flag relevant changes, map them to your clauses or policies, and assemble a short "what changed/so what" brief with links back to the text.
- **Discovery and investigations.** Triage collections, de-duplicate, suggest targeted searches, cluster documents by issue, and produce a daily status note that a lawyer can scan in minutes.
- **Knowledge and precedent.** Pull comparable matters, surface relevant clauses and filings, and build a quick binder for the team—citations included.
- **Legal operations and billing.** Check invoices against outside-counsel guidelines, spot variances, draft polite notes, and queue them for approval—tightening hygiene without adding headcount.

**Why it helps.**

Agents compress the **swivel-chair work** between systems, eliminate dead time in handoffs, and produce consistent checklists and summaries that are easy to verify. That combination—**speed + traceability**—lets teams respond faster without lowering the bar. Over time, repeatable agent-handled tasks open the door to **fixed-fee or hybrid pricing** for review and research, reserving hourly time for judgment and strategy.

**What to watch.**

- **Hype vs. reality.** Not every "agent" is truly capable of finishing multi-step work. Start with a **narrow, valuable use case**, define "done," and measure outcomes.
- **Permissions and privacy.** Agents need access to mail, calendars, DMS/CLM, and billing. Keep them on a tight leash: least-privilege access, action logs, and clear boundaries.
- **Reliability.** Agents still make confident mistakes. Time-box runs, require **human approval** for anything client-facing and insist they **show their work** (quotes or links to the source text they used).
- **Workflow fit.** The tech fails when the process is fuzzy. Spell out where the agent starts, what it hands off, and who **owns the decision**.

**The safe pattern (as we write this book).**

Adopt a "**copilot with chores**" mindset. Let agents handle the steps—collect, compare, compile, route—while attorneys make the calls. Keep the loop simple: **do → show → ask**. When an agent finishes a task, it shows the evidence, proposes next actions, and asks for approval. That's how you gain speed without sacrificing trust.

**Bottom line.**

Agentic AI is the natural next step in machine-assisted law. It doesn't replace lawyers; it **clears the deck** so lawyers can practice at the top of their license. Start small, keep it verifiable, and make the human the hero.

## AUTONOMOUS LEGAL REASONING

The frontier of legal AI research points toward systems that are capable of more sophisticated legal reasoning—technologies that may fundamentally reshape aspects of the profession over the next decade. These emerging capabilities extend beyond current efficiency gains toward limited autonomy in legal analysis and decision support.

Researchers are developing hybrid systems that combine neural networks' pattern recognition with symbolic AI's logical reasoning capabilities, creating approaches better suited for legal tasks that require both factual analysis and application of principles. Experimental platforms explore how multiple specialized AI agents might collaborate on complex matters, with different agents handling research, drafting, and risk assessment functions. These developments could eventually support mediators and arbitrators by suggesting compromise positions based on case law and party preferences, advance "law as code" approaches for regulatory compliance, and enable sophisticated scenario analysis for litigation strategy.

The trajectory toward more autonomous legal systems raises profound governance questions that the profession must address proactively. As AI systems take on increasingly significant roles in legal analysis, standards for algorithmic accountability, transparency, and fairness become essential. Without careful design and oversight, autonomous systems risk embedding and amplifying existing biases in legal practice and case law—potentially at scale and with the veneer of technological objectivity. This creates both ethical and liability concerns that require attention well before widespread deployment.

The boundaries between AI assistance and human decision-making require equally careful consideration. Legal organizations must establish clear domains where AI acts autonomously, where it provides recommendations subject to human approval, and where human judgment remains primary. This is particularly crucial for matters involving ethical considerations, novel legal questions, or significant client impact. The profession's core values of judgment, confidentiality, and loyalty to client interests should guide these boundaries.

While true autonomous legal reasoning remains aspirational, incremental advances are already influencing how forward-thinking legal organizations plan their technology strategies. Legal leaders should monitor these developments not just as technological innovations but also as catalysts for evolving professional practices and responsibilities.

## THE COMPETITIVE NECESSITY OF AI ADOPTION

If you're still debating whether AI adoption is essential for your legal organization, consider this: Your competitors are already using it, your clients increasingly expect it, and the efficiency and strategic advantages are becoming impossible to ignore. The legal profession is at an inflection point—organizations that proactively integrate AI will lead, while those that resist risk obsolescence.

## Market Pressures: Client Expectations Are Shifting

Legal clients—both corporate and individual—are demanding faster, more cost-effective, and data-driven legal services. Increasingly, they expect:

- Expedited turnaround times that AI-assisted workflows enable.
- Cost efficiency in routine legal work, driven by automation.
- Data-driven insights that go beyond traditional legal advice.
- Innovation from their legal service providers, not just legal expertise.

Many corporate clients are already adopting AI internally and will expect their legal partners to keep pace. If they haven't already, they will soon require specific AI capabilities and compliance measures in outside counsel guidelines. Firms that fail to demonstrate AI competency risk losing business to more agile competitors.

## The Efficiency Imperative: Staying Competitive on Quality and Cost

AI's impact on legal efficiency is no longer theoretical; it is measurable and significant. Tasks that once took weeks now take days, those that took days now take hours, and contract reviews that once consumed hours now require only minutes.

- Document review at scale is dramatically accelerated.
- Legal research is faster, more comprehensive, and less prone to oversight.
- Contract analysis and due diligence are more consistent and data driven.

The bottom line? Organizations that fail to integrate AI will struggle to remain competitive on both quality and price. Those that resist AI adoption risk higher costs, slower turnaround times, and declining client satisfaction, making them increasingly unviable in a profession that values precision and efficiency.

## Risk Management: AI as a Necessity, Not a Luxury

Beyond efficiency, AI is becoming indispensable for risk management in modern legal practice.

- **Litigation and e-discovery:** The sheer volume of documents in modern litigation often exceeds what human reviewers alone can handle. AI-assisted e-discovery tools ensure critical information isn't overlooked in massive datasets.

- **Comprehensive legal research:** Given the ever-growing complexity of laws and regulations, AI-driven research ensures nothing critical is missed.
- **Contract risk detection:** AI enhances contract consistency and risk flagging, reducing errors and omissions at scale.

Increasingly, AI isn't just an efficiency tool—it's a risk mitigation necessity. Legal professionals who ignore AI tools may find themselves at a competitive and professional disadvantage.

## Talent Considerations: The Next Generation of Lawyers

For legal organizations looking to attract and retain top talent, AI adoption is no longer optional.

- Young lawyers expect to work with modern technology. Many law schools are integrating AI into legal education, and new graduates will increasingly view AI proficiency as part of professional competence.
- Firms that lag in technology adoption may struggle to attract and retain talent. Lawyers who are forced to work with outdated, inefficient processes may seek opportunities at more forward-thinking organizations.

Technical competence is becoming a core professional expectation. Just as legal professionals are expected to understand precedent and statutory interpretation, they will increasingly be expected to navigate AI-powered legal tools effectively.

## Data as the Competitive Differentiator

As AI capabilities become more widely available, sustainable competitive advantage will increasingly depend on data readiness rather than technology selection. Organizations with well-structured, semantically rich, and consistently maintained data assets will extract significantly more value from any AI system than competitors using the same technology against unprepared data.

This creates what data strategists call "data network effects"; organizations with better data infrastructure see compounding returns from AI investments, while those with poor data preparation experience diminishing returns regardless of their technology spending. Forward-thinking legal organizations are recognizing that data architecture represents a strategic asset that requires the same level of attention and investment as traditional legal expertise.

The implications extend beyond efficiency gains. In an increasingly competitive legal marketplace, the ability to generate unique insights from proprietary data, including client patterns, matter outcomes, regulatory trends, and market intelligence, becomes a sustainable differentiator that competitors cannot easily replicate.

## LOOKING AHEAD: THE FUTURE BELONGS TO THE STRATEGICALLY PREPARED

The legal profession is at an inflection point, where AI adoption is becoming a competitive necessity rather than merely an option. As AI technologies continue advancing exponentially, legal organizations must prepare for both immediate impacts and longer-term transformations.

### Near-Term Evolution and Strategic Imperatives

Over the next few years, we can expect AI to develop increasing sophistication in legal reasoning. While still requiring human oversight, AI will improve its handling of complex legal concepts, analyze case law with greater nuance, and minimize errors in routine tasks such as contract review and compliance analysis. Legal professionals will spend less time correcting AI outputs and more time leveraging these tools for higher-value work.

The early applications in document automation, contract analysis, and legal research represent only the beginning. As technology evolves, AI will expand into regulatory compliance monitoring, real-time risk assessment, dispute resolution, and sophisticated predictive analytics. We'll also see AI seamlessly integrate into everyday legal software, blurring the lines between traditional legal work and AI-powered automation. Future platforms will incorporate AI-driven drafting, knowledge retrieval, and analytics as standard features rather than optional add-ons. Even as these capabilities are expanded and become more sophisticated, the need for strong human oversight will remain, as concerns about professional responsibility and liability are sure to expand.

### The Data Infrastructure Imperative

Successful AI adoption requires more than selecting the right tools—it demands building data infrastructure that can evolve with advancing AI capabilities. Organizations that treat data preparation as a one-time project rather than an ongoing strategic capability will find themselves constantly struggling to leverage new AI technologies as they emerge.

The most successful legal organizations will implement "AI-ready data architectures"—unified information systems that maintain semantic relationships, consistent quality standards, and flexible integration capabilities. This type of infrastructure enables organizations to adopt new AI capabilities rapidly while maintaining data sovereignty and ensuring that their most valuable information assets remain under their direct control.

## Long-Term Transformation and the Human–AI Partnership

Looking further ahead, we can anticipate more fundamental changes as autonomous reasoning capabilities mature. These developments will enable new models for regulatory compliance, dispute resolution, and access to justice. The most successful legal organizations will prepare for these shifts by developing comprehensive AI strategies addressing technology selection, talent development, knowledge management, ethical governance, and client communication.

Despite advances in automation, the most successful implementations will focus not on replacing lawyers but on creating effective human–AI teams that leverage complementary strengths. Technology will increasingly handle routine tasks and initial analysis, while human professionals provide judgment, creativity, ethical reasoning, and emotional intelligence that AI cannot replicate.

As AI continues to transform legal practice, the organizations that thrive will be those that thoughtfully integrate these technologies while maintaining their core professional values of judgment, ethics, and client service. The future of legal practice will be neither fully automated nor unchanged by technology, but rather a carefully balanced collaboration between human expertise and artificial intelligence—one that legal professionals must begin preparing for today.

# CONCLUSION

The AI revolution in legal practice presents both unprecedented opportunities and complex challenges for legal professionals. As we've explored throughout this chapter, AI is not merely transforming how legal tasks are performed—it's reshaping the fundamental economic and competitive dynamics of legal service delivery.

The evidence is compelling: AI-powered technologies are already delivering measurable benefits in document analysis, legal research, contract management, and predictive analytics. Early adopters are gaining significant advantages in efficiency, quality, and risk management. Meanwhile, client expectations continue to evolve, with increasing demands for speed, cost-effectiveness, data-driven insights, and technological sophistication.

For legal leaders, the question is no longer whether to embrace AI but how to do so responsibly, effectively, and strategically. This requires:

1. **Honest assessment** of your organization's current technological capabilities and readiness for AI adoption.
2. **Strategic prioritization** of use cases that deliver meaningful value while managing implementation risks.
3. **Thoughtful governance** that ensures responsible use aligned with professional obligations.
4. **Investment in talent development** to build necessary skills and competencies.
5. **Client engagement** about how AI enhances service delivery and value.

The competitive dynamics are clear; organizations that thoughtfully integrate AI while maintaining their core professional values will thrive, while those that resist adoption risk being outpaced by more technologically advanced competitors. The efficiency and quality advantages of AI adoption are simply too significant to ignore in an increasingly competitive legal marketplace.

Yet amidst this technological transformation, we must remember that the core of legal practice remains distinctly human. The most successful implementations will focus not on replacing legal professionals but on creating effective human-AI partnerships that leverage complementary strengths. AI excels at pattern recognition, data processing, and routine analysis; humans provide judgment, creativity, ethical reasoning, and emotional intelligence that AI cannot replicate, yet.

The future of legal practice will be neither fully automated nor unchanged by technology, but rather a carefully balanced collaboration between human expertise and artificial intelligence. Legal organizations that develop a clear strategic vision for this collaboration—one that embraces technological innovation while preserving the judgment, ethics, and client service that define the profession—will be best positioned to lead in this new era.

## Building the Foundation for AI Success

As legal organizations develop their AI strategies, they must recognize that technology selection represents only one component of successful implementation. The organizations that will lead in the AI-enabled future are those that invest equally in data readiness, governance frameworks, and organizational capabilities that enable sustainable AI adoption.

This means treating data architecture as a strategic priority rather than a technical afterthought. It requires developing comprehensive data governance that ensures quality, consistency, and accessibility while maintaining appropriate security and confidentiality protections. Most importantly, it demands recognizing that in an AI-driven competitive landscape, data preparation and management capabilities represent core competencies that directly impact organizational success.

As we turn to the next chapter, we'll explore specific AI applications across different practice areas, providing concrete guidance on implementation approaches, governance considerations, and practical strategies for maximizing value while managing risks. The AI revolution in legal practice has begun—and forward-thinking legal professionals must be prepared to lead rather than follow as this transformation continues to unfold.

CHAPTER 2

# Using AI Tools in Your Legal Practice

## INTRODUCTION

*The future belongs to organizations that can effectively leverage AI while maintaining their professional obligations and ethical standards.*

Have you heard stories about what it was like when automated legal research first arose? If you attended law school or started your legal practice after 1980, you won't remember the days of doing all your research by using a keyword system and a library of hard-bound books filled with court rulings and daily paper records of legislative and administrative actions. When an automated approach was first introduced, some insisted nothing could replace books and manual research. Today, imagine trying to compete without electronic research tools. We're at a similar inflection point with AI in legal practice—but the stakes are even higher.

As a law firm leader or legal department director, you're facing decisions about AI applications that will fundamentally reshape how your organization delivers legal services. The range of available AI tools is expanding rapidly, from document review to predictive analytics. But here's the challenge: Each application brings its mix of opportunities and risks, particularly in this highly regulated profession where mistakes can have serious consequences.

You need to understand not just what these applications can do but how to implement them in ways that enhance rather than compromise your professional obligations. This chapter explores the major AI application areas transforming legal practice today, including:

- Document review and analysis tools that are reshaping discovery and due diligence.
- Legal research and analytics platforms that enhance case preparation and strategy.
- Contract analysis and management systems that streamline transactional work.
- Litigation analytics and prediction tools that inform case strategy and client counseling.
- AI-powered knowledge management that preserves and leverages institutional expertise.
- Administrative and business operations applications that improve firm management.

For each application area, we'll examine what's working in practice, what risks you need to manage, and how to implement these tools successfully while maintaining the highest standards of legal practice. Throughout this chapter, we'll provide practical examples and implementation guidance to help you navigate this rapidly evolving landscape.

## DOCUMENT REVIEW AND ANALYSIS

If there's one area where AI is already transforming legal practice, it's document review. But let's be clear about what this means for your organization.

### The Reality of AI-Powered Document Review

Think about your last major document review project without the use of AI tools. How many attorney and paralegal hours did it consume? What was the cost to your client? How confident were you in the consistency of the review? AI is dramatically changing these calculations, but not in the way many people think.

Here's what's really happening in leading legal organizations: AI isn't replacing attorneys—it's transforming their role in the review process. Instead of junior lawyers and paralegals spending countless hours on initial document sorting, AI systems do the first pass, allowing lawyers to focus on analysis and strategy. Document review teams can now handle vastly greater volumes of documents while improving accuracy rates.

Here's what many organizations get wrong: They treat AI document review as a simple automation tool rather than a sophisticated system requiring proper governance and oversight. The result? They miss both opportunities and risks.

## Technical Spotlight: Leading Document Review Platforms

Today's market offers several sophisticated AI-powered document review platforms, each with distinct strengths. For example, a system might:

- Combine traditional e-discovery with AI capabilities like active learning and concept clustering.
- Emphasize intuitive AI with continuous learning from reviewer decisions.
- Focus on accessible predictive coding and visualizations for complex document sets.
- Offer pre-built AI models for specific practice areas and document types.

The most effective implementations typically integrate systems that offer these aspects with robust workflow management and quality control processes.

## Practice-Specific Applications

Document review AI is being deployed differently across various practice areas:

- **Litigation:** In litigation contexts, AI review tools excel at identifying responsive documents, flagging privilege issues, and organizing evidence themes. Leading firms are using tiered approaches where AI confidence scores determine human review requirements.
- **Transactional:** For due diligence and M&A work, AI systems can rapidly identify key provisions, potential risks, and inconsistencies across document sets. Some firms now offer fixed-fee due diligence services based on AI-enhanced efficiency.
- **Regulatory/compliance:** When facing regulatory investigations, organizations are using AI to quickly identify potential violations and prepare responses, often reducing response time by 50–70%.

## Making It Work in Your Organization

Success with AI document review requires thinking through critical elements, including:

- **Quality control and professional responsibility:** How do you maintain appropriate attorney oversight when AI is handling the initial review? Smart organizations are developing tiered review protocols where AI confidence scores determine the level of human review required. For instance, documents flagged as potentially privileged always get human eyes, while routine commercial documents might use sampling approaches.

- **Consider this example:** A major corporate legal department implemented AI document review but found their quality control process was creating a bottleneck. Their solution? They developed a risk-based protocol that adjusted review requirements based on document type and potential impact. High-risk documents such as board materials or regulatory filings get 100% attorney review, while routine documents use statistical sampling approaches. This approach reduced review time by 60% while improving accuracy and consistency.
- **Measuring return on investment (ROI) and performance:** Organizations successfully implementing AI document review establish clear metrics to track impact, including:
  - Efficiency metrics: Document review time, attorney hours per gigabyte of data.
  - Quality metrics: Accuracy rates, consistency scores, error identification.
  - Financial metrics: Cost per document, budget predictability, project timelines.

Law firms using AI document review have indicated cost savings of 35% or more, while simultaneously increasing accuracy on complex matters—a compelling case for both the firm and its clients.

## Protecting Client Confidentiality in AI Document Review

Here's a scenario that keeps many legal leaders awake at night: Your team is using a cloud-based AI document review tool, and a client asks, "Where exactly is our confidential information going?" Do you have a good answer?

The reality is that many third-party AI tools raise significant confidentiality concerns. Your ethical obligations don't change just because you're using AI. The American Bar Association (ABA) specifically addresses lawyer obligations regarding technology use in its Model Rules of Professional Conduct, Rule 1.1 (Competence), Comment 8, emphasizing the need to "keep abreast of changes in the law and its practice, including the benefits and risks associated with relevant technology." Additionally, Model Rule 1.6 (Confidentiality of Information) underscores the lawyer's duty to implement reasonable measures to safeguard client confidentiality when employing technological tools. Organizations leveraging AI must, therefore, actively align their policies and procedures with these explicit ethical standards:

- **Data protection protocols:** Establishing clear rules about what can and cannot be processed through third-party AI tools. Some firms create "clean rooms" where sensitive data never leaves their control.
- **Vendor management:** Developing rigorous evaluation processes for AI vendors, focusing on data security, confidentiality protections, and privilege maintenance. It is always prudent to treat AI vendor contracts as seriously as client engagements.
- **Documentation:** Create clear audit trails of how AI tools are used in document review, including what protections were in place. This isn't just good practice; it is necessary for ethical compliance.

### Implementation Pitfalls to Avoid

- **The "black box" problem:** Implementing AI without understanding how it makes decisions.
- **Inadequate training:** Deploying technology without properly training legal teams.
- **Poor integration:** Failing to integrate AI review with existing legal workflows.
- **Overreliance:** Treating AI determinations as definitive without appropriate validation.
- **Inadequate disclosure:** Not properly informing clients about AI use in their matters.

## LEGAL RESEARCH AND ANALYTICS

Remember when legal research meant hours or even days in the library? Today's AI-powered research tools don't just find cases—they help predict how courts might rule. But this power comes with both opportunities and obligations.

### Transforming Research Practices

Let's be honest. Traditional legal research was never perfectly comprehensive. There was always the nagging question: "Did I miss something important?" AI is changing this equation, but not in the way many expect.

Modern AI research platforms can:

- Understand legal concepts even when expressed differently.
- Identify relevant cases that traditional keyword searches might miss.
- Analyze judicial writing patterns overall as well as prior decisions of a particular judge to predict likely outcomes.
- Flag new developments that might affect your analysis.

But here's the catch: These capabilities don't reduce professional obligations for thorough research. Rather, they raise the bar for what's considered reasonable diligence.

## Technical Spotlight: Advanced Legal Research Platforms

Today's market leaders offer increasingly sophisticated capabilities. Here are some examples of what they can do:

- Incorporate advanced natural language processing and predictive analytics.
- Use generative AI to draft research memos and analyze documents.
- Combine AI with global legal content for cross-jurisdictional research.

Most significant is the shift from keyword-based to concept-based search, allowing attorneys to find relevant precedents even when key terminology differs.

## Cost Considerations and Billing Practices

AI research tools are reshaping billing practices:

- **Fixed-fee research:** Some firms now offer fixed-fee research packages based on AI-enhanced efficiency.
- **Value-based billing:** Some are moving from hourly to value-based models for research tasks.
- **Transparency requirements:** Clients increasingly demand clarity on how AI tools factor into research billing.

Firms are finding that AI research tools substantially reduce associate research time, which means they need to restructure their research billing approach to maintain profitability while sharing efficiency benefits with clients.

## Managing Professional Obligations

Consider this scenario: Your associate uses an AI research tool that misses a key contrary authority. The oversight leads to an embarrassing court appearance. Who's responsible? The AI? The associate? You? The answer, of course, is that professional responsibility still rests with the lawyers. You can address this through a combination of:

- **Clear research protocols:** Establishing when and how AI tools should be used, including requirements for traditional research validation.
- **Training programs:** Teaching lawyers not just how to use AI research tools but also their limitations and the need for critical analysis.
- **Quality control:** Implementing review processes that ensure AI-assisted research meets professional standards.

## International and Cross-Jurisdictional Research

AI is proving particularly valuable for cross-border legal work:

- **Language translation:** Advanced systems can identify relevant foreign-language precedents.
- **Jurisdictional comparison:** AI tools can highlight similarities and differences in legal treatment across borders.
- **Regulatory tracking:** Global regulatory changes can be monitored and analyzed in almost real time.

Global firms are implementing AI systems that standardize research approaches across many jurisdictions, ensuring consistent quality while accommodating local legal differences—a capability that was practically impossible with traditional research methods.

## Implementation Pitfalls to Avoid

- **Overreliance syndrome:** Accepting AI research outputs without critical analysis
- **"Set and forget" approach:** Not updating AI tools as laws and regulations evolve
- **Inadequate training:** Assuming lawyers intuitively understand AI research limitations
- **Poor integration:** Failing to connect AI research with knowledge management systems

## CONTRACT ANALYSIS AND MANAGEMENT

If you're not using AI for contract work yet, you're likely falling behind. However, implementing contract AI tools requires careful attention to both efficiency and professional obligations.

### The Reality of AI Contract Tools

Here's what's possible today:

- Automated identification of key terms and obligations
- Risk flagging in complex agreements
- Pattern recognition across contract portfolios
- Obligation tracking and compliance monitoring

But some organizations get this wrong. They treat AI contract tools as simple automation rather than sophisticated systems requiring proper governance.

### Technical Spotlight: Contract AI Capabilities

Today's leading contract AI platforms offer capabilities tailored to different needs. Example capabilities include:

- Due diligence and provision extraction across multiple languages.
- End-to-end contract life cycle with AI at each stage.
- Smart workflows with analytics for contract creation and management.
- AI-powered contract management with risk scoring and analytics.

Most advanced implementations combine pre-trained AI models with custom training for organization-specific provisions and risk factors.

### Industry-Specific Applications

Contract AI is being adapted to specific industry needs:

- **Financial services:** Focus on regulatory compliance terms and risk provisions.
- **Healthcare:** Emphasis on privacy, compliance, and specialized terminology.
- **Technology:** Attention to intellectual property provisions, licensing terms, and service level agreement commitments.
- **Real estate:** Concentration on property-specific provisions and obligations.

## Pre-Execution and Post-Execution Management

The most comprehensive implementations address the entire contract life cycle:

### *Pre-Execution Contract Analysis*

- Automated drafting assistance and template selection
- Clause libraries and playbooks with AI recommendation engines
- Negotiation guidance based on historical outcomes
- Risk scoring and approval routing

### *Post-Execution Contract Management*

- Automatic obligation extraction and tracking
- Compliance monitoring and alerting
- Amendment and renewal management
- Performance analytics and optimization

## Implementation That Works

Consider this example of how one corporate legal department transformed its contract process. They conducted an initial AI review of all contracts using customized risk criteria and then automated routing based on risk level and contract type. Attorney review focused on high-risk provisions and strategic issues while ensuring continuous monitoring of obligations and compliance. The key to their success? They didn't just implement technology—they redesigned their entire contract process around appropriate human oversight and risk management.

## Integration with Existing Systems

Successful implementations connect contract AI with:

- Document management systems
- E-signature platforms
- Financial management/ERP systems
- CRM and business intelligence tools

Integrating contract AI with the ERP system has been seen to eliminate many hours of monthly manual reporting while dramatically improving compliance tracking, creating value far beyond just the legal department.

### Implementation Pitfalls to Avoid

- **Tool-first thinking:** Implementing technology without redesigning processes
- **Insufficient training data:** Not providing enough examples for AI to learn the organization-specific needs
- **Siloed implementation:** Failing to integrate with broader business systems
- **Inadequate change management:** Not preparing users for new workflows and responsibilities

## LITIGATION ANALYTICS AND PREDICTION

Imagine having data-driven insights into how specific judges tend to rule, how long cases typically take, and what arguments are most likely to succeed. That's the promise of litigation analytics—but realizing it requires careful implementation.

### Beyond Basic Analytics

Today's litigation analytics can:

- Predict likely case outcomes based on historical data.
- Analyze judicial tendencies and preferences.
- Track opposing counsel patterns and strategies.
- Estimate timelines and costs with increasing accuracy.

But here's a crucial point: These tools should inform, not replace, professional judgment.

### Technical Spotlight: Litigation Analytics Platforms

Leading platforms offer increasingly sophisticated capabilities. For example:

- Providing detailed judge, party, and counsel analytics with outcome predictions
- Considering judicial analytics and motion outcomes
- Analyzing lawyer and law firm performance metrics across jurisdictions
- Evaluating motion language and argument effectiveness metrics

The most valuable implementations combine these external analytics with internal case data to create proprietary insights.

## Applications Throughout the Litigation Life Cycle

Litigation analytics add value at every stage of litigation:

### *Case Evaluation*

- Outcome prediction
- Risk assessment
- Settlement value estimation
- Budget forecasting

### *Strategic Planning*

- Judge-specific strategy development
- Motion practice optimization
- Opposing counsel analysis
- Argument effectiveness assessment

### *Trial Preparation*

- Witness performance analytics
- Jury selection assistance
- Trial theme testing
- Evidence presentation optimization

### *Settlement and Alternative Dispute Resolution*

- Settlement timing analysis
- Mediator selection optimization
- Settlement value validation
- Negotiation strategy guidance

## Ethical Considerations in Litigation Analytics

The use of predictive analytics raises important ethical questions:

- **Disclosure obligations:** When and how should you disclose analytics use to clients, courts, and opposing counsel?
- **Maintaining independent judgment:** How do you ensure analytics inform rather than dictate professional judgment?
- **Avoiding bias amplification:** How do you guard against analytics reinforcing existing biases in the legal system?

One proven approach is to establish a detailed analytics governance framework that requires:

- Regular validation of prediction models against actual outcomes.
- Explicit documentation of how analytics informed strategy recommendations.
- Mandatory professional judgment override capabilities.
- Clear client disclosure about analytics uses and limitations.

Consider these key questions:

- How do you use predictive analytics without compromising independent judgment?
- When should you disclose AI use to clients?
- How do you ensure predictions don't create unrealistic client expectations?

Leading organizations are addressing these challenges by establishing clear guidelines on how analytics inform strategy, ensuring transparent client communication about AI use, and regularly validating analytical models and predictions.

## Managing Limitations and Client Expectations

Current litigation analytics tools have important limitations:

- Data gaps in certain jurisdictions or practice areas
- Limited ability to account for unique case facts
- Challenges with rapidly evolving areas of law
- Difficulty modeling novel legal theories

Successful organizations are developing clear client communication strategies that:

- Explain both the capabilities and limitations of analytics.
- Set appropriate expectations for prediction accuracy.
- Position analytics as decision support rather than a crystal ball.
- Maintain emphasis on professional judgment and expertise.

## Implementation Pitfalls to Avoid

- **Overreliance on predictions:** Treating analytics as deterministic rather than probabilistic
- **Confirmation bias:** Using analytics selectively to support predetermined positions

- **Inadequate validation:** Failing to validate analytical models against actual outcomes
- **Poor integration:** Not connecting analytics with existing litigation management processes

# KNOWLEDGE MANAGEMENT AND AI

Your organization's collective knowledge is one of its most valuable assets. AI is transforming how this knowledge is captured, organized, and leveraged—but implementation requires careful attention to ethical obligations.

## Beyond Traditional Knowledge Management

Modern AI knowledge management systems can:

- Automatically categorize and tag documents.
- Identify relevant precedents and work product.
- Surface insights from past matters.
- Enable more efficient knowledge sharing.

But they also raise important questions about confidentiality and privilege.

## Technical Spotlight: AI Knowledge Management Approaches

Leading knowledge management implementations use several AI approaches:

- Natural language processing for automatic document classification and tagging
- Machine learning for relevance ranking and recommendation systems
- Entity recognition to identify key parties, concepts, and relationships
- Content generation to create knowledge summaries and practice guides

Most sophisticated systems combine these technologies with robust workflow integration.

## Change Management Challenges

The human aspect of AI knowledge management is often the most challenging:

- **Cultural resistance:** Knowledge sharing often conflicts with traditional "knowledge is power" mindsets.

- **Workflow disruption:** New systems require changes to established work patterns.
- **Quality concerns:** Attorneys may question AI-driven recommendations.
- **Time investment:** Immediate pressures compete with long-term knowledge benefits.

Successful organizations address these challenges through:

- Partner-level champions and accountability.
- Clear demonstration of practical benefits.
- Integration with performance evaluation.
- "Frictionless" capture of work product.

## Measuring Success in AI Knowledge Management

You can track several key metrics to demonstrate value as your use of AI knowledge management systems expands:

### *Efficiency Metrics*

- Research time reduction
- Template usage rates
- Knowledge reuse statistics
- Expertise location time

### *Quality Metrics*

- Work product consistency
- Error reduction rates
- Client satisfaction scores
- Knowledge currency measurements

### *Financial Metrics*

- Knowledge management ROI
- Matter profitability impact
- Client retention effects
- New business attribution

Successful organizations develop clear protocols for what can be included in AI knowledge bases, implement robust anonymization procedures, and maintain appropriate access controls and audit trails. Most importantly, they are ensuring proper attorney oversight of knowledge sharing.

### Implementation Pitfalls to Avoid

- **Technology-only thinking:** Implementing systems without addressing culture
- **Poor content governance:** Not establishing clear protocols for knowledge inclusion
- **Inadequate privacy protection:** Failing to anonymize confidential information properly
- **Lack of integration:** Creating knowledge systems disconnected from daily workflows

## ADMINISTRATIVE AND BUSINESS OPERATIONS

AI isn't just transforming legal work—it's revolutionizing how legal organizations operate. From resource allocation to client relationship management, AI tools are creating new opportunities for efficiency and insight.

### Operational Applications

Operational activities include:

- Predictive staffing and resource allocation.
- Financial forecasting and budget management.
- Client relationship analytics.
- Performance monitoring and optimization.

Even in these generally administrative applications, professional obligations matter. You must maintain confidentiality in operational data and protect client information in analytics. You also must ensure ethical billing practices with transparency and policy implementation that includes appropriate oversight.

### Technical Spotlight: Business Operations AI

Effective operational implementations leverage several AI approaches:

- Predictive analytics for financial forecasting and resource planning
- Natural language processing for client communication analysis and feedback
- Machine learning for performance optimization and pattern detection
- Process automation for routine administrative tasks and workflow

The most valuable implementations integrate these capabilities with existing practice management systems.

## Client Intake and Relationship Management

AI is transforming client-facing operations:

### *Enhanced Client Intake*

- Automated conflict checking with higher accuracy
- Sophisticated client risk assessment
- Efficient onboarding workflow automation
- Matter scoping and budget prediction

### *Relationship Analytics*

- Client communication pattern analysis
- Satisfaction prediction and early warning systems
- Cross-selling opportunity identification
- Client team optimization

Implementing AI-driven client intake has been seen in some instances to reduce onboarding time by as much as 60% while simultaneously improving conflict detection and risk assessment—creating both efficiency and risk management benefits.

## Professional Development and Talent Management

Forward-thinking organizations use AI for talent optimization:

### *Performance Analytics*

- Work product quality assessment
- Efficiency and productivity analysis
- Skill gap identification
- Development recommendation engines

### *Career Path Optimization*

- Success pattern identification
- Mentor matching algorithms
- Specialized skill development tracking
- Retention risk prediction

Many global law firms have implemented AI systems that analyze associate work products, identify skill development needs, and automatically recommend targeted training and mentoring, improving both development outcomes and retention rates.

### Financial Management and Optimization

AI is bringing new sophistication to legal financial management:

#### *Budget Development*

- Matter cost prediction based on historical patterns
- Resource requirement forecasting
- Pricing optimization models
- Profitability simulation tools

#### *Operational Efficiency*

- Automated time capture and analysis
- Billing optimization and compliance
- Collection probability prediction
- Resource utilization optimization

AI financial analytics can increase realization rates while reducing write-offs, translating directly to bottom-line improvement.

### Implementation Pitfalls to Avoid

- **Data silos:** Implementing disconnected systems that can't share insights
- **Poor change management:** Failing to prepare stakeholders for new approaches
- **Inadequate privacy protection:** Not properly securing sensitive operational data
- **Missing the human element:** Overemphasizing metrics without addressing cultural factors

## THE INTEGRATED VIEW: HOW APPLICATIONS INTERSECT

While we've examined each application area separately, the greatest value comes from understanding how they intersect and reinforce each other. Leading organizations develop integrated AI strategies that leverage connections between different applications.

### Key Integration Points

- **Document review and knowledge management:** Review insights become knowledge assets when properly captured and organized.
- **Contract analysis and litigation analytics:** Contract patterns inform litigation risk assessment and strategy.
- **Research tools and practice management:** Research efficiency directly impacts financial performance and client value.
- **Business intelligence and talent development:** Performance analytics guide professional development and staffing strategies.

It is clear that an integrated AI strategy, connecting document review, knowledge management, and financial analytics, will create compound benefits exceeding the sum of individual initiatives.

## CONCLUSION

The AI revolution in legal practice isn't coming—it's here. Success requires thoughtful implementation that balances innovation with professional obligations. If you get this right, you will gain significant competitive advantages while maintaining the highest standards of legal practice.

Key success factors include:

- Clear governance frameworks for AI use.
- Robust training and oversight mechanisms.
- Strong data protection and confidentiality protocols.
- Regular validation and quality control processes.
- Transparent client communication about AI use.

The future belongs to those who can effectively leverage AI while maintaining their professional obligations and ethical standards. The applications discussed in this chapter represent just the beginning of AI's transformation of legal practice. In subsequent chapters, we'll explore how to build the organizational capabilities needed to implement these technologies successfully while maintaining the highest professional standards.

## ACTION ITEMS

1. **Audit Current AI Applications**
   - Inventory existing AI tools across practice areas
   - Assess application-specific effectiveness and risks
   - Evaluate integration with current workflows
2. **Select Priority AI Applications**
   - Identify high-value use cases for document review, research, and contract analysis
   - Evaluate vendor solutions for specific applications
   - Conduct pilot programs for selected tools
3. **Implement Application-Specific Controls**
   - Establish validation protocols for each AI application type
   - Create oversight mechanisms appropriate to application risk
   - Define quality assurance procedures
4. **Integrate AI Applications**
   - Connect AI tools with existing practice management systems
   - Design workflows incorporating AI-assisted processes
   - Establish handoffs between AI and human work
5. **Measure Application Performance**
   - Track efficiency gains and accuracy improvements
   - Monitor user adoption and satisfaction
   - Assess impact on client service delivery
6. **Scale Successful Applications**
   - Expand proven AI applications across practice areas
   - Standardize implementation approaches
   - Share best practices organization-wide

CHAPTER 3

# Practice-Specific AI Applications

## INTRODUCTION

*By focusing on practice-specific applications that address concrete challenges, legal organizations can move beyond general AI experimentation to deliver measurable value through thoughtfully designed and implemented solutions.*

Imagine this scenario: Your organization has just completed a successful implementation of AI-powered contract analysis. The initial results are impressive—faster review times, more consistent analysis, and reduced costs. Then the questions start coming. The litigation team wants to know if they can use the tool for discovery. The M&A group wonders about due diligence applications. The IP team asks about patent analysis. Each practice group sees the potential but needs something different from the technology.

According to the 2025 Report on the State of the U.S. Legal Market, published by the Thomson Reuters Institute and the Georgetown Law Center on Ethics and the Legal Profession, the rapid emergence of generative AI is poised to fundamentally reshape law firm operations and business models, including the need for new pricing models.[1] While law firms have long used AI in various forms, the latest advances in generative AI and large language models could have a profound impact on areas such as lawyer headcount, service delivery, and pricing. Rather than being solely a technical challenge, the adoption of AI requires

[1] THOMSON REUTERS INST., 2025 REPORT ON THE STATE OF THE US LEGAL MARKET (Jan. 7, 2025), https://www.thomsonreuters.com/en-us/posts/legal/state-of-the-us-legal-market-2025/.

law firms to rethink how technology can best support diverse types of legal work and client needs.

Despite ongoing concerns about accuracy and professional responsibility, the 2024 Wolters Kluwer Future Ready Lawyer Survey Report[2] found that generative AI is rapidly being integrated into legal practice: 76% of lawyers in corporate legal departments and 68% of those in law firms reported using generative AI at least once a week. Looking ahead, 73% of legal departments and 58% of law firms expect to increase their investment in AI technology over the next three years. However, while more than half of respondents feel well-prepared to adjust their business practices and workflows in response to AI, significant challenges remain around integration, ethical considerations, and maximizing the technology's potential.

A critical challenge is the need to customize AI tools to effectively serve different practice areas. Experts in the use of generative AI for law practice note the importance of training models to better determine relevant data in case law, statutes, and contracts to ensure precise insights relevant to specific practice areas and support strategy development.

Practice-specific customization is what distinguishes truly transformative AI implementations from basic tool adoption. Generic AI tools might offer marginal improvements, but tailored implementations that address the unique workflows, terminology, and requirements of specific practice areas deliver substantially greater value. This requires more than technical expertise—it demands a deep understanding of practice-specific challenges and opportunities.

Practice group leadership involvement is essential for successful AI implementation. When practice leaders actively engage in AI initiatives, they help ensure alignment with practice-specific priorities and pain points, appropriate customization for specialized workflows, effective change management and attorney adoption, and realistic expectations with appropriate success metrics.

This chapter explores how different practice areas can leverage AI while addressing their unique challenges and requirements. We'll examine specific applications in litigation, transactional work, and regulatory compliance, then briefly describe how AI can assist in several other specialized practices, providing practical guidance for implementing AI in ways that enhance rather than disrupt specialized legal work.

---

[2] Wolters Kluwer, 2024 Future Ready Lawyer Survey Report (2024), https://www.wolterskluwer.com/en/know/future-ready-lawyer-2024.

# LITIGATION PRACTICE

The application of AI in litigation represents perhaps the broadest range of opportunities and challenges in legal practice. From initial case assessment through trial preparation and appeals, AI tools can transform how litigators work—but only if implemented with careful attention to practice-specific needs.

## Early Case Assessment and Strategy

**Illustrative scenario.** A litigation team receives a complex commercial dispute involving allegations of breach of contract and fraud. Traditionally, partners would spend days reviewing similar cases from their experience, consulting with colleagues, and making educated guesses about likely outcomes. With AI tools, they can transform this process.

The team might use AI analytics to scan thousands of similar cases, identifying patterns that human analysis might miss. The system could reveal that cases combining contract and fraud claims have significantly different settlement patterns than pure contract disputes. It might show that specific fact patterns—like the timing of alleged fraudulent statements—correlate strongly with particular outcomes.

Next, they could analyze judicial tendencies. The AI system might reveal that their assigned judge has historically favored early mediation in similar cases and typically rules for defendants on certain types of preliminary motions. This intelligence would help shape early strategy decisions.

Implementing such capabilities requires careful attention to practice-specific factors. Smart organizations develop what we might call "litigation-specific AI frameworks" that address data quality, context analysis, and integration points.

Data quality programs are required to ensure that the historical case data used for analysis is both comprehensive and relevant. This might mean combining public court records with published decisions and internal case data while maintaining appropriate confidentiality. Context analysis teaches AI systems to understand the nuances of different types of litigation. A breach of contract in a construction dispute, for instance, might have very different patterns than one in a software licensing case. Integration points identify where in the litigation workflow AI insights can most effectively support attorney decision-making. This might include creating standardized points in the case assessment process where teams consult AI analytics.

## Discovery and Document Review

While document review represents one of the most mature AI applications in legal practice, litigation-specific implementation requires sophisticated approaches to maintain defensibility while maximizing efficiency.

**Illustrative scenario:** A litigation team faces document review for a complex antitrust matter. The collection includes millions of documents in multiple languages, involving technical industry terminology and complex business relationships. The smart approach would involve several strategic layers of analysis and review.

First, an initial assessment would utilize AI to analyze the document population before beginning the review. This would reveal document clusters that help identify key issues, communication patterns that highlight key players, timeline anomalies that warrant closer investigation, and language and format distributions that inform staffing needs.

Next would come review protocol development that creates sophisticated protocols combining AI capabilities with human expertise. This involves training AI systems on industry-specific terminology, developing custom models for identifying potentially privileged documents, creating issue-specific coding protocols that align with case strategy, and implementing quality control processes that satisfy court requirements.

Throughout the review process, real-time analysis would use AI to continuously monitor review progress and identify potential issues. This includes pattern detection to flag inconsistent coding, productivity analysis to optimize reviewer assignments, coverage analysis to ensure thorough review, and cost projection to manage budgets effectively.

## Deposition Preparation and Analysis

AI is increasingly transforming how litigators prepare for and analyze depositions.

**Illustrative scenario:** A complex product liability case involves dozens of fact witnesses and multiple experts. Traditionally, preparing for and analyzing these depositions would consume hundreds of attorney hours. AI tools can significantly enhance this process across all stages of deposition work.

During deposition preparation, AI systems can assist with automated identification of critical documents for each witness and generate witness-specific chronologies and document sets. They can suggest question development based on document analysis and identify potential inconsistencies in prior statements.

This comprehensive preparation allows attorneys to spend more time on strategy and less time on document organization.

When it comes to real-time deposition support, AI tools provide live transcription with key term highlighting, instant document retrieval based on testimony references, inconsistency flagging compared to documents or prior statements, and automated tracking of admission and concession points. These capabilities allow the attorney taking the deposition to focus on questioning strategy rather than document management.

For post-deposition analysis, AI systems can generate automated deposition summarization with key point extraction, compare testimony across multiple witnesses, integrate testimony with document evidence, and identify gaps requiring further discovery. This comprehensive analysis provides a foundation for case strategy development and subsequent deposition planning.

## Settlement Valuation and Negotiation Strategy

AI analytics are transforming settlement practices by providing data-driven insights into case valuation and negotiation approaches.

**Illustrative scenario:** Traditional settlement analysis relied heavily on attorney experience and limited historical data. Today's AI-enabled approaches offer far more sophisticated analysis.

In terms of case valuation enhancement, AI systems can analyze settlement patterns in similar cases, identify key factors driving settlement values, quantify risk factors and probability distributions, and model various scenarios for different litigation outcomes. This data-driven approach provides a more objective foundation for valuation discussions.

For negotiation strategy development, AI tools can optimize offer timing and amounts, analyze opposing counsel settlement patterns from previous cases, predict likely counteroffers and responses, and identify leverage points and risk factors. These insights help attorneys develop more effective negotiation strategies based on data rather than intuition alone.

## Trial Preparation and Strategy

AI can transform trial preparation through sophisticated analysis and prediction.

**Illustrative scenario:** A team preparing for a major jury trial might use AI to enhance several aspects of trial preparation and execution.

For jury selection support, AI systems can identify demographic patterns in similar cases, analyze response patterns to specific questions, predict likely receptiveness to key arguments, and optimize juror profiles based on case specifics. These insights help attorneys make more informed decisions during the jury selection process.

When developing arguments, AI tools can analyze successful argument patterns in similar cases, identify judge-specific preferences for presentation style, evaluate the effectiveness of different evidence ordering strategies, and predict opposing counsel's likely counterarguments. This analysis helps attorneys craft more compelling and effective arguments.

For evidence organization, AI systems can create dynamic trial outlines that adapt to developments in the courtroom, organize exhibits for maximum impact, identify the most effective demonstrative aids, and track witness testimony for consistency. These capabilities streamline the trial presentation process and help attorneys maintain focus on advocacy rather than document management.

### Litigation ROI Analytics

Measuring return on investment (ROI) from AI implementations in litigation practices requires tracking both efficiency and effectiveness metrics. Efficiency metrics include document review time and cost reduction, brief preparation time savings, research time optimization, and resource allocation improvements. These metrics quantify the direct cost and time savings from AI implementation.

Effectiveness metrics focus on outcomes, including improved settlement values, higher success rates in motion practice, better trial win rates, and reduced unfavorable surprise events. These metrics capture the quality improvements from AI implementation.

Client value metrics measure the impact on client relationships, including total cost reduction per matter, improved outcome predictability, faster case resolution, and enhanced client satisfaction scores. These metrics help quantify the business development and client retention benefits of AI implementation.

## TRANSACTIONAL PRACTICE

Transactional practice presents different challenges and opportunities for AI implementation. The focus shifts from adversarial analysis to facilitation and risk management. The complexity of modern transactions, combined with intense time pressure and high stakes, creates unique opportunities for AI to enhance legal service delivery.

## Due Diligence Applications

M&A due diligence is a complex and labor-intensive process, often requiring analysis of thousands of documents across multiple jurisdictions for contractual obligations, regulatory compliance issues, litigation risks, and financial exposures—all under intense deadline pressure. AI transforms this landscape by automatically categorizing and extracting key provisions from vast document repositories, identifying anomalies and inconsistencies across contracts, detecting regulatory compliance gaps in target companies, and performing risk assessment across jurisdictions. Advanced systems can also analyze historical transaction data to better predict post-merger integration challenges and valuation impacts of discovered issues.

By automating these document-intensive tasks, AI not only accelerates the due diligence timeline but enables legal teams to shift their focus from mechanical review to strategic risk analysis and transaction structuring advice—delivering both efficiency gains and enhanced decision-making support throughout the M&A life cycle.

**Illustrative scenario:** An M&A team faces a due diligence project for a global acquisition target with operations in 12 countries. The data room contains over 50,000 contracts in multiple languages, along with corporate records, employment agreements, and regulatory filings. The client expects initial findings within two weeks.

Traditional approaches would require dozens of attorneys working around the clock. But a sophisticated AI implementation could transform this process through a multilayered approach.

Initial data assessment would use AI to analyze document types and languages to inform staffing decisions, identify document families and relationships, conduct preliminary risk scoring based on document characteristics, and generate timeline and resource requirement projections. This initial analysis provides a foundation for efficient review planning.

A systematic review process would then implement automated extraction of key terms and obligations, risk-based prioritization of document review, real-time issue spotting and escalation, and multi-language analysis with consistency checking. These capabilities ensure comprehensive review while focusing attorney attention on high-risk areas.

Quality control integration would implement automated cross-reference checking across documents, anomaly detection in contract terms, consistency verification across document sets, and validation of machine translations. These safeguards ensure accuracy and reliability of the review findings.

## Deal Management and Execution

Modern transactions require sophisticated management of multiple workstreams, numerous parties, and complex documentation. AI can transform how deals are managed and executed.

**Illustrative scenario:** A corporate team is managing a complex carve-out transaction involving multiple business units across jurisdictions, hundreds of transitional service requirements, thousands of contracts requiring assignment or replication, and dozens of regulatory approvals. AI might enhance the process across several dimensions of transaction management.

Transaction planning and coordination would benefit from automated dependency mapping between workstreams, resource allocation optimization across teams, real-time progress tracking and reporting, and early warning systems for potential delays. These capabilities help ensure efficient coordination among multiple workstreams and parties.

Document generation and management would be enhanced through intelligent template selection and customization based on transaction requirements, automated first drafts of transaction documents, consistency checking across document sets, and version control with comprehensive change tracking. These tools reduce drafting time while improving document quality.

Closing management would be streamlined with automated closing checklist generation and maintenance, real-time status tracking of conditions precedent, signature page organization and tracking, and post-closing obligation management. These capabilities ensure smoother closings with fewer errors and omissions.

## Technical Integration in Transactional Practice

Effective transactional AI implementations require thoughtful integration with existing systems to maximize value. Virtual data room (VDR) integration is often a critical starting point, requiring secure API connections to popular VDR platforms, automated document categorization and organization, intelligent access management and tracking, and real-time analytics dashboard integration. These connections ensure seamless information flow between the data room and AI analysis tools.

Document management system connectivity is equally important, involving bidirectional synchronization with DMS platforms, version control and change tracking, automated document categorization and tagging, and template management with governance controls. These connections ensure that AI insights and work product are properly captured and managed within the firm's information systems.

# REGULATORY COUNSELING

Regulatory practice presents a particularly compelling opportunity for AI implementation. The volume, complexity, and constant evolution of regulations across industries create significant challenges that AI is uniquely positioned to address. From financial services to healthcare, energy to telecommunications, organizations face an ever-expanding regulatory landscape that demands sophisticated monitoring and analysis capabilities.

## Regulatory Monitoring and Analysis

**Illustrative scenario:** A financial services institution must track regulatory developments across multiple jurisdictions, agencies, and product lines. Traditional approaches require teams of attorneys constantly monitoring multiple sources and manually assessing relevance and impact. AI-enhanced approaches can transform this process fundamentally.

When it comes to comprehensive monitoring, AI systems can continuously scan thousands of regulatory sources including agency websites, Federal Register publications, legislative developments, and industry publications. They can automatically categorize and tag regulatory developments by topic, jurisdiction, and business line relevance. These systems can also maintain historical tracking of regulatory evolution with version comparison and track informal guidance alongside formal regulations.

For impact assessment, AI tools can analyze new regulations against existing business operations to identify potential compliance gaps, quantify implementation costs and timeframes, generate preliminary compliance checklists, and assess relative risk levels across regulatory changes. This analysis helps organizations prioritize their compliance efforts effectively.

Notification and escalation workflows benefit from AI through automated alerts to relevant stakeholders based on regulatory relevance, prioritized regulatory updates based on business impact, executive dashboard reporting with visualization of regulatory trends, and integration with compliance management systems. These capabilities ensure timely awareness and response to regulatory developments. Beyond scanning sources, AI agents could maintain the watch list, de-duplicate overlapping updates, draft a short "what changed/so what" note with links to source text, and automatically open a ticket in the compliance system. They schedule the briefing, assign an owner, and set follow-ups—so the alert becomes an action plan, not another email.

## Compliance Risk Assessment

AI is transforming how organizations assess and manage regulatory compliance risk across their operations.

**Illustrative scenario:** A healthcare organization with operations across multiple states must ensure compliance with federal regulations, state-specific requirements, and industry standards. Traditional approaches rely on periodic manual audits and institutional knowledge. AI-enhanced approaches offer more comprehensive and continuous risk assessment.

For operational risk mapping, AI systems can analyze business processes against regulatory requirements to identify compliance touchpoints, continuously monitor process changes that might create new compliance obligations, generate comprehensive compliance maps across the organization, and identify control gaps or redundancies. This mapping provides a foundation for targeted risk management efforts.

When it comes to violation pattern detection, AI tools can analyze historical compliance incidents to identify common risk factors, predict potential compliance failures based on leading indicators, monitor communication patterns for potential compliance issues, and detect unusual patterns that might indicate developing problems. These capabilities enable more proactive risk management.

Compliance maturity assessment benefits from AI through benchmarking against industry standards and best practices, quantitative scoring of compliance program elements, identification of improvement opportunities with prioritization, and tracking of maturity evolution over time. These insights help organizations target their compliance investments effectively.

Agents can keep a live map of compliance touchpoints and watch for process changes that create new obligations. When a control gap appears, they pre-fill a remediation task with context and evidence, assign it to the right team, chase attestations, and escalate if deadlines slip—keeping momentum without adding meetings.

## Policy Development and Management

AI is fundamentally transforming organizational policy management by converting what was once a static, reactive process into a dynamic, proactive system aligned with evolving legal requirements. Advanced AI tools continuously monitor regulatory changes across jurisdictions, automatically identifying which organizational policies require updates and generating amendment recommendations that maintain compliance while preserving operational flexibility.

These systems can analyze policies against organizational objectives and industry benchmarks, detect internal inconsistencies across policy documents, and evaluate implementation effectiveness through analysis of employee interactions and compliance data. When new policies are drafted, AI ensures clarity through readability assessment, consistency with existing frameworks, and identification of potential unintended consequences.

Most significantly, AI enables personalized policy delivery—automatically generating role-specific summaries and interactive guidance tailored to individual employees' responsibilities and locations. This comprehensive approach not only reduces compliance risks and administrative burden but transforms policies from mere risk management documents into strategic assets that support informed decision-making throughout the organization.

**Illustrative scenario:** A multinational corporation must maintain policies that comply with regulations across dozens of jurisdictions while ensuring consistent application where possible. Traditional approaches result in policy fragmentation, inconsistencies, and ineffective implementation. AI-enhanced approaches offer more sophisticated policy management.

For policy drafting and review, AI systems can generate initial policy drafts based on regulatory requirements, analyze existing policies against new regulations to identify gaps, ensure consistent terminology and approach across the policy portfolio, and maintain appropriate localization for jurisdictional requirements. These capabilities streamline the policy development process while improving quality.

When it comes to policy implementation, AI tools can generate role-specific guidance and training materials, create automated workflows for policy attestation and exception management, maintain audit trails of policy communication and acknowledgment, and track policy effectiveness through compliance metrics. These capabilities improve policy adoption and effectiveness.

Policy maintenance benefits from AI through automated flagging of policies requiring review based on regulatory changes, version control with comparison capabilities, policy optimization based on implementation data, and streamlined approval workflows for updates. These capabilities ensure policies remain current and effective with minimal manual effort.

## Regulatory Reporting Enhancement

AI is transforming regulatory reporting through automation and enhanced analytics.

**Illustrative scenario:** A financial institution must submit dozens of regulatory reports to multiple agencies on varying schedules with different data requirements. Traditional approaches involve manual data gathering, validation, and formatting, creating significant compliance burden and risk. AI-enhanced approaches offer more efficient and accurate reporting.

For data aggregation and validation, AI systems can automate data collection from multiple systems of record, identify anomalies and inconsistencies before submission, validate calculations against regulatory formulas, and maintain audit trails of data sources and transformations. These capabilities improve reporting accuracy while reducing manual effort.

Report generation and submission benefit from AI through automated formatting according to regulatory requirements, comparative analysis against prior submissions, explanatory note generation for significant variances, and streamlined electronic filing processes. These capabilities reduce the administrative burden of reporting while improving quality.

Trend analysis and forecasting are enhanced through historical pattern identification across reporting periods, early warning indicators for potential compliance issues, simulation of future reporting based on business projections, and scenario analysis for regulatory changes. These insights help organizations anticipate and manage regulatory reporting challenges more effectively.

Agents can run the reporting calendar, pull required data on schedule, validate against the rule set, and assemble the filing package. They draft variance explanations, route for sign-off, e-file where permitted, and store the evidence log alongside the submission—turning month-end into a predictable, auditable routine.

## Regulatory Counseling ROI Analysis

Measuring ROI from AI implementations in regulatory practice includes multiple dimensions of value. Efficiency metrics focus on monitoring time reduction, policy development acceleration, risk assessment streamlining, and reporting automation. These metrics quantify the direct cost and time savings from AI implementation.

Quality metrics include improved regulatory coverage, more consistent policy implementation, more accurate risk identification, and enhanced reporting accuracy. These metrics capture the quality improvements from AI implementation.

Risk reduction metrics measure decreased regulatory violations, reduced audit findings, faster remediation of issues, and improved examination outcomes. These metrics help quantify the risk management benefits of AI implementation.

Strategic metrics include improved product launch timelines, more effective innovation within regulatory constraints, enhanced regulatory relationship management, and competitive advantage through compliance excellence. These metrics capture the strategic business benefits of AI implementation in regulatory practice.

The combination of these metrics provides a comprehensive view of AI's impact on regulatory counseling effectiveness and efficiency, helping organizations justify continued investment in regulatory technology while demonstrating value to stakeholders.

Layer in agent-specific metrics: time-to-awareness, time-to-first-action, % straight-through filings, exception/rework rate, and evidence completeness. These numbers make the business case visible and prove that alerts are becoming outcomes.

## EMERGING AI APPLICATIONS IN OTHER SPECIALIZED PRACTICE AREAS

While we have explored AI applications in a few key practice areas in detail, numerous other specialized practice areas are also experiencing transformative AI implementations. These applications demonstrate how AI can be tailored to address unique practice-specific challenges and requirements.

### Labor and Employment Practice

AI is useful in labor and employment practice by assisting comprehensive compliance monitoring and strategic risk management. Advanced systems track employment law changes across multiple jurisdictions, automatically flag policies requiring updates, and analyze HR data to identify potential compliance issues before they escalate. For litigation risk management, AI analyzes communication patterns and historical cases to predict potential claims, quantify exposure across different claim types, and develop optimal defense strategies—enabling organizations to shift from reactive responses to proactive risk mitigation.

Beyond compliance, AI transforms employee relations management and labor relations activities. Intelligent systems standardize complaint intake, support thorough investigations through communication pattern analysis, and recommend appropriate resolutions based on similar cases. For unionized workforces,

AI enhances collective bargaining by extracting and comparing key provisions across agreements, analyzing grievance patterns to identify systemic issues, and modeling the potential impacts of various proposals. These capabilities not only streamline operations but deliver measurable ROI through reduced compliance violations, decreased claim frequency, improved documentation quality, and enhanced consistency in employment decisions.

## Intellectual Property Practice

AI aids intellectual property practice through enhanced search capabilities and sophisticated content creation tools. For patent work, AI enables semantic search beyond keywords, identifies conceptually similar inventions across languages, and analyzes non-patent literature—dramatically improving prior art search efficiency and comprehensiveness. In trademark practice, AI detects image and conceptual similarities, conducts cross-category risk assessments, and performs global database searches with localized relevance scoring. These technologies help attorneys identify potential conflicts and opportunities with unprecedented precision while significantly reducing research time.

Beyond search functions, AI transforms IP portfolio management and enforcement through intelligent drafting assistance and strategic analysis. Patent drafting benefits from claim language optimization based on historical success patterns, consistent terminology enforcement, and automated drawing generation. For copyright holders, AI streamlines infringement detection through web monitoring, image matching across platforms, and content modification identification. These capabilities deliver measurable ROI through reduced application preparation time, higher success rates, better infringement detection, and enhanced IP asset value—allowing legal teams to focus on strategic advisory work while AI handles routine analysis and documentation tasks.

## Tax Practice

AI revolutionizes tax practice through advanced regulatory monitoring and compliance management. Systems can track multi-jurisdictional tax law changes with automatic relevance assessment, analyze regulatory guidance for implementation implications, and generate jurisdiction-specific compliance calendars. For compliance, AI automates data collection from multiple sources, identifies anomalies requiring attention, and maintains comprehensive audit trails—significantly improving accuracy while reducing administrative burden.

For multinational enterprises, AI transforms international tax planning by enabling dynamic structure optimization and treaty analysis. AI tools can model alternative legal structures with tax implications, evaluate base erosion and profit sharing (BEPS) compliance, quantify effective tax rate impacts across jurisdictions, and assess sustainability against evolving regulatory landscapes. Additionally, AI enables automated interpretation of treaty provisions, identifies planning opportunities within treaty networks, and monitors treaty developments—helping organizations navigate complex international tax challenges with greater precision and foresight.

## International Trade Practice

AI supports international trade practice by automating complex compliance processes while enhancing strategic decision-making across global regulatory frameworks. For trade compliance management, AI systems analyze product specifications against harmonized tariff schedules, screen transactions against restricted party lists with fuzzy matching capabilities, identify dual-use items based on technical specifications, and generate appropriate documentation tailored to jurisdiction-specific requirements. In sanctions compliance, advanced AI tools analyze transaction patterns for risk indicators, map corporate structures to identify ultimate beneficial owners despite complex arrangements, and score entities based on multiple risk factors. These capabilities dramatically improve compliance accuracy while reducing false positives and manual effort.

Beyond compliance, AI transforms how organizations leverage trade agreements and navigate disputes. Intelligent systems analyze bills of materials against agreement-specific rules of origin, model alternative sourcing scenarios with duty impact analysis, and identify process adjustments to achieve preferential status. For trade remedies, AI analyzes pricing data across markets to identify vulnerabilities, evaluates alternative explanations for industry conditions, and assesses precedents across similar disputes. The ROI from these implementations spans multiple dimensions: organizations report efficiency gains through classification time reduction and documentation streamlining; financial impact through duty savings and penalty avoidance; and strategic advantages through improved market access and enhanced reputation with customs authorities.

## Healthcare Law Practice

AI elevates healthcare legal practice by empowering attorneys to navigate the sector's uniquely complex regulatory landscape with unprecedented precision. Advanced systems continuously monitor evolving healthcare regulations—including Centers for Medicare and Medicaid Services (CMS) rules, state licensing requirements, and fraud and abuse laws—automatically identifying compliance gaps and risk exposure. For healthcare transactions, AI analyzes provider contracts for Stark Law and Anti-Kickback Statute compliance, evaluates medical necessity documentation for reimbursement risk, and identifies potential corporate practice of medicine violations across multiple states.

Beyond compliance, AI transforms strategic capabilities through sophisticated analytics and predictive insights. For litigation, AI evaluates historical case outcomes to develop evidence-based strategies and assesses settlement values based on jurisdiction-specific variables. When advising on healthcare business models, AI helps attorneys simulate regulatory implications across structural options, evaluate multi-state telemedicine requirements, and assess fraud and abuse risks for innovative payment arrangements. These applications fundamentally enhance healthcare attorneys' ability to deliver value beyond traditional legal services—positioning them as strategic advisors who leverage data-driven insights to guide organizations through complex regulatory landscapes.

## Environmental Law Practice

Environmental practice combines scientific complexity with evolving regulatory frameworks. AI systems in this area support permit compliance monitoring through automated reporting analysis, environmental impact assessment through predictive modeling, due diligence through comprehensive record analysis, and enforcement action defense through pattern recognition in compliance data. Firms specializing in environmental law report using AI to identify non-obvious relationships between operational activities and environmental impacts, enabling more proactive compliance approaches.

## Banking and Financial Services Practice

The highly regulated banking sector presents unique challenges that specialized AI tools address through AML/KYC (anti-money laundering/know your customer) process automation with enhanced pattern detection, consumer protection compliance monitoring across digital channels, capital adequacy analysis with scenario modeling, and automated regulatory reporting with validation controls. Major financial institutions have deployed AI systems that specifically address the technical requirements of regulations like the Bank Secrecy Act, Dodd-Frank, and Basel III.

## Real Estate and Land Use Practice

Real estate practice benefits from specialized AI applications in title search automation with enhanced defect detection, zoning compliance analysis through document interpretation, environmental risk assessment through data integration, and lease portfolio management with obligation tracking. These tools address the document-intensive nature of real estate practice while incorporating spatial analysis capabilities for land use applications.

### Cybersecurity and Data Privacy Practice

The rapidly evolving landscape of data protection regulations has spurred development of specialized AI applications for General Data Protection Regulation (GDPR) and California Consumer Privacy Act (CCPA) compliance monitoring across enterprise systems, breach risk assessment with vulnerability identification, data governance automation with classification and tracking, and privacy impact analysis for new initiatives. These tools help organizations navigate the complex matrix of global privacy requirements while managing the technical aspects of data protection.

## IMPLEMENTATION CONSIDERATIONS

Implementing AI in specialized practice areas requires careful attention to several factors. Domain-specific expertise integration is essential, requiring collaboration between legal specialists and technologists to ensure AI systems properly reflect practice nuances. This collaboration ensures that the technology addresses genuine practice challenges while incorporating appropriate domain knowledge.

Specialized data requirements must be addressed, often involving unique data types, controlled access requirements, and specialized reference databases. Successful implementations develop appropriate data governance frameworks that balance accessibility with security and privacy requirements.

Regulatory acceptance considerations may apply in certain practice areas, requiring transparency in methodology and human oversight to ensure AI applications meet regulatory expectations. Organizations should engage with regulators early in the implementation process to address potential concerns.

Small market dynamics can create implementation challenges due to the limited availability of specialized solutions and smaller user communities for knowledge sharing. Organizations in these specialized areas may need to consider custom development approaches or adapt more general tools to their specific requirements.

If you deploy AI that can take actions on your behalf (an "agent"), start with a narrow, well-defined task and least-privilege access, and require it to show its sources before anything goes to a client. Keep an audit trail and clear human approval points so alerts become accountable actions rather than invisible automation.

The diversity of specialized AI applications demonstrates the flexibility of these technologies to address unique practice challenges. As technology continues to evolve, we can expect further innovation in specialized applications that transform even the most distinctive practice areas.

## CONCLUSION

As we've explored throughout this chapter, successful AI implementation requires careful attention to practice-specific needs and workflows. Generic approaches yield limited benefits, while tailored implementations that address the unique challenges of different practice areas deliver transformative results.

The evolution of practice-specific AI applications shows several emerging trends:

Integration across practice areas is accelerating as organizations recognize that legal matters often cross traditional practice boundaries. Next-generation systems will likely provide more seamless capabilities across domains while maintaining practice-specific expertise.

Deeper workflow integration is improving user experience by embedding AI capabilities directly into existing processes rather than creating separate tools. This approach increases adoption while enhancing productivity.

Collaborative intelligence models are emerging that optimize the human–AI partnership by focusing machines on pattern recognition, data analysis, and routine tasks while leveraging human judgment for strategic decisions, contextual understanding, and relationship management.

Looking ahead, organizations should approach practice-specific AI implementation with both strategic vision and practical grounding. The most successful implementations will combine ambitious goals with realistic implementation plans, deep practice expertise with technical capabilities, and careful measurement with continuous improvement.

By focusing on practice-specific applications that address concrete challenges, legal organizations can move beyond general AI experimentation to deliver measurable value through thoughtfully designed and implemented solutions. The organizations that master this approach will establish significant competitive advantages in efficiency, quality, and client service.

# CHAPTER 4

# Managing Your Firm's Knowledge with AI

## INTRODUCTION

*Rather than relying on periodic manual updates, AI systems can continuously analyze matter outcomes, identify successful approaches, and automatically suggest updates to best practices.*

Consider this scenario playing out at a large law firm: After 30 years of leading the firm's securities practice, a senior partner announces her retirement. The firm has six months to capture three decades of expertise—including her nuanced understanding of SEC enforcement patterns, relationships with key regulators, and strategies that have consistently delivered superior outcomes for financial institution clients. Meanwhile, that same week, a seven-partner healthcare regulatory practice group unexpectedly departs for a competitor, taking with them not just clients but the collective wisdom developed during a decade of helping clients navigate the Affordable Care Act implementation and subsequent reforms.

These two situations—one predictable and one sudden—illustrate the vulnerability of traditional knowledge management approaches. Virtually every law firm can report significant knowledge loss from partner retirements or team departures. Despite investing in document management systems and maintaining practice guides, organizations struggle to capture and preserve the deep expertise that makes their practices valuable.

Traditional approaches to knowledge management, focused primarily on document storage and retrieval, simply cannot meet the demands of modern legal practice. AI offers an effective and efficient way to transform knowledge management from passive document storage to active knowledge capture and deployment. But realizing this potential requires rethinking how organizations approach knowledge management at a fundamental level.

### The Data Foundation Challenge

Before exploring AI's transformative potential for legal knowledge management, law firms must confront a fundamental reality: Most legal organizations possess vast amounts of data but lack AI-ready information architecture. Legal knowledge exists in fragmented silos—document management systems, email archives, practice databases, client files, and individual practitioner expertise—without the semantic relationships and contextual frameworks that enable AI systems to generate meaningful insights.

This fragmentation creates what data scientists call the "semantic gap," that is, the disconnect between how legal professionals conceptualize knowledge relationships and how AI systems process information. A retiring partner's decades of securities law expertise encompasses not just documents she created, but the contextual relationships between regulatory changes, market conditions, client needs, and strategic responses. Traditional data storage captures the documents; AI-ready data architecture preserves the relationships and context that make the knowledge valuable.

Most firms have repositories; few have a substrate. A knowledge substrate is a governed semantic layer—an ontology and set of machine-interpretable relationships (matters, parties, issues, authorities, jurisdictions, timelines, outcomes)—that lets AI *reason with* legal knowledge rather than merely *retrieve* documents. In practice, this means linking work product, cited authorities, client constraints, and jurisdictional rules to the facts and issues in each matter, with provenance, temporal context, and policy constraints.

## EVOLUTION OF LEGAL KNOWLEDGE MANAGEMENT

The evolution of knowledge management in legal practice reflects the profession's changing understanding of what constitutes valuable knowledge. Early systems focused almost exclusively on document management—storing and retrieving precedents, memoranda, and research. While valuable, these systems captured only the most visible forms of organizational knowledge.

Traditional knowledge management approaches face several fundamental limitations. They typically capture only formal work products, missing the context and reasoning behind decisions. They rely heavily on manual tagging and categorization, leading to inconsistent organization and difficult retrieval. Perhaps most importantly, they struggle to capture the tacit knowledge—the judgment, experience, and practical insights—that often proves most valuable in legal practice.

AI technology changes this equation fundamentally. Rather than simply storing documents more efficiently, AI systems can actively analyze work patterns, identify relationships between matters, and surface insights that might otherwise remain hidden. They can capture not just what was done, but how and why decisions were made, preserving crucial context for future use.

## AI-Enhanced Precedent Systems

Consider how AI transforms precedent management in practice. In our scenario of the retiring securities partner, a traditional system might preserve her final versions of documents and perhaps some practice notes. An AI-enhanced system could do much more.

By analyzing patterns across her 30 years of work, the system could identify how her approach to particular issues evolved in response to changing market conditions and regulatory requirements. It could recognize relationships between different types of transactions that might not be obvious from document classifications alone. Most importantly, it could capture the context of decisions—why particular approaches were taken in specific situations. As organizations expand their use of AI-supported knowledge management systems, they gain better retention and faster access to relevant expertise, but achieving these benefits requires careful attention to several key factors:

- **Document intelligence:** Modern AI systems can understand documents at a deeper level than traditional keyword-based systems. They can identify subtle patterns in drafting choices, recognize when similar concepts appear in different forms, and understand how different documents relate to one another. This enables much more sophisticated analyses and retrieval of precedents.
- **Context preservation:** Perhaps most valuable is AI's ability to preserve context. When analyzing a partner's work history, the system can identify not only what documents were created but also what factors influenced

key decisions. It might be able to recognize patterns in how different situations were handled and preserve these insights for future use.

- **Market intelligence integration:** AI systems can automatically connect internal precedents with external market information, helping organizations understand how their approaches compare to market standards and evolving practices. This dynamic updating helps keep knowledge current and relevant.

## Illustrative Case Study: A Knowledge Management Transformation

Consider this hypothetical scenario: A global law firm with more than 10,000 lawyers in 80 countries implements an AI-powered knowledge management system that transforms how it preserves and deploys expertise across its global practice. The system reduces the time required to locate relevant precedents by 70% while simultaneously improving the contextual relevance of search results by 80%.

The implementation focuses on three key elements:

First, deep document analysis goes beyond keywords to understand substantive legal concepts and drafting patterns. This enables the system to recognize similar legal approaches even when expressed in different terminology or document structures.

Second, automated tagging and classification that maintained consistent organization without burdening attorneys. The system could analyze new documents and automatically apply appropriate tags and classifications, ensuring consistent organization without requiring manual input.

Third, contextual relationship mapping that preserved connections between related matters and practice areas. This helped maintain the broader context of how different matters and practices relate to each other, preserving crucial institutional knowledge.

Most significantly, the system could identify and flag "high-value knowledge assets"—documents representing novel approaches or significant innovations—and automatically route them for more detailed analysis and preservation. The firm is no longer dependent on individual attorneys remembering to share important innovations because the system identifies valuable approaches automatically and ensures they become part of the collective knowledge.

## Technical Spotlight: AI Technologies Transforming Knowledge Management

Modern knowledge management systems employ several key AI technologies:

- **Natural language processing (NLP)** enables systems to understand legal documents at a conceptual level. Advanced NLP models can identify legal concepts even when expressed in different terminology, enabling much more sophisticated analysis than traditional keyword systems.
- **Machine learning classification** automates document categorization while maintaining consistency. These systems learn from expert-classified examples to recognize patterns and apply appropriate tags, reducing the burden on legal professionals while improving organization.
- **Knowledge graph technology** creates sophisticated maps of relationships between concepts, matters, and documents, which improves relevant document retrieval compared to traditional taxonomies.
- **Generative AI** can synthesize knowledge from multiple sources to create summaries, practice guides, and initial drafts. While requiring appropriate oversight, these capabilities dramatically accelerate knowledge deployment in practice situations.

## Experience Capture and Analysis

The sudden departure of a practice group highlights another crucial aspect of knowledge management: the need to capture and preserve experience-based knowledge. Consider how an AI-enhanced system might help organizations maintain continuity in such situations.

Instead of relying solely on documented procedures and saved work product, AI systems can analyze historical matter patterns to identify successful strategies, common pitfalls, and effective approaches to particular types of problems. They can map relationships between matters, clients, and regulatory developments, preserving crucial context that might otherwise be lost.

Some organizations are developing what we might call "experience mapping" systems that go beyond traditional experience databases. These systems actively analyze work patterns to identify expertise, track successful approaches, and capture decision-making patterns. When a team departs, the organization retains not just its documents but a deeper understanding of its practice approaches and successful strategies.

# IMPLEMENTATION REALITY CHECK

## The Implementation Gap: From Data to Knowledge

Many law firms assume that implementing AI knowledge management is primarily a software selection and deployment challenge. In reality, the most significant barriers are data related. Organizations typically discover that 60–80% of their implementation timeline involves data preparation, cleaning, and restructuring rather than AI system configuration.

- **The hidden data debt:** Most legal organizations carry substantial "data debt"—years of inconsistent data practices, incomplete metadata, and fragmented information architecture. This debt must be addressed before AI systems can generate reliable insights. Organizations that attempt to implement AI knowledge management without first addressing data readiness often experience disappointing results, leading to the common misconception that AI technology is overhyped rather than recognizing the underlying data preparation challenges.
- **Incremental data transformation:** Rather than attempting comprehensive data remediation before implementing AI systems, successful organizations adopt incremental approaches that improve data quality while simultaneously deploying AI capabilities. This might involve starting with well-structured practice areas, implementing automated data quality monitoring, and gradually expanding to more complex knowledge domains as data maturity improves.

## Best Practices Evolution

Traditional best practices documentation often becomes outdated quickly, requiring constant manual updating to maintain relevance. AI transforms this static approach into a dynamic, self-updating system.

Consider how this might work in practice. Rather than relying on periodic manual updates, AI systems can continuously analyze matter outcomes, identify successful approaches, and automatically suggest updates to best practices. For example, when a new regulatory interpretation emerges, the system can automatically identify relevant practice documents and suggest necessary updates.

One law firm implemented such a system for their global tax practice, using AI to track regulatory changes across dozens of jurisdictions and automatically identify affected advice documents and practice guides. Reportedly, this approach reduced update lag time by roughly 90% while significantly improving accuracy and consistency.

The key lies in creating what we might call "living best practices"—frameworks that automatically evolve based on actual practice experience while maintaining appropriate human oversight. This combines the efficiency of automated analysis with the crucial element of professional judgment.

## Institutional Memory Preservation

The departure of experienced practitioners, whether through retirement or team moves, highlights the crucial importance of institutional memory preservation. Organizations need approaches that capture not just documented knowledge, but the deeper insights and understanding that experienced practitioners develop over years of practice.

Consider again our retiring securities partner. Beyond her formal work product lies decades of accumulated wisdom about market practices, regulatory approaches, and client relationships. Traditional knowledge management systems struggle to capture this tacit knowledge. AI-enhanced systems can help preserve these insights by analyzing patterns in her work, identifying successful strategies, and capturing the context of key decisions.

The challenge becomes even more acute with team departures. When an entire practice group departs, organizations lose not just individual expertise but the collective knowledge and synchronized workflows that make teams effective. AI systems can help preserve this collective knowledge by mapping team interactions, identifying successful collaboration patterns, and preserving insights about how different team members' skills complement each other.

Successful organizations are developing what we might call "knowledge continuity frameworks" that combine AI analysis with structured knowledge capture. These frameworks typically build on several key capabilities:

- **Active pattern recognition:** Rather than relying solely on practitioners to document their knowledge, AI systems can supplement knowledge capture by analyzing work patterns and surfacing potential insights. These analyses may identify correlations in how experienced practitioners structure documents, sequence tasks, or respond to particular situations. However, current AI struggles to reliably infer the strategic thinking or domain expertise behind observed patterns. At the time of this writing, combining AI pattern detection with targeted human verification is still good practice to distinguish meaningful approaches from coincidental correlations, thus creating a hybrid knowledge capture system.

- **Decision context preservation:** By analyzing patterns across matters, AI systems can help identify correlations between case factors and approaches taken, though inferring the precise reasoning behind decisions remains challenging. While current AI can recognize when certain approaches are used in specific situations, capturing the nuanced decision-making process of experienced attorneys represents an ongoing technological challenge. Organizations should combine AI pattern recognition with structured knowledge capture methods that explicitly document decision rationales when possible.
- **Relationship mapping:** AI systems can help preserve understanding of complex relationship networks such as which attorneys work effectively together, which approaches work best with particular clients, and how different practice areas complement each other. This insight helps organizations maintain effectiveness even if and when key team members depart.

The legal landscape regarding AI analysis of attorney work products remains in flux. While firms generally own the work product created by their attorneys during employment, the application of intellectual property principles to AI analysis of that work creates novel questions. Former members challenging such use would need to navigate several complex considerations.

First, copyright protection for legal documents is limited to creative elements rather than factual or standard components, with many routine legal documents receiving thin copyright protection at best. Second, while firms likely have contractual rights to use work products developed during employment, employee agreements may not explicitly address AI analysis capabilities that weren't contemplated when those agreements were drafted. Third, the distinction between using documents as training data versus extracting specific advice presents different legal considerations around fair use and derivative works.

To mitigate potential disputes, forward-thinking firms should implement several protective measures: update partnership and employment agreements to explicitly address AI analysis rights, implement technical safeguards preventing extraction of client-specific or individually attributable information, focus analytical systems on identifying generalizable patterns rather than individual approaches, and consider implementing attribution systems that acknowledge contributions while respecting ownership boundaries.

As courts continue to address the intersection of AI and intellectual property, organizations should stay attuned to evolving standards while developing governance frameworks that balance knowledge preservation with appropriate respect for individual contributions.

## ETHICAL CONSIDERATIONS AND GOVERNANCE FOR AI KNOWLEDGE MANAGEMENT

The application of AI to knowledge management raises important ethical considerations that demand structured governance frameworks. Recent guidance from bar associations and legal ethics scholars provides essential guardrails for implementing these systems responsibly.

### Professional Responsibility Framework

AI knowledge management systems must operate within established professional responsibility requirements. The American Bar Association's Formal Opinion 512 (July 2024) on generative AI emphasizes several key principles that apply directly to knowledge management:

- **Competence obligation:** Attorneys must understand both the capabilities and limitations of the AI systems they implement. This includes awareness of potential inaccuracies, bias risks, and appropriate verification processes.
- **Confidentiality requirements:** Knowledge systems must implement robust safeguards to protect client information from unauthorized access or disclosure, including technical security, data minimization, and access controls.
- **Supervision responsibility:** Managing attorneys have obligations to ensure appropriate oversight of AI systems, particularly those that analyze client information. This includes establishing clear policies, training requirements, and review protocols.
- **Independent judgment:** Knowledge systems should support rather than supplant attorney judgment, with appropriate emphasis on professional evaluation of AI-generated insights.

## Structured Privacy Governance

Knowledge management systems require specific privacy governance addressing several key dimensions:

- **Data minimization strategies:** Systems should collect and retain only information necessary for legitimate knowledge management purposes, implementing anonymization processes for client information and sensitive details.
- **Informed consent protocols:** Organizations should establish clear policies regarding when and how client consent is obtained for knowledge extraction, including both general terms of engagement and matter-specific consent for sensitive situations.
- **Access control frameworks:** Knowledge systems should implement sophisticated access controls ensuring information is available only to appropriate personnel with legitimate needs, including role-based access, practice area restrictions, and client-specific limitations.
- **Audit and monitoring systems:** Organizations should maintain comprehensive audit trails documenting how knowledge systems are used, what information they process, and who accesses their outputs.
- **Data security measures:** Technical safeguards should reflect the sensitivity of information processed, with encryption, access monitoring, and breach response protocols proportionate to potential risks.

## Client Communication and Transparency

Organizations implementing AI knowledge management should develop thoughtful approaches to client communication, including:

- Clear explanations in engagement letters regarding knowledge management practices.
- Specific disclosures when client matters may inform broader knowledge initiatives.
- Opt-out provisions for clients with heightened confidentiality concerns.
- Transparent descriptions of anonymization and protection measures.

## Preventing Algorithmic Bias

Knowledge systems may inadvertently prioritize certain types of information or approaches, potentially reinforcing existing biases or overlooking valuable innovations. Legal organizations should implement regular audits to identify and address potential biases in their knowledge systems.

### Attribution and Recognition

AI knowledge systems should maintain appropriate connections between analyses, innovations, and their creators, both to recognize contributions and to enable follow-up questions when needed.

## TIERED KNOWLEDGE FRAMEWORK

The most efficient implementations create tiered knowledge frameworks with different governance requirements based on information sensitivity:

- General legal knowledge receives minimal restrictions.
- Client-specific insights require robust protections.
- Highly sensitive information remains completely segregated from knowledge systems.

By establishing comprehensive ethical and privacy frameworks at the outset, organizations can realize the benefits of AI knowledge management while maintaining the highest standards of professional responsibility and client protection. These frameworks should evolve as bar associations and courts continue developing more specific guidance on AI applications in legal practice.

## INTEGRATION OF PRACTICE GROUPS

Different practice groups have distinct knowledge management needs and challenges. Successful organizations develop approaches that recognize these differences while maintaining consistent overall frameworks.

Litigation groups often need to preserve knowledge about successful strategies, judicial tendencies, and opposing counsel patterns. Some firms have established their own systems to analyze historical data and identify what approaches worked best before specific judges and against particular opposing counsel, helping preserve crucial tactical knowledge even when experienced litigators depart.

Preserving knowledge about market terms, negotiation strategies, and deal structures is crucial for transactional practices. AI can be used to analyze historical transactions and identify term evolution, negotiation patterns, and successful closing strategies across different market conditions and jurisdictions.

Regulatory practices need to maintain a deep understanding of agency approaches, enforcement patterns, and compliance strategies. Regulatory knowledge systems can track enforcement actions across a multitude of federal agencies, automatically identifying pattern shifts and updating compliance guidance.

## MULTIMODAL KNOWLEDGE CAPTURE AND MANAGEMENT

While text-based knowledge has dominated legal knowledge management, the profession increasingly generates and utilizes valuable knowledge in multiple formats. Modern AI is advancing rapidly in its ability to process and analyze diverse information types, creating opportunities for more comprehensive knowledge capture.

### Audiovisual Knowledge Preservation

Consider how audio and video recording can preserve knowledge that might otherwise be lost. For example, a retiring partner's client consultation approach—including verbal cues, questioning techniques, and rapport building—represents valuable tacit knowledge that text alone cannot capture. Implementation approaches include:

- **Meeting and deposition analysis:** AI systems can transcribe, analyze, and extract key insights from recorded client meetings, depositions, and internal discussions. These systems identify not just what was said, but significant patterns in questioning techniques, negotiation approaches, and persuasive strategies.
- **Training and mentoring preservation:** Recording training sessions and mentoring conversations preserves pedagogical approaches that might otherwise be lost. AI analysis can identify effective teaching methods and create indexed, searchable resources that new attorneys can access for just-in-time learning.
- **Oral history initiatives:** Structured interviews with senior practitioners about landmark matters can capture experiential wisdom in rich detail. AI tools can analyze these recordings to extract insights about problem solving approaches, relationship management strategies, and professional development paths.

When implementing audiovisual knowledge capture, organizations must address significant confidentiality, privacy, and ethical considerations. All systems require robust governance frameworks including:

- Clear consent protocols for all recorded participants.
- Sophisticated access controls limiting material to appropriate audiences.
- Data minimization practices ensuring only necessary information is preserved.
- Strong security measures protecting sensitive content.
- Retention policies balancing knowledge preservation with privacy considerations.

## Visual Knowledge Management

Legal practice involves significant visual knowledge that traditional systems often overlook, such as:

- **Document layout analysis:** The visual structure of complex legal documents often embodies sophisticated expertise. AI systems can now analyze document layouts to identify structural patterns, visual hierarchies, and organizational approaches that reflect practice wisdom.
- **Diagrammatic knowledge:** Complex legal concepts are frequently represented visually through charts, diagrams, and visual models. Advanced knowledge systems can extract, categorize, and make searchable the conceptual frameworks embedded in these visual representations.
- **Spatial relationship mapping:** In complex litigation, investigations, and transactions, spatial relationships between entities, events, and documents often represent crucial insights. Visual knowledge systems can preserve these spatial maps and the expertise they represent.

## Multimodal Integration Strategies

The greatest value comes from integrating multiple knowledge formats within unified systems that preserve connections between related content:

- **Cross-modal linking:** Advanced systems maintain relationships between text documents, audio and video recordings, and visual materials, allowing practitioners to access all relevant knowledge regardless of format.

- **Contextual retrieval:** When an attorney searches for information on a particular topic, modern systems can return relevant text, audio clips, video segments, and visual materials, providing comprehensive knowledge access.
- **Format-appropriate analysis:** Different knowledge types require specialized analytical approaches. Sophisticated systems employ specific AI models optimized for each format while maintaining integrated retrieval and presentation.
- **Knowledge translation:** Sometimes the most valuable capability is translating knowledge between formats—creating textual summaries of audio recordings, visual representations of textual concepts, or audio explanations of visual materials.

The most advanced implementations create what we might call "knowledge ecosystems" where insights in one format inform and enrich understanding in others. For example, analysis of successful negotiation recordings might enhance document drafting approaches, while document pattern analysis might inform training program design.

As AI capabilities continue advancing in multimodal processing, you have unprecedented opportunities to capture and deploy knowledge in its most natural and complete forms. Those that successfully implement these comprehensive approaches gain significant advantages in knowledge preservation, professional development, and client service.

## KNOWLEDGE BEYOND ORGANIZATIONAL BOUNDARIES

The future of legal knowledge management extends beyond organizational boundaries. While traditionally law firms have jealously guarded their institutional knowledge, emerging AI technologies are creating new possibilities for selective knowledge sharing with appropriate protections. Consider these evolving models:

- **Client collaboration platforms:** Advanced firms are developing secure knowledge-sharing environments where client-specific expertise can be jointly developed and preserved. These systems can use sophisticated permissioning and confidentiality protections to maintain appropriate boundaries while allowing collaborative knowledge development. For example, a financial services regulatory practice might establish a secure platform where regulatory interpretation knowledge is collaboratively built with key banking clients, with each participant maintaining control over their contributed insights while benefiting from the collective expertise.

- **Industry knowledge networks:** In specialized practice areas, some competing firms are exploring limited knowledge-sharing arrangements that benefit all participants while preserving competitive advantages. These carefully structured networks typically focus on foundational knowledge rather than strategic approaches. For instance, several firms with life sciences practices might jointly develop and maintain a knowledge base of regulatory requirements across jurisdictions, with appropriate technological and contractual safeguards preventing misuse.
- **Academic-practitioner exchanges:** The traditional divide between legal academia and practice is diminishing through AI-facilitated knowledge exchanges. Forward-thinking firms are establishing structured knowledge partnerships with law schools, where anonymized practice insights inform academic research while theoretical frameworks enhance practical approaches. These partnerships often focus on emerging areas where both practitioners and academics benefit from collaborative knowledge development.
- **Public-private knowledge partnerships:** Government agencies and private firms are exploring new models for knowledge sharing around regulatory compliance and public interest law. These partnerships use sophisticated AI tools to extract generalizable insights while protecting confidential information. For example, a consortium of environmental law practices might develop a shared knowledge base with environmental protection agencies, enhancing regulatory compliance while advancing environmental protection goals.

Each of these cross-boundary knowledge models requires careful governance frameworks addressing confidentiality, intellectual property, competitive concerns, and professional obligations. Organizations exploring these approaches need robust technological safeguards, clear contractual frameworks, and appropriate ethical guidelines. Despite these challenges, the potential benefits in enhanced expertise, efficiency, and client service make cross-boundary knowledge sharing an important frontier in legal knowledge management.

## IMPLEMENTATION CHALLENGES AND SOLUTIONS

Implementing AI-enhanced knowledge management systems requires careful attention to several key challenges:

- **Data quality and standardization:** AI systems require high-quality data to generate valuable insights. Organizations need to develop approaches for ensuring consistent data quality while minimizing the burden on practitioners.
- **Privacy and confidentiality:** Knowledge capture must respect client confidentiality and practitioner privacy. Organizations need sophisticated approaches to anonymizing sensitive information while preserving valuable insights.
- **Integration with existing systems:** New knowledge management approaches need to work seamlessly with existing practice tools. Success requires careful attention to workflow integration and user experience.
- **Cultural adaptation:** Creating cultures that support effective knowledge sharing often presents the greatest challenge and requires thoughtful change management. Organizations need approaches that encourage knowledge contribution while respecting practitioners' time and expertise.
- **Measuring success and ROI:** Organizations need sophisticated approaches to measuring the effectiveness of their knowledge management initiatives. Asking the following questions is a start:
    - **Knowledge retention:** How effectively does the organization maintain crucial knowledge when key practitioners depart?
    - **Knowledge access:** How quickly and effectively can practitioners find relevant knowledge when needed?
    - **Knowledge application:** How successfully does the organization apply preserved knowledge to new situations?
    - **Knowledge evolution:** How effectively does the organization's knowledge base adapt to changing circumstances?

Despite the challenges, organizations implementing sophisticated AI knowledge management systems report significant measurable benefits including speeding up new associate knowledge, reducing response time on routine questions, cutting research time on jurisdiction-specific questions, and maintaining knowledge continuity after an expert's departure or during a temporary absence.

## CONCLUSION

As AI technology continues to evolve, organizations need to prepare for several emerging capabilities:

- **Enhanced natural language understanding:** Better ability to capture and analyze unstructured knowledge sharing will enable more sophisticated preservation of tacit knowledge.
- **Predictive knowledge delivery:** More sophisticated approaches to anticipating knowledge needs will help organizations deploy their knowledge more effectively.
- **Cross-organization knowledge sharing:** New frameworks for sharing knowledge across organizational boundaries while maintaining appropriate protections could transform how organizations collaborate.
- **Automated expertise networks:** More sophisticated approaches to connecting practitioners with relevant expertise might enhance knowledge deployment and transform how organizations leverage their collective knowledge.

## ACTION ITEMS

1. **Identify Critical Knowledge at Risk**
   - Map tacit knowledge from senior practitioners
   - Assess knowledge loss risks from retirements/departures
   - Inventory institutional memory and expertise
2. **Implement AI Knowledge Capture**
   - Deploy AI systems for automatic document classification and tagging
   - Establish multimodal capture (audio, video, text analysis)
   - Create AI-powered precedent and work product analysis
3. **Build Tiered Knowledge Framework**
   - Create confidentiality-based knowledge classification
   - Establish privilege protection protocols for AI analysis
   - Design access controls for sensitive knowledge
4. **Deploy Experience Capture Systems**
   - Implement AI analysis of historical matter patterns
   - Create systems to preserve decision-making context
   - Establish knowledge extraction from departing practitioners

5. **Enable AI-Powered Knowledge Discovery**
   - Implement intelligent search with legal concept understanding
   - Deploy recommendation systems for relevant precedents
   - Create expertise location and matching capabilities
6. **Monitor Knowledge Transformation Impact**
   - Track knowledge reuse and accessibility improvements
   - Measure retention of critical expertise during transitions
   - Assess AI effectiveness in knowledge preservation and deployment

# CHAPTER 5
# Professional Responsibility and AI

## INTRODUCTION

*It's not enough to know how to use AI tools; you must understand how to use them responsibly within the bounds of professional obligations.*

Ask any lawyer about their core professional obligations, and they can recite them without hesitation: competence, confidentiality, avoiding conflicts, and maintaining independence of judgment. But when artificial intelligence enters the equation, these familiar duties suddenly demand new interpretations and safeguards.

Consider this scenario playing out in law firms today: A prestigious law firm implements an AI document analysis platform to enhance efficiency across practice groups. Partners routinely upload client materials, including confidential litigation documents and strategic planning materials. Unknown to them, the vendor's terms of service permit the AI provider to retain and learn from all uploaded content. This seemingly minor oversight could create two profound ethical breaches.

First, sensitive client information is exposed to third parties without consent, potentially violating confidentiality under Rule 1.6 of the ABA's Model Rules of Professional Conduct. Second, when the same AI analyzes documents from competing clients, it potentially creates an algorithmic conflict of interest, as insights from one client's strategy subtly influence recommendations for another—a new form of conflict that traditional detection systems aren't designed to identify.

*Note: While courts and bar associations have not yet formally addressed this type of algorithmic conflict, legal leaders must proactively consider the potential ethical implications of such implicit cross-contamination to prevent future conflicts or regulatory scrutiny. While some experts share this concern, others argue that proper AI system design can prevent such transfer through technical controls like data segregation, context boundaries, and selective training. We acknowledge that there are ongoing debates about the extent of this risk and the effectiveness of technical solutions to prevent such conflicts.*

The consequences of AI misuse aren't theoretical. In the landmark *Mata v. Avianca* case, attorneys received court sanctions after submitting a brief containing fabricated case citations generated by an LLM.[1] Despite being confronted by the court, one attorney compounded the error by again using the same unreliable technology to "verify" the false citations, revealing a fundamental failure of both technological competence and independent judgment.

This pattern repeated in 2025 when, during motions practice in Coomer v. Lindell, the court identified approximately 30 defective citations in an opposition brief.[2] Only when directly questioned did counsel admit to using generative AI without verification, triggering potential sanctions and disciplinary proceedings.

These cases demonstrate the dangers at the intersection of AI and professional responsibility: Without technological competence, attorneys cannot properly evaluate AI outputs; without maintaining independent judgment, they risk surrendering their core professional obligations to algorithms.

As a legal leader, you face decisions about AI implementation that carry profound ethical implications. Your challenge isn't merely understanding new technologies; it's ensuring these tools enhance rather than undermine your professional obligations. This chapter provides a framework for maintaining the highest ethical standards while leveraging AI's benefits.

## FOUNDATIONAL ETHICAL OBLIGATIONS IN THE DIGITAL AGE

### The Evolving Nature of Professional Responsibility

Remember when "competence" meant knowing the law and keeping up with legal developments? Today, it means something more. ABA Model Rules of

[1] Mata v. Avianca, Inc., 678 F. Supp. 3d 443 (S.D.N.Y. 2023).

[2] Coomer v. Lindell, No. 1:22-cv-01129, ECF No. 309 (D. Colo. Apr. 23, 2025), https://cases.justia.com/federal/district-courts/colorado/codce/1:2022cv01129/215068/309/0.pdf.

Professional Conduct, Rule 1.1, Comment 8, specifically requires keeping up with and understanding the "benefits and risks associated with relevant technology."[3] But what does that really mean for your AI use?

Bar associations across the U.S. are actively developing guidance on AI use that not only controls the use but may actually require it. For example, the New York State Bar Association's 2024 Task Force on Artificial Intelligence notes that "When utilizing generative AI tools such as ChatGPT, attorneys need to be knowledgeable about the technology they are using and/or ask for assistance from those lawyers or trusted technology experts who do understand its use and limitations, including IT personnel. If none of these options is possible, then the attorney should not utilize such technologies until they are competent to do so per the duty of competency."[4]

The Task Force further states that compliance with the rules of professional conduct establishes a "Duty of Competency/Techno-solutionism" that establishes the principle that "A refusal to use technology that makes legal work more accurate and efficient may be considered a refusal to provide competent legal representation to clients," while at the same time, Rule 5.3 of the rules of professional conduct requires attorneys to supervise nonlawyer work, which would establish human oversight of AI tools. The report further addresses how the use of AI implicates rules addressing the duty of confidentiality and privacy and the unauthorized practice of law.[5]

*Note: The view that refusing to use AI might violate competence obligations represents an aggressive interpretation that some traditional practitioners might challenge. We acknowledge it represents one end of a spectrum of views on technology adoption obligations.*

Consider the example of a midsize law firm that recently implemented an AI contract analysis tool. Initially, they thought technical competence meant simply teaching lawyers how to use the tool to select and review contract clauses. After six months of use, they realized technical competence runs much deeper. Their attorneys needed to understand not just how to operate the tool but also its limitations, potential biases, and appropriate use cases.

---

[3] Model rules are adopted state-by-state; consult your jurisdiction's versions and ethics opinions.

[4] N.Y. State Bar Ass'n Task Force on Artificial Intelligence, Report and Recommendations (Apr. 2024), https://nysba.org/wp-content/uploads/2022/03/2024-April-Report-and-Recommendations-of-the-Task-Force-on-Artificial-Intelligence.pdf.

[5] Keep in mind that state rules vary and that firms should structure self-service tools to avoid unauthorized practice exposure (e.g., disclaimers, supervision, jurisdictional checks).

This realization led them to develop a comprehensive competence framework. Rather than focusing solely on tool operation, they emphasized understanding when and how to effectively oversee the use of AI. Junior attorneys learned not just how to use the tools but also how to spot potential errors and when to seek additional review. Partners focused on developing oversight skills specific to AI-assisted work.

The key insight? Technical competence serves professional duties. It's not enough to know how to use AI tools; you must understand how to use them responsibly within the bounds of professional obligations. While most U.S. state bar associations require continuing education, including a requirement for one hour on "ethics," it seems that the need for deep training on the ethical and effective use of AI may far exceed this requirement.

### Maintaining Independence of Judgment

Your duty to exercise independent professional judgment is central to legal practice. AI tools, while powerful, can create subtle threats to this independence if not managed properly. Consider how you might be prone to excessive deference to AI outputs, especially when they seem authoritative or align with your initial thinking.

The *Mata* case showed how easily attorneys can surrender their verification responsibilities to AI tools. This is problematic on its own, but independence issues extend beyond verification. You face risks of confirmation bias when AI outputs align with your preferences, automation bias when you defer to AI recommendations without critical evaluation, and anchoring effects when AI-generated options frame subsequent discussions.

Leading organizations preserve independence by treating AI as a consultation tool rather than a decision-maker. They design workflows where AI can inform analysis, but attorneys must independently articulate reasoning and conclusions. This intentional separation helps maintain the critical independent judgment that defines professional legal service.

## EMERGING ETHICAL CHALLENGES IN AI-ASSISTED LEGAL PRACTICE

### The Challenge of Overseeing AI Systems

Think about how you typically supervise junior attorneys. You review their work, provide feedback, and guide their development. But how do you supervise an AI system? What does appropriate oversight look like when the "junior associate" is an algorithm?

This isn't a theoretical question. Courts and ethics committees are already weighing in on what constitutes reasonable supervision of AI tools. In *Mata v. Avianca, Inc.*, the judge emphasized that while AI tools can be used legitimately in legal practice, they require appropriate supervision and verification of all factual and legal content.[6] Other opinions have similarly stated that attorneys must have reasonable supervision over AI tools, commensurate with the complexity and potential risks of the specific application.

Leading organizations have learned from such cautionary tales. They understand that supervision requirements should scale with risk, giving careful consideration to how AI use is governed and overseen on a day-to-day basis.

Consider a hypothetical example of how one corporate legal department transformed its approach to AI supervision after a close call with an AI contract analysis tool. They had assumed the tool's high accuracy ratings meant minimal oversight was needed. That assumption lasted until the system missed a critical change-of-control provision in a major agreement.

The oversight nearly resulted in the company proceeding with a significant acquisition without recognizing that the target company's key supplier contract would terminate automatically upon a change of ownership. Had this error not been caught by a junior attorney who happened to manually review the document days before closing, the company would have lost a supplier relationship representing 30% of the target's revenue stream—potentially transforming a strategic acquisition into a value-destroying transaction. The $50 million deal, priced based on future cash flows that included this supplier relationship, would have immediately lost approximately $15 million in value while simultaneously requiring emergency sourcing alternatives.

This near miss served as a sobering reminder that even as AI tools advance, the fundamental professional duty of competent representation cannot be outsourced to technology.

## Client Communications

When do you need to tell clients you're using AI? The question seems simple, but the answer can be surprisingly complex. Consider these scenarios:

[6] Mata v. Avianca, Inc., 678 F. Supp. 3d 443 (S.D.N.Y. 2023).

- Your firm uses AI for initial document review in a major litigation matter. The tool significantly reduces costs and improves accuracy. Do you need to disclose this to the client? What if you find that the tool made a significant mistake?
- Your legal department employs AI-powered research tools that influence strategy recommendations. Should you explain how these tools affect your advice? What level of detail is appropriate?
- Your firm implements an AI drafting assistant that generates the first version of a complex merger agreement, which attorneys then heavily edit and finalize. The AI significantly accelerates the drafting process but also introduces subtle terminology differences from your firm's standard templates. Should you inform the client about this drafting approach, particularly if it affects your billing or timeline representations?
- You use a third-party AI tool to analyze past judicial decisions to predict likely outcomes in a client's case, and these predictions substantially influence your settlement recommendations. The AI's methodology is proprietary and not fully transparent even to your firm. What obligation do you have to disclose the role this "black box" analysis played in forming your professional judgment?

The answers often depend on materiality, impact on legal strategy, and potential risks. But there's a broader principle at stake: maintaining client trust through appropriate transparency.

While routine AI use, such as standard legal research, generally requires minimal disclosure, more significant reliance—particularly where AI substantially shapes case strategies, settlement recommendations, or complex document drafting—should be transparently communicated to maintain client trust and informed consent.

Even beyond maintaining trust, you can turn AI disclosure into a competitive advantage. Rather than treating it as a compliance burden, use it as an opportunity to demonstrate innovation and responsibility. Ensure your client engagement letters clearly explain how you use AI to enhance service delivery while maintaining professional standards.

You will find that proactive communication about your use of AI strengthens client relationships. Clients appreciate understanding how technology helps deliver more efficient service as long as they also understand the oversight measures in place and the cost savings they may realize. The key is striking the right balance—providing enough information to maintain transparency without overwhelming clients with technical details.

*Note: While many ethics opinions support our recommended approach, some practitioners argue that routine AI use (e.g., using AI-powered legal research tools) doesn't require specific disclosure any more than using other technologies. We acknowledge the range of views but maintain our recommendation for transparency.*

## Maintaining Attorney–Client Privilege

Picture this scenario: Your team uses a popular AI platform to analyze privileged documents in a major transaction without redacting the names of the parties. A month later, you learn the platform retains data to improve its models. Has privilege been waived? Who else might have access to insights derived from your confidential documents?

The potential negative outcomes extend far beyond theoretical considerations:

First, courts could find that privilege has been waived through disclosure to a third-party vendor without adequate safeguards. This could render previously protected communications suddenly discoverable, fundamentally altering the evidence available in pending or future litigation. In a worst-case scenario, smoking-gun communications about transaction weaknesses, litigation vulnerabilities, or negotiation strategies could become available to opposing parties.

Second, competitors using the same AI platform might benefit from insights derived from your confidential information without ever seeing the original documents. The AI might generate an improved analysis of certain clause types or transaction structures based partly on learning from your privileged materials, effectively transferring competitive legal intelligence without direct document sharing. For instance, if the AI analyzed your unique approach to addressing a regulatory concern, that approach might influence recommendations made to your direct competitors facing similar issues.

Third, the lack of transparency around data retention creates regulatory exposure. In regulated industries or cross-border transactions, unauthorized data transfers could trigger notification requirements, regulatory penalties, or even deal-breaking compliance violations. A financial services client might face regulatory scrutiny if confidential customer information within privileged documents was inadvertently processed and retained by an AI vendor without appropriate controls.`

These aren't hypothetical concerns. Standard privilege protections may not adequately address AI's unique challenges. When an AI contract analysis tool identifies patterns across multiple clients' privileged documents, you will face difficult questions about information segregation and privilege maintenance. Although current court decisions have not yet definitively addressed privilege waiver through AI vendor data retention, the uncertainty itself warrants proactive safeguards. Until clearer legal guidance emerges, firms should assume heightened caution and implement robust privilege protection protocols.

## Data Privacy and Security Challenges

Traditional data security focuses on preventing unauthorized access. But AI introduces fundamentally new challenges: What happens when authorized access includes machine learning? How do you protect client data when AI systems are designed to find patterns across multiple matters?

Consider this scenario: A mid-sized law firm implemented an AI research tool to enhance their case analysis capabilities. Six months after deployment, a partner discovered the tool had begun making connections across supposedly segregated client matters, identifying litigation strategy patterns that spanned multiple cases. While no confidential information was leaked externally, the internal pattern recognition effectively breached the information barriers between clients with potentially adverse interests.

The discovery triggered an urgent review of all AI tools in use. What they found was concerning—their confidentiality framework addressed who could access information but failed to account for how AI systems learn from and apply that information. The firm's carefully constructed ethical walls had become permeable through AI's ability to extract and generalize patterns across matters.

This incident highlights how AI requires you to think differently about data protection. Traditional security models focused on access control (who can see what) are insufficient in an AI context. You must now also control how data is used, what patterns can be recognized across datasets, and how insights derived from one matter can influence analysis in another.

## Preventing Bias

When using AI tools, the possibility of creating or reinforcing bias is a serious issue. When we think about bias in legal practice, we typically focus on human bias. But AI introduces new forms of bias that can be harder for you to detect and correct.

Based on our reading of ABA Model Rule 1.1 and its comments, ABA Formal Opinion 512, several U.S. state bar opinions and guidance documents on the need to understand AI's capabilities and limitations, and the EU AI Act references to controlling high-risk AI systems, we believe that legal professionals have an ethical duty to actively seek out, monitor, and mitigate biases within AI systems to the extent practical. Regular audits and transparent procedures demonstrate reasonable efforts to uphold ethical standards.

AI systems learn from historical data—including past legal decisions, briefs, and agreements—which may contain embedded societal or systemic biases. Unlike human bias, which might be conscious or unconscious, AI bias manifests through mathematical patterns that can appear objective while perpetuating or amplifying existing inequities.

Consider this scenario: Your litigation practice implements an AI case prediction tool to assess settlement values for personal injury claims. After months of use, data analysis reveals the tool consistently recommends lower settlement values for plaintiffs from certain zip codes or demographic groups, even when controlling for all other case factors. The bias isn't immediately apparent in any single case recommendation but emerges clearly in aggregate pattern analysis.

This bias can stem from multiple sources: The historical case data used to train the system may reflect decades of systemic disparities in damage awards; the features the AI prioritizes might inadvertently correlate with protected characteristics; or the model's design might fail to account for important contextual factors that human attorneys would recognize.

The discovery highlights an important truth: AI bias in legal practice isn't just a technical issue—it's a professional responsibility concern. When AI tools reflect or amplify existing biases in the legal system, they can compromise your fundamental obligation to promote justice and equal treatment under law. When you unknowingly rely on biased AI recommendations, you may violate your ethical duties without realizing it.

## PRACTICAL FRAMEWORKS FOR ETHICAL AI GOVERNANCE

### Oversight and Supervision Frameworks

A tiered classification system for AI applications based on potential risk exposure is an essential part of your AI Use Policy. For example, a three-tiered categorization might identify:

- Low-risk applications (e.g., email drafting assistance) that require standard quality checks.

- Medium-risk applications (e.g., document summarization) that require validation protocols.
- High-risk applications (e.g., legal analysis or strategy) that require comprehensive review processes with documented oversight.

For routine matters, you must implement standard quality control through sampling and spot-checking. Higher-risk applications should trigger mandatory attorney review and enhanced documentation requirements. Critical applications require comprehensive oversight with multiple levels of review and detailed audit trails. The key is matching the level of supervision with the potential consequences of errors.

This approach treats AI oversight as an integral part of legal practice. Supervising attorneys understand they're responsible not just for the final work product but also for ensuring the appropriate use of AI tools throughout the process. They develop clear protocols for when and how AI can be used, how outputs should be validated, and how to document oversight activities.

Most importantly, effective AI governance creates a culture where questioning AI outputs is expected and valued. Junior attorneys know they won't be criticized for flagging potential AI errors or asking for additional review. This combination of clear protocols and a supportive culture makes AI oversight both more effective and more consistent.

## Safeguards for Independence of Judgment

Address independence of judgment challenges by implementing specific safeguards:

- Establish explicit verification requirements for all AI outputs.
- Create regular process checks that require attorneys to articulate independent reasoning.
- Design workflows where AI tools inform but don't direct decision-making.
- Implement "alternative consideration" protocols that require exploring options beyond AI recommendations.
- Train attorneys to recognize cognitive biases when using AI tools.

## Privilege and Data Protection Strategies

### *Privilege Protection Approaches*

Advanced law firms are implementing specialized technologies to maintain privilege when using AI tools, including the following examples:

- **Clean room implementations:** Some firms have developed "AI clean rooms" where privileged information is processed in isolated environments that prevent model training or data retention. These environments apply technical safeguards like data tokenization and ephemeral processing that eliminate persistent storage of sensitive information.

- **Private cloud deployments:** You can implement private cloud versions of AI tools that operate solely within your own security perimeter. This may include deploying a customized LLM that operates exclusively on firm infrastructure, ensuring no client data leaves your control. This can address the risk that uploading confidential client information to third-party tools may constitute disclosure to a third party that waives privilege absent a confidentiality agreement.
- **Privilege detection systems:** Automated systems that identify potentially privileged information before it reaches external AI tools provide another layer of protection. For example, you might implement an automated privilege detection system that scans all documents before they reach AI processing, flagging sensitive content for attorney review.

These technical approaches complement policy measures to create comprehensive privilege protection frameworks suitable for the AI era.

Forward-thinking organizations will develop even better approaches to privilege protection in the AI era. Large law firms will redesign their privilege protection frameworks after realizing their existing protocols don't adequately address AI-specific risks. They will need to create a comprehensive system that considers not just data access but also model training, pattern recognition, and cross-matter insights.

This approach begins with careful vendor evaluation. Before using any AI tool that might encounter privileged information, you should conduct detailed assessments of how the tool handles data, what it retains, and how it uses information for model training. You will need to establish specific contractual provisions requiring vendors to protect privilege and limit data retention.

Most importantly, you must create clearly defined protocols for different types of privileged information. Some categories must never touch external AI tools, while others will require specific technical safeguards and oversight measures. The result will be a nuanced approach that maintains privilege protection while allowing appropriate AI use.

### *Multidimensional Data Governance*

Leading organizations are developing multidimensional data governance frameworks specifically for AI use. Rather than treating all client data the same way, you should implement a tiered classification system that addresses both access and utilization rights:

- **Restricted data:** Highly sensitive information that should never be processed by external AI tools and requires specialized containment even with internal systems
- **Controlled data:** Information that can be processed by carefully selected AI tools but with strict limitations on model training and pattern extraction
- **Standard data:** Information that can be used more broadly but still requires appropriate anonymization and technical safeguards

For each tier, you need to establish clear protocols addressing not just who can access the information but also:

- Which AI systems can process it.
- Whether it can be used for model training.
- What types of pattern recognition are permitted across matters.
- How derivative insights can be applied.
- What technical safeguards must be implemented.

Forward-thinking legal organizations will supplement policy controls with technical measures like differential privacy techniques, federated learning approaches, and specialized data tokenization. These technologies allow AI systems to learn from data without creating privacy or confidentiality risks.

Rather than treating data security as a separate concern from ethical obligations, you should integrate security considerations directly into your professional responsibility framework. By reconceptualizing data protection to address AI's unique characteristics, you can maintain information barriers even as AI tools become more sophisticated in recognizing patterns across seemingly unrelated matters.

## Bias Mitigation Strategies

Addressing AI bias requires both technical solutions (diverse training data, algorithmic fairness measures) and professional vigilance (regular auditing, critical evaluation of recommendations). You must implement governance structures that regularly test for bias and establish clear protocols for when human judgment should override AI recommendations, particularly in high-stakes decisions affecting client interests.

Effective bias mitigation requires both technical and procedural controls. Consider the example of a corporate legal department that regularly runs "bias audits" of its AI tools, testing them against diverse scenarios to identify potential prejudices. But they don't stop at testing. They've developed clear protocols for what happens when bias is detected. This includes not just technical corrections but also reviews of how the bias might have affected past work. They've created a culture in which identifying and addressing bias is seen as a professional obligation, not just a technical issue.

## Joint Responsibility with AI Vendors

The use of AI in legal practice often involves shared responsibility with technology vendors. You need to develop comprehensive approaches to vendor management that consider both ethical considerations and technical capabilities. Assess vendors based on technical proficiency and their handling of ethical issues, such as confidentiality, bias mitigation, and transparency.

Key elements of effective AI vendor management include:

- **Contractual safeguards:** You should include specialized contract provisions addressing data handling, model training limitations, and confidentiality requirements. These go beyond standard confidentiality clauses to address AI-specific concerns like preventing client data from being used for model training.
- **Ongoing monitoring:** Rather than treating vendor assessment as a one-time event, you should implement continuous monitoring of AI vendor practices. This includes regular audits, performance reviews, and updates on vendor policies and practices.
- **Collaborative problem solving:** When issues arise, you should work collaboratively with your vendors to develop solutions. This might include creating custom implementations, modifying standard offerings, or developing specialized protocols for sensitive matters.
- **Clear expectations:** Effective vendor relationships start with clear communication about performance and ethical requirements. Before implementation begins, you should articulate specific expectations regarding data handling, confidentiality, bias mitigation, and transparency.
- **Independence protection:** You must maintain your independent judgment even when relying on vendor expertise. This includes preserving the ability to question vendor recommendations and maintaining ultimate responsibility for all legal work.

## Professional Development Approaches

Instead of treating AI competence as a one-time training issue, you need to weave it into your professional development framework. New associates should receive foundational training in AI concepts and ethical implications before touching specific tools. Mid-level attorneys must learn advanced concepts about AI limitations and oversight. Partners need to focus on governance, ethics, and risk management aspects.

Additionally, you should tie everything back to professional responsibility. When introducing new AI tools, instead of starting with education about features and functions, begin with discussions about professional responsibility implications and oversight requirements. This approach will transform how your attorneys think about AI—not as just another technology tool but as a capability that must be thoughtfully integrated into an ethical legal practice.

## FUTURE CONSIDERATIONS

The pace of AI advancement in legal practice shows no signs of slowing. New capabilities emerge almost weekly, from increasingly sophisticated document analysis to AI-powered legal reasoning. Each advance brings new ethical challenges you need to prepare for.

As AI capabilities evolve, your professional responsibilities will face increasingly complex challenges:

- **Evolving duty of competence:** The definition of technological competence will continue to expand. You must stay informed about AI advancements that impact legal practice, requiring ongoing education beyond traditional legal updates. Soon, competence may include understanding concepts like model validation, prompt engineering, and AI governance—areas previously considered purely technical. Some might argue this sets an unreasonably high bar for technical knowledge. We acknowledge that different roles may require different depths of technical understanding, and that many attorneys might satisfy their duty through appropriate delegation and oversight rather than personal technical expertise.
- **Redefining supervision requirements:** As AI systems become more autonomous, your supervision obligations will evolve. You'll need new frameworks for providing appropriate oversight when AI performs increasingly complex tasks with less human intervention. This may include developing specialized audit protocols, statistical quality controls, and automated oversight mechanisms.
- **Independence and AI co-counseling:** Future AI systems may function more like collaborative partners than passive tools. You'll need to establish

clear boundaries that maintain your independent judgment while leveraging AI capabilities. This might involve creating explicit decision protocols that clearly delineate human versus AI responsibilities.

- **Cross-border ethical considerations:** AI tools will increasingly operate across jurisdictional boundaries, creating complex professional responsibility questions. You'll need to navigate different ethical standards for AI use across jurisdictions, potentially requiring comprehensive conflict-of-law analyses for AI applications.
- **Transparency and explainability obligations:** As clients become more sophisticated about AI use, your disclosure obligations may expand. You might face requirements to explain AI decision-making processes to clients in comprehensible terms, even when dealing with complex "black box" systems.
- **New forms of unauthorized practice:** Future AI capabilities will blur traditional boundaries of legal practice, requiring you to establish clear protocols for distinguishing between permissible automation and impermissible practice delegation. This may involve creating detailed taxonomies of legal tasks and appropriate automation levels.

The most successful organizations will develop flexible approaches that can evolve with technology. Rather than creating rigid rules, you should build principles-based frameworks that can adapt to new challenges while maintaining core ethical values. One approach is to use an ethical innovation committee. This cross-functional team regularly reviews emerging AI capabilities against professional obligations, updating guidance and controls as needed. This proactive approach can help you stay ahead of ethical challenges while maintaining innovation.

## CONCLUSION

Managing ethical obligations in the AI era requires a fundamental rethinking of how you approach professional responsibility. Success requires more than updating existing policies; it demands creating new frameworks that preserve core ethical principles while embracing technological innovation.

The organizations that will thrive are those that treat AI ethics not as a compliance burden but as an opportunity to enhance professional practice. By developing comprehensive approaches that address both current and emerging challenges, you position yourself to leverage AI's benefits while maintaining the highest ethical standards.

The future of legal practice will belong to organizations that can effectively navigate this balance by embracing AI's capabilities while upholding the fundamental ethical obligations that have always defined the profession.

## ACTION ITEMS

1. **Establish AI Competence Requirements**
   - Define technological competence standards for AI tool use
   - Create attorney oversight protocols for AI-assisted work
   - Implement validation requirements for AI outputs
2. **Protect Independence of Judgment**
   - Design workflows that preserve attorney decision-making authority
   - Create safeguards against excessive deference to AI recommendations
   - Establish critical evaluation requirements for AI-generated content
3. **Maintain Attorney–Client Privilege**
   - Implement privilege protection protocols for AI data processing
   - Create information barriers preventing cross-client contamination
   - Establish audit systems for privileged information handling
4. **Address Professional Responsibility in AI Supervision**
   - Define supervision requirements for AI-assisted work by experience level
   - Create escalation protocols for AI-related ethical concerns
   - Establish documentation standards for professional oversight
5. **Implement Ethical AI Use Frameworks**
   - Create ethics consultation processes for novel AI applications
   - Establish bias detection and mitigation protocols
   - Design ethical decision trees for AI tool selection and use
6. **Develop Client Disclosure Protocols**
   - Create materiality assessment frameworks for AI use disclosure
   - Establish consent procedures for AI processing of client information
   - Design transparency frameworks balancing disclosure with practical efficiency

# CHAPTER 6

# Managing Legal and Compliance Risks with AI

## INTRODUCTION

*The risks from using AI aren't just theoretical, they're immediate, significant, and often not obvious until something goes wrong.*

Picture this scenario: You've just learned that an associate used a public AI tool to analyze a confidential merger agreement. The tool's terms of service grant it rights to use uploaded content for model training. Your client is a public company, and the agreement contained material nonpublic information. In one seemingly innocent action, you're now facing potential securities law violations, breach of client confidentiality, and malpractice exposure.

As AI tools become more integrated into legal practice, scenarios like this play out in law firms and legal departments across the United States and around the world. The risks from uses of AI aren't just theoretical, they're immediate, significant, and often not obvious until something goes wrong.

Here's the challenge: AI can dramatically improve legal service delivery, but it also introduces novel risks that many traditional risk management approaches weren't designed to address. You need to understand what can go wrong, and how to protect your organization while still capturing AI's benefits.

# DATA PRIVACY AND SECURITY

## The New Data Security Landscape

Traditionally, data security focused on keeping unauthorized users out. AI changes this equation fundamentally. You need to worry about what authorized AI systems are doing with your data. Consider what happens when a law firm discovers that its AI research system uses client matter information to improve its algorithms—creating potential privacy violations across multiple jurisdictions.

The challenge is particularly acute for international practices navigating multiple regulatory regimes. The EU's GDPR defines AI systems as processors that trigger specific requirements, while the UK Data Protection Act imposes different standards. Meanwhile, China's Personal Information Protection Law (PIPL) creates yet another framework for AI data processing. Organizations find themselves trying to comply with overlapping—and sometimes conflicting—requirements.

Recent surveys of in-house legal professionals highlight that legal departments face significant challenges related to data privacy, security, and regulatory complexity when adopting AI tools. Key concerns include data governance, cross-border data transfers, and risks tied to training AI on confidential documents. In response, some organizations are developing "regulatory heat maps" for AI data transfers, mapping requirements across dozens of jurisdictions to enable implementation of jurisdiction-specific controls while maintaining a consistent overall framework.

The challenge isn't just about data access anymore. It's about data use, retention, and learning. When an AI system processes your documents, it's not just reading them—it's learning from them. This learning capability creates new privacy and security risks that many organizations aren't prepared to handle.

The data readiness challenges we discuss in Chapter 7 create specific security vulnerabilities that legal organizations must address. When AI systems attempt to learn from fragmented, inconsistently structured data, the reality in many legal organizations, they may require broader data access permissions than necessary, increasing security exposure. Systems struggling with poor data quality often implement workarounds that bypass security controls, creating hidden vulnerabilities that traditional security audits miss.

Organizations are developing new approaches to data protection that specifically address AI risks. Different types of data have different AI handling requirements. Not all data needs the same level of protection, but you need clear protocols for determining appropriate handling.

## Technical Spotlight: Advanced Data Protection for AI Systems

Some legal organizations are implementing sophisticated technical controls for AI data protection:

- **Privacy-preserving machine learning (PPML):** Techniques like federated learning allow AI systems to learn from data without direct access to raw information. In 2025, Apple developed and deployed a private federated learning (PFL) framework to enhance user experiences while maintaining data privacy.[1] This approach allows machine learning models to be trained directly on users' devices, ensuring that personal data remains local and is not transmitted to central servers. Only essential model updates are shared in a privacy-preserving manner, enabling collective learning without compromising individual privacy.
- **Differential privacy:** This mathematical framework adds calibrated noise to data, protecting individual records while preserving overall analytical value. In the 2020 Census, the U.S. Census Bureau adopted differential privacy (DP) to protect individual respondent data. They developed the Disclosure Avoidance System (DAS), which includes the TopDown Algorithm (TDA), to add statistical noise to census data. This approach ensures that published statistics do not compromise the confidentiality of individual responses while maintaining the overall utility of the data. The implementation of DP in the 2020 Census represents one of the largest-scale applications of this privacy-preserving technique.[2]
- **Synthetic data:** Some organizations are creating synthetic datasets that reflect the statistical properties of real data without containing actual client information. Synthetic data is increasingly utilized in legal AI to mitigate privacy concerns and enhance model training. For instance, researchers have demonstrated that generating synthetic queries for legal documents can significantly improve retrieval accuracy in legal information systems. This approach enables the development of robust AI models without compromising sensitive client information.

---

[1] An Ji et al., *Private Federated Learning in Real World Application—A Case Study*, Apple Machine Learning Rsch. (Feb. 2025), https://machinelearning.apple.com/research/learning-real-world-application.

[2] U.S. Census Bureau, Disclosure Avoidance and the 2020 Census: How the TopDown Algorithm Works (Mar. 2023), https://www2.census.gov/library/publications/decennial/2020/census-briefs/c2020br-04.pdf.

- **Homomorphic encryption:** This advanced technique allows computation on encrypted data without decryption. Though computationally intensive, limited implementations are emerging for high-sensitivity applications. Some large firms are piloting homomorphic encryption, including for analyzing highly confidential M&A data.
- **Data governance as security foundation:** The enterprise data governance frameworks outlined in Chapter 8 serve a dual purpose: enabling AI effectiveness while creating security boundaries. Organizations with mature data governance—including semantic data modeling and intelligent data classification—can implement more granular security controls because they understand precisely what data exists, where it's located, and how it should be protected.
- **Risk-based data classification for AI:** Rather than applying uniform security controls, we recommend you implement risk-based data classification that determines appropriate AI processing levels. Client merger documents require different AI security protocols than general legal research materials, but these distinctions are only possible with the semantic data frameworks discussed in Chapter 7.

### Implementing Effective Controls

The most successful approaches to AI data protection combine technical controls with operational safeguards. Consider an example of how a regional law firm might approach this challenge. After a close call with an AI tool that was saving client documents, they developed a comprehensive protection framework.

Their system starts with technical controls: encryption for data in transit and at rest, access controls based on user roles, and monitoring systems to track AI tool usage. But they don't stop there. They recognize that technical controls alone aren't enough.

The firm also implements operational safeguards: clear protocols for which AI tools can be used with which types of data, training programs to help lawyers understand data protection requirements, and regular audits to ensure compliance. Most importantly, they create a culture where people feel comfortable raising concerns about data handling.

## CONFIDENTIALITY CONCERNS

### Beyond Traditional Confidentiality

Client confidentiality has always been a cornerstone of legal practice. But AI introduces new challenges to maintaining this fundamental obligation. When you use an AI tool, you could possibly be sharing client information with a third party in ways that may not be obvious.

Consider this example: A litigation team uses an AI tool to analyze deposition transcripts, not realizing the tool's terms of service allowed it to use uploaded content to train its models. Effectively, they are sharing confidential client information not just with the vendor but potentially with future users who might benefit from the model's learning. Additionally, this sharing may include a methodology the firm uses in its analyses, effectively sharing the firm's confidential IP.

Some AI tools have terms of service that permit using customer data for model training unless the users explicitly opt out. This potentially creates confidentiality risks that organizations might fail to recognize until it is too late.

We acknowledge that the extent of information transfer between client matters depends on the specific AI architecture, model training approach, and vendor safeguards. While some systems may pose this risk, others implement technical controls specifically designed to prevent cross-client contamination.

## Managing Modern Confidentiality Risks

Some organizations are developing new approaches to confidentiality that specifically address AI risks. One innovative approach is to create a "confidentiality impact assessment" for AI tools. Before any AI tool can be used with client information, the legal department evaluates:

- How the tool handles and stores information.
- What rights the vendor has over uploaded content.
- How the tool uses data for model training.
- What happens to information after analysis is complete.

The data preparation and quality management processes described in Chapter 8 become critical confidentiality controls. When organizations attempt to use AI systems with unprepared data—documents with inconsistent metadata, unclear provenance, or mixed sensitivity levels—they risk accidentally exposing confidential information to AI processing that exceeds authorized access levels. Proper data tokenization and semantic classification, as outlined in Chapter 8, ensures that confidentiality boundaries are maintained throughout AI processing workflows.

Going beyond assessment, you can develop specific protocols for different types of confidential information, allowing some information to only be used with AI tools that provide contractual guarantees against retention or model training and identifying other information that requires specific technical safeguards like encryption or data masking.

Law firms are increasingly developing structured protocols to manage the use of AI tools while safeguarding client confidentiality. For instance, the American Bar Association (ABA) has issued Formal Opinion 512, which emphasizes the importance of protecting client information when using generative AI tools. The opinion advises lawyers to understand how AI tools handle data, including storage, retrieval, and retention, and to ensure that any use complies with their duty of confidentiality. It also recommends that lawyers obtain informed consent from clients when necessary and implement appropriate safeguards, such as data encryption and secure access controls. By adopting such structured approaches, law firms can leverage the benefits of AI technologies while maintaining their ethical obligations to protect client confidentiality.

## BIAS AND DISCRIMINATION RISKS

### Understanding AI Bias in Legal Context

AI bias in legal practice isn't just a technical issue; it's a serious risk that can lead to discrimination claims, ethical violations, and reputational damage. Law firms have learned this lesson the hard way when their AI-powered hiring tools have shown systematic bias against certain candidate demographics.

The risk of bias extends beyond hiring. AI tools used in legal practice can reflect and amplify existing biases in the legal system. Think about prediction tools that draw conclusions based on historical case outcomes, potentially perpetuating past patterns of discrimination.

Studies have shown that algorithmic tools used in the legal system can exhibit significant biases, particularly affecting marginalized groups. For instance, the Correctional Offender Management Profiling for Alternative Sanctions (COMPAS) system, widely used in U.S. courts to assess the likelihood of a defendant re-offending, has been found to disproportionately assign higher risk scores to Black defendants compared to White defendants, even when controlling for prior offenses and other relevant factors.[3] Such disparities raise concerns about the potential for biased outcomes in legal decision-making processes when relying on predictive algorithms.

[3] Julia Angwin et al., *Machine Bias*, ProPublica (May 23, 2016), https://www.propublica.org/article/machine-bias-risk-assessments-in-criminal-sentencing.

### Effective Bias Mitigation

Leading organizations have developed comprehensive strategies to manage bias risks in AI tools. One effective approach involves implementing a "bias testing protocol" that evaluates AI systems against diverse scenarios before deployment to identify potential biases.

However, testing alone isn't sufficient. It's crucial to establish clear protocols for addressing detected biases, including rectifying immediate issues and reviewing past decisions that may have been affected. Cultivating a culture in which identifying and addressing bias is a shared responsibility is essential.

## REGULATORY COMPLIANCE

### Navigating Complex Requirements

The regulatory landscape for AI in legal practice is becoming increasingly complex. From data privacy regulations to emerging AI-specific rules, organizations face a growing web of compliance obligations. The challenge isn't just understanding current requirements—it's preparing for what's coming.

Rather than waiting for regulations to be finalized, effective lawyers typically monitor regulatory developments and begin preparing early. When the European Union's AI Act was still in draft form, some but not all firms started analyzing its potential implications and adjusting their practices proactively.

### Emerging AI Regulatory Frameworks

The regulatory landscape for AI in legal practice is rapidly evolving across multiple jurisdictions.

#### *The EU Approach*

The EU AI Act establishes a comprehensive, risk-based framework for regulating AI systems. AI is classified into four categories: unacceptable risk, high risk, limited risk, and minimal risk. Legal research and analytics tools generally fall under the limited risk category, requiring transparency measures such as disclosing AI-generated content and informing users about the system's capabilities and limitations. In contrast, AI systems that make decisions affecting legal rights—such as those used in judicial decision-making, legal interpretation, or migration and asylum processes—are classified as high risk. These high-risk systems must comply with stringent requirements, including robust risk management, high-quality and representative training data, detailed documentation, registration in an EU database, and meaningful human oversight. Legal organizations must assess and classify their AI applications accordingly and implement the appropriate controls to ensure compliance as the act's provisions are phased in between 2025 and 2027.

## *U.S. Sector-Specific Approach*

Rather than comprehensive, cross-industry legislation, the United States has adopted a sector-specific approach to AI regulation. Federal agencies such as the Federal Trade Commission (FTC) and the Consumer Financial Protection Bureau (CFPB) have each issued guidance for their respective domains. The FTC's 2023 guidance on AI emphasizes transparency, explainability, fairness, and the avoidance of deceptive or discriminatory practices. The CFPB has set forth requirements for the use of AI in consumer financial services, clarifying that all AI-driven products must comply with existing consumer protection laws and be subject to ongoing risk management and monitoring for bias.

While there is no comprehensive U.S. federal law specifically governing AI in legal practice, the ABA issued Formal Opinion 512 in July 2024, providing formal guidance on the use of generative AI by lawyers. The opinion highlights that lawyers must ensure competence (Model Rule 1.1), protect client confidentiality (Model Rule 1.6), maintain effective client communication (Model Rule 1.4), and charge reasonable fees (Model Rule 1.5) when using AI tools. Additionally, several states and courts have issued their own guidelines for responsible AI use in legal practice. Legal organizations serving financial or other regulated clients must ensure their AI implementations comply with both sector-specific regulatory standards and the ethical obligations set forth by professional legal bodies.

## *International Standards*

The ISO/IEC 42001:2023 standard provides a comprehensive framework for AI management systems, establishing requirements for trustworthy, transparent, and ethical AI governance.[4] While some legal technology providers have publicly announced ISO/IEC 42001 certification for their AI solutions, as far as we know, the number of law firms that have achieved this certification remains very limited. Most law firms are still in the early stages of evaluating or adopting the standard, and widespread certification in the legal sector has not yet occurred.

---

[4] Int'l Org. for Standardization, *ISO/IEC 42001:2023—Artificial Intelligence Management System Requirements* (2023), https://www.iso.org/standard/81230.html.

As client expectations and regulatory pressures increase, it is anticipated that more law firms will pursue ISO/IEC 42001 certification to demonstrate responsible AI management and build client trust.

Recent research from Thomson Reuters highlights the evolving awareness and risk posture of law firms regarding AI regulation and compliance. According to a Thomson Reuters summary of its research, a vast majority (93%) of professionals—including those in the legal sector—recognize the need for regulation of AI in professional practice.[5] This high level of awareness signals that regulatory compliance is top of mind for legal professionals as AI adoption accelerates in the industry.

Thomson Reuters' 2024 Future of the Professionals Report, which focused on generative AI use in law firms, indicates that the top negative consequence of its use is identified as overreliance on generative AI at the expense of skill development.[6] Other top noted concerns include AI use for malicious purposes, and privacy or confidentiality concerns. This statistic underscores that risk management is a significant priority for legal organizations, particularly as generative AI introduces new challenges related to data privacy, confidentiality, and ethical obligations.

While many law firms are actively considering these risks, a substantial portion of firms have not yet established clear policies or fully assessed their risk posture regarding AI. This uncertainty highlights the need for proactive, flexible compliance frameworks that can adapt to evolving regulatory requirements and best practices. Forward-thinking organizations are responding by developing such frameworks, ensuring they can meet both current and future compliance demands as AI regulation in the legal sector continues to develop.

## Building Adaptable Compliance

We recommend that legal organizations develop flexible AI governance frameworks that can adapt to new requirements. One effective approach involves creating layered compliance protocols in which core requirements apply to all AI use with additional controls based on specific regulatory demands, including flexible components that can be adjusted as requirements change.

---

[5] Thomson Reuters, Navigate Ethical and Regulatory Issues of Using AI (Aug. 15, 2024), https://legal.thomsonreuters.com/blog/navigate-ethical-and-regulatory-issues-of-using-ai/.

[6] Thomson Reuters, Future of Professionals Report 2024 (2024), https://www.thomsonreuters.com/en/c/future-of-professionals.

The key is building systems that can evolve without requiring a complete redesign. One way is to use a modular AI compliance framework, which separates requirements into core, jurisdictional, and sector-specific components. This structure allows an organization to maintain consistent baseline controls while adapting to regional variations or client-specific requirements. When new regulations emerge, they can update specific modules without redesigning the entire framework.

Effective compliance frameworks must account for the data infrastructure requirements. Organizations with AI-ready data architectures—including automated lineage tracking, semantic classification, and intelligent data agents—can demonstrate compliance more effectively because they maintain comprehensive records of how data is processed, transformed, and accessed. Conversely, organizations attempting to achieve AI compliance without proper data governance face exponentially higher compliance costs and risks.

## Cross-Border Considerations

For organizations operating across multiple jurisdictions, AI use presents unique cross-border challenges that extend beyond data privacy concerns.

Legal organizations must navigate different standards for AI use in legal practice across jurisdictions. While some bar associations have explicitly authorized certain AI applications, others have imposed significant restrictions or special disclosure requirements.

Global law firms addressed this challenge by developing a jurisdiction-specific AI protocol map. The system classifies AI applications based on their function and then applies appropriate controls based on local requirements. They needed a system that could accommodate everything from one country's strict oversight requirements to another's regulatory sandbox approach.

Key cross-border considerations include:

- **Licensing requirements:** Some jurisdictions may classify certain AI systems as providing legal services, triggering licensing requirements or unauthorized practice concerns.
- **Disclosure obligations:** Requirements for disclosing AI use to clients or courts vary significantly across jurisdictions, necessitating tailored approaches.
- **Local storage requirements:** Data localization laws may require keeping certain information within specific geographic boundaries, affecting cloud-based AI implementations.

- **Evidence standards:** Different jurisdictions have varying standards for the admissibility and weight of AI-generated analysis, potentially affecting litigation strategy.

Organizations operating internationally should develop flexible frameworks that can accommodate these variations while maintaining consistent core principles. This might include jurisdiction-specific protocols, localized training, and adaptable validation requirements.

# MALPRACTICE CONSIDERATIONS

## New Frontiers in Professional Liability

AI use introduces novel malpractice risks that many lawyers haven't considered. What happens when an AI tool provides incorrect guidance that an attorney relies on? What if an AI system misses a critical provision during contract review? These aren't theoretical questions; they're already appearing in malpractice claims.

Consider a hypothetical scenario in which a firm faced this reality when their AI contract analysis tool missed a critical change-of-control provision. The oversight wasn't discovered until after the deal closed, leading to significant client losses and a malpractice claim. The case highlighted how AI use can create new forms of professional liability exposure.

## AI and Malpractice Risks: Emerging Trends

While medical malpractice claims involving AI tools have risen by 14% between 2022 and 2024 (primarily in diagnostic fields like radiology and oncology), we are not aware that any comparable data exists yet for legal malpractice claims.[7] However, legal experts anticipate similar risks as AI adoption grows in legal practice. The ABA and legal risk management firms warn that inadequate supervision of AI tools, failure to validate outputs, and overreliance on automated systems could lead to an increase in malpractice claims.

---

[7] B.J. Broderick, Medical Malpractice in 2025: How AI in Healthcare Is Changing Lawsuits (2025), https://www.brandonjbroderick.com/medical-malpractice-2025-how-ai-healthcare-changing-lawsuits.

### *Countervailing Potential*

While risks are emerging, AI could also *reduce* malpractice claims over time by minimizing human error in tasks like contract review, legal research, and deadline tracking. Improved accuracy and consistency in routine processes may lower traditional error rates, though this depends on robust implementation and human–AI collaboration.

## Building Protective Frameworks

We recommend legal organizations develop comprehensive approaches to manage AI-related malpractice risks. Such a framework typically addresses three key areas: prevention, detection, and response.

Prevention starts with clear protocols for AI use. Smart organizations establish guidelines for when and how AI tools can be used, what level of attorney oversight is required, and how results should be validated. They train their lawyers not just in tool operation but also in understanding limitations and potential failure points.

Detection involves systematic quality control and validation procedures. Leading organizations implement regular audits of AI-assisted work, looking for potential issues before they become problems. They also create clear channels for reporting concerns about AI outputs.

The data quality monitoring and validation frameworks discussed in Chapter8 provide essential malpractice protection by creating audit trails that demonstrate appropriate AI oversight. When AI systems operate with well-prepared, semantically structured data with proper governance controls, legal organizations can more easily demonstrate that they exercised reasonable professional judgment in their AI implementation and oversight decisions.

Response protocols ensure that issues are identified and addressed quickly and effectively. This includes procedures for correcting errors, notifying affected clients, and updating practices to prevent recurrence.

# INSURANCE CONSIDERATIONS FOR AI RISK MANAGEMENT

Traditional legal malpractice policies often do not explicitly cover AI-related risks, leaving potential coverage gaps—especially for claims involving technology services, third-party software, or automated systems. To the contrary, many malpractice policies contain exclusions or ambiguous language that could limit or deny coverage for AI-related claims unless specifically addressed.

Some law firms are working with insurers to develop specialized endorsements or hybrid policies that explicitly cover AI use in legal practice. These endorsements typically address claims arising from AI-generated content, technology errors, supervision failures, and third-party vendor issues. In exchange, insurers often require firms to implement risk controls such as documented validation procedures, clear supervision protocols, and regular audits of AI use.

Key considerations for evaluating AI insurance coverage include:

- **Exclusion review:** Scrutinize policy language for exclusions related to technology, automation, or third-party software.
- **Vendor coverage:** Assess how your policy addresses claims from errors by AI vendors.
- **Documentation:** Maintain robust records of AI governance and oversight, as required by many carriers.
- **Risk control credits:** Some insurers offer premium discounts for strong AI risk management practices.

# VENDOR DUE DILIGENCE

## Beyond Traditional Vendor Assessment

Selecting AI vendors for legal work requires a different level of scrutiny than traditional legal technology providers. You're not just buying a tool—you're often entering into a relationship where the vendor will have access to sensitive client information and may be integral to your service delivery.

Consider the hypothetical example of a firm that selected an AI vendor based primarily on features and price. Six months later, they discovered the vendor was using client data to train models sold to other customers, creating potential confidentiality breaches across multiple clients.

## Creating Effective Vendor Management

Some organizations have developed sophisticated approaches to AI vendor assessment. One particularly effective framework examines vendors across multiple dimensions:

- **Technical capability:** Beyond basic functionality, how does the vendor handle data security, model training, and quality control?
- **Data architecture compatibility:** How well does the vendor's system align with the data readiness requirements, as outlined in Chapters 7 and 8? Can the vendor work effectively with your existing data governance

frameworks, or will implementation require compromising security and governance standards to accommodate vendor limitations?

- **Legal compliance:** What are the vendor's data handling practices? How do they address privacy regulations? What rights do they claim over uploaded content?
- **Business stability:** What's the vendor's financial position? What happens to your data if they're acquired or go out of business?
- **Risk management:** How does the vendor handle security incidents? What liability protections do they offer? How do they manage model drift and quality issues?

But due diligence doesn't stop at selection. Smart organizations create ongoing monitoring programs to ensure vendors maintain appropriate standards over time. This includes regular audits, performance reviews, and updates to security assessments.

Some international law firms developed comprehensive AI vendor management programs. Their approach combines detailed initial assessment with ongoing monitoring and governance. Key elements include:

- Specialized contract provisions addressing model training rights, data retention, and confidentiality.
- Regular security and compliance audits of key AI vendors.
- Clear procedures for handling vendor-related incidents or breaches.
- Executive-level oversight of critical AI vendor relationships.

They treat critical AI vendors as strategic partners rather than commodity providers. This required deeper engagement but delivered better risk management and performance outcomes.

## CONCLUSION

Managing legal and compliance risks in AI adoption requires a fundamental rethinking of traditional risk management approaches. The risks are real and significant, but they can be managed effectively with the right frameworks and protocols.

Success requires more than just updating existing policies; it demands creating new approaches that specifically address AI's unique challenges. Organizations that get this right will be positioned to leverage AI's benefits while protecting themselves and their clients from emerging risks.

The key is developing comprehensive, adaptable risk management frameworks that:

- Address current and emerging risks.
- Provide practical guidance for day-to-day operations.
- Support innovation while maintaining appropriate protections.
- Evolve as AI capabilities and regulations change.

As AI technology continues to advance, the organizations that thrive will be those that combine innovation with thoughtful risk management. By developing robust frameworks now, you position your organization to leverage AI's benefits while avoiding its pitfalls.

## ACTION ITEMS

1. **Implement Data Privacy and Security Controls**
   - Establish AI-specific data protection protocols
   - Create cross-border data transfer compliance frameworks
   - Implement technical safeguards for AI data processing
2. **Protect Client Confidentiality in AI Systems**
   - Design confidentiality safeguards for AI vendor relationships
   - Create information barriers preventing cross-client contamination
   - Establish incident response procedures for confidentiality breaches
3. **Establish Bias Detection and Mitigation**
   - Implement systematic bias testing protocols for AI outputs
   - Create bias monitoring and correction procedures
   - Design fairness assessment frameworks for AI decisions
4. **Ensure Regulatory Compliance**
   - Map applicable AI regulations across jurisdictions
   - Create compliance monitoring and reporting systems
   - Establish regulatory change tracking and adaptation processes
5. **Mitigate Malpractice and Insurance Risks**
   - Assess malpractice coverage for AI-related claims
   - Implement risk management protocols for AI use
   - Create documentation standards for AI oversight and validation
6. **Conduct Comprehensive Vendor Due Diligence**
   - Develop AI vendor risk assessment frameworks
   - Establish ongoing vendor security and compliance monitoring
   - Create vendor incident response and liability management procedures

# CHAPTER 7

# Creating Your AI Strategy

## INTRODUCTION

*The "implementation gap" isn't due to technology limitations but to inadequate strategic planning.*

Picture two large law firms, both deciding to implement AI tools in their practice. The first rushes to adopt the latest AI technology because competitors are using it. They buy several tools, announce their AI initiative to clients, and expect magic to happen. Six months later, they're dealing with underutilized tools, frustrated attorneys, and questioning clients.

The second firm takes a different approach. It starts by understanding its readiness for AI adoption. Then, it identifies specific problems AI could solve, builds clear business cases, and creates realistic implementation plans. A year later, it systematically expands its AI capabilities while delivering measurable value to clients.

The difference? Strategy. Survey after survey finds that at least three-quarters of legal professionals believe AI will have a high or transformational impact on their work within the next five years. However, a 2024 study revealed that while AI adoption in the legal sector surged from 19% to 79% in just one year, a minority of legal departments foresee generative AI being truly transformative.[1] There is a gap between the widespread use of AI tools and their truly transformative impact on legal practice. The Clio report highlighted that many firms were still struggling with how to effectively implement, integrate, and realize the full value of AI, especially generative AI.

[1] Clio, Legal Trends Report 2024 (2024), https://www.clio.com/resources/legal-trends/2024-report/.

The "implementation gap" isn't due to technology limitations but to inadequate strategic planning. Most studies find that legal organizations with documented AI strategies are more likely to report successful implementations than those without strategic frameworks.

In the rush to adopt AI, some legal organizations skip the crucial step of developing a comprehensive strategy. They treat AI adoption as a technology project rather than a fundamental transformation of how legal work gets done. The results are predictable: wasted resources, missed opportunities, and increased risks.

This chapter will explain how to develop a successful AI strategy. We'll explore how to assess your organization's readiness, identify the right opportunities, build compelling business cases, set achievable goals, and manage the change that AI inevitably brings. Most importantly, we'll focus on practical approaches that work in the real world of legal practice.

## ASSESSING ORGANIZATIONAL READINESS

### Beyond the Technology Checklist

When most organizations assess their AI readiness, they focus on technical capabilities: Do we have the right infrastructure? Do we have data scientists? Can we afford the tools? While these technical questions are essential foundation elements, a comprehensive readiness assessment must go beyond them. While technical capabilities provide the foundation for AI implementation, cultural readiness often determines whether that implementation will deliver sustained value. Both dimensions are critical—technical readiness enables implementation while cultural readiness ensures adoption and value realization.

Consider this scenario as an example of what can go wrong. The global law firm planning to implement AI tools had the budget, the technology team, and the infrastructure. What they didn't have was a culture ready to embrace AI-enabled change. Their first major AI initiative failed not because of technology but because their attorneys didn't trust the tools and weren't prepared to change how they worked.

### The Cost of Strategic Failure: A Case Study

A mid-sized law firm's AI implementation serves as a cautionary example of strategic planning failures. The firm invested over $500,000 in AI contract analysis technology without proper readiness assessment or strategic alignment.

The implementation encountered multiple challenges:

- Incompatible document management systems required extensive manual preparation.
- Partner resistance emerged when the system changed established review practices.
- Inconsistent metadata made AI analysis unreliable without significant human oversight.
- Training costs exceeded initial estimates by 300%.

After six months, the firm abandoned the implementation, having achieved only 15% of anticipated efficiency gains while creating significant internal friction. Post-implementation analysis revealed that a proper readiness assessment would have identified these barriers early, allowing for appropriate preparation before technology deployment.

This example illustrates how even promising AI technology can fail without a proper strategic foundation.

## The Measures of Readiness

Smart organizations will evaluate AI readiness across multiple dimensions. A practical approach is to use a five-pillar AI readiness framework that assesses these crucial areas:

1. Cultural Readiness
   How open is your organization to change, and do your people trust technology? Are they willing to learn new ways of working? Different practice groups may have vastly different attitudes toward AI adoption. Understanding these differences helps you tailor your approach to each group and foster a supportive environment for change.
2. Process Maturity
   Do you have well-defined, documented processes that could benefit from AI? Can you clearly articulate how work gets done now? Organizations with mature processes find it much easier to identify AI opportunities and implement solutions effectively.
3. Data Readiness
   Data is the foundation of AI success, yet legal organizations often face unique challenges due to diverse and inconsistently organized data. Assess these elements of data readiness:

- **Data accessibility:** Can systems securely access needed data? Establishing secure data pipelines between document management systems and AI platforms is often necessary.
- **Data architecture and integration:** Evaluate how effectively your current data infrastructure supports AI workloads across organizational silos. Most legal organizations discover that their data exists in dozens of disconnected systems, each optimized for specific functions but lacking integration capabilities that AI systems require.
- **Semantic context and relationships:** Assess the availability of semantic models and ontologies that provide meaning to your data. Legal knowledge operates through complex conceptual relationships—how regulatory changes connect to client risks, how matter types relate to resource requirements, how precedents inform current strategies. AI systems require explicit semantic frameworks to understand these relationships.
- **Data quality and completeness:** Analyze data accuracy, consistency, and completeness for AI model development. This includes standardizing metadata schemas, implementing consistent tagging protocols, and establishing automated validation processes that maintain data integrity at scale.
- **Data governance and ethics:** Review frameworks for ensuring data compliance, privacy, and ethical use in AI applications. This includes data classification systems, access controls, retention policies, and lineage tracking that enables transparency and accountability.
- **AI pipeline readiness:** Evaluate data preparation pipelines, automation capabilities, and data transformation processes. Most legal organizations need sophisticated data preparation capabilities that clean, enrich, and contextualize information before AI analysis.
- **Data sovereignty and security:** Assess your ability to maintain complete control over sensitive data while enabling AI capabilities. This includes secure data processing environments, vendor data policies, and technical safeguards that keep confidential information within your control.

Organizations discovering significant data readiness gaps should treat data infrastructure development as a prerequisite investment rather than a parallel activity. Organizations that invest in specialized data management platforms and tools can better identify inconsistencies, standardize formats, and create appropriate training datasets for AI systems.

4. Skills Base
   Does your team have the right mix of skills? Success often depends on having people who can bridge the gap between legal practice and technology. The most effective organizations nurture "bridge builders": lawyers with a strong interest in technology or technologists who understand legal workflows.
5. Governance Capability
   Can you effectively oversee AI systems? Do you have frameworks for managing risks and ensuring ethical use? Building governance capabilities early—including risk management, ethical guidelines, and regular audits—positions organizations for safer and more successful AI adoption.

   This five-pillar framework draws on widely accepted industry best practices for AI readiness, ensuring your organization is well-prepared for responsible and effective AI integration.

## CONDUCTING AN EFFECTIVE ASSESSMENT

Leading organizations approach readiness assessment as a structured process, not a one-time checklist. One particularly effective approach is to apply "readiness sprints"—focused two-week periods where you deeply examine one aspect of readiness.

This type of sprint process involves:

Week one: Data gathering through surveys, interviews, and process analysis.
Week two: Assessment, gap analysis, and action planning.

You can repeat these sprints for each readiness dimension, building a comprehensive picture of your AI preparation needs.

### From Assessment to Action

The value of an effective AI readiness assessment is enhanced by connecting it directly to action. When you identify gaps, create specific plans to address them. You should create a "readiness road map" that maps out exactly what your firm or department needs to do to prepare for AI adoption across each dimension. The road map should include specific initiatives like:

- **Cultural preparation:** A series of AI awareness sessions and hands-on demonstrations to build trust and understanding.
- **Process documentation:** A systematic effort to document and standardize key processes before introducing AI.

- **Data cleanup:** A focused project to organize and standardize your document management system.
- **Skills development:** A training program that combines technical skills with practical application in legal work.

Most importantly, you must treat these preparation activities as essential investments, not as "overhead." Recognize that building readiness is as important as the eventual AI implementation.

## THE DATA EXCELLENCE FRAMEWORK: A STRATEGIC APPROACH

Beyond basic data readiness, you should implement what we call a "data excellence framework"—a comprehensive methodology that transforms raw enterprise data into AI-ready information assets. We propose this framework; it aligns with core data-governance tenets (quality, lineage, semantics) while adding legal-specific structure. This framework addresses three critical transformation requirements:

### Enterprise Knowledge Model Development

Create semantic frameworks that bridge business and technical perspectives on data. For legal organizations, this means developing ontologies that capture how legal concepts, matter types, client relationships, and regulatory requirements interconnect. Rather than treating documents as isolated files, knowledge models preserve the contextual relationships that make information valuable.

### Intelligent Data Agent Implementation

Deploy specialized AI components that automate data preparation, cleaning, enrichment, and monitoring. These autonomous agents form an intelligent workforce that scales beyond manual capabilities, continuously improving data quality while embedding governance and compliance requirements into automated processes.

### Data Tokenization Strategy

Transform raw data into standardized, modular "data tokens" that enable three critical advantages: (1) acceleration through eliminated data preparation bottlenecks, (2) governance by design through embedded compliance and lineage tracking, and (3) complete data sovereignty by keeping sensitive information entirely within secure environments.

This framework enables legal organizations to move beyond traditional data management approaches—focused primarily on storage and access—toward semantic intelligence systems that understand context, relationships, and meaning.

**What "AI-ready Data" Really Means in Law (four non-negotiables)**

1. **Semantics, not just storage** Adopt/align to a legal ontology (e.g., matter type, issue, cause of action, forum, authority, clause function). This closes the "semantic gap" by making legal reasoning structures explicit for machines.
2. **Provenance & citation-binding** Every AI answer must trace back to sources with citations, versions, and dates. In legal domains, explainability is inseparable from admissibility and professional duty.
3. **Temporal and jurisdictional versioning** Laws, regulations, policies, and templates evolve. Models and retrieval pipelines need time-aware and locale-aware indexing.
4. **Privilege-aware governance** Confidentiality, legal hold, ethical walls, retention, data minimization, and cross-border transfer rules should be enforced at query time and training time—not documented only in manuals.

# IDENTIFYING PRIORITY USE CASES

## Finding the Right Starting Point

One of the biggest mistakes legal organizations make with AI is trying to do too much too soon. They see dozens of potential applications and want to tackle them all. The result? Resources are spread too thin, implementation teams are overwhelmed, and results don't meet expectations.

Consider this scenario about a regional law firm. Their initial AI strategy identified 15 different use cases, all labeled "high priority." Six months into implementation, they had made minimal progress on all of them but hadn't fully succeeded with any. The lesson? Success with AI requires focus and prioritization.

## Systematic Use Case Prioritization: A Framework

Employ a structured framework for AI use case selection. There are publicly available resources that discuss AI implementation and prioritization in legal organizations that you can draw on. For instance, the Liquid Legal Institute's First Global Report on the State of Artificial Intelligence in Legal Practice (2023) provides insights into how law firms are adopting AI technologies and prioritizing use cases.[2] This report includes survey results from over 200 law firms globally, as well as references to numerous academic studies and articles, offering a useful view of AI integration in legal practice as of 2023. While we know that adoption has exploded since this report was issued, and at the time of this writing, Liquid Legal Institute is preparing its second global report with input from 1,000 law firms, the 2023 report provides valuable information for developing a framework for AI use case selection and prioritization.

Your use case assessment methodology might examine potential AI applications across multiple dimensions:

### *Impact Dimensions*

- Financial impact: Direct revenue increase or cost reduction
- Client value: Enhanced service quality or delivery
- Strategic alignment: Contribution to organizational goals
- Scale potential: Applicability across practice areas

### *Effort Dimensions*

- Technical complexity: Required technology capabilities
- Process change: Workflow modifications needed
- Integration requirements: Connections with existing systems
- Skills gap: New capabilities required

### *Risk Dimensions*

- Implementation risk: Likelihood of project challenges
- Adoption risk: Potential resistance or acceptance issues
- Ethical risk: Professional responsibility considerations
- Regulatory risk: Compliance implications

This framework can produce a comprehensive evaluation that balances multiple factors rather than focusing solely on ROI or technical feasibility. Done well, the framework should prevent organizations from pursuing a technology-first implementation.

---

[2] Liquid Legal Inst., First Global Report on the State of Artificial Intelligence in Legal Practice (2023), https://liquid-legal-institute.com/wp-content/uploads/2024/03/E-Book-First-Global-Report-on-AI-in-Legal-Practice.pdf.

## The Art of Use Case Selection

It is important to approach use case selection systematically. We suggest using a framework like one we call "Impact vs. Effort vs. Risk" analysis. For each potential AI application, you evaluate:

- **Impact:** How much value would successful implementation create? This includes both quantitative measures like time savings and qualitative benefits like improved accuracy or reduced risk.
- **Effort:** How difficult would implementation be? This considers technical complexity, process changes required, and resources needed.
- **Risk:** What could go wrong? This examines both implementation risks and ongoing operational risks.

But go beyond simple scoring. Look for use cases that can create early wins and build momentum. These "lighthouse projects" share certain characteristics:

- **Clear problem definition:** There's a specific, well-understood problem to solve.
- **Measurable outcomes:** Success can be clearly defined and measured.
- **Manageable scope:** The project can be completed in a reasonable timeframe.
- **Limited risk:** Initial failure wouldn't create significant problems.

## Making Selection Work

One approach to use case selection offers valuable lessons. You can create what some call "AI opportunity workshops"—structured sessions where practice groups identify and evaluate potential AI applications.

The workshops follow a specific format such as:

First hour: Problem identification. What challenges could AI help solve?
Second hour: Impact analysis. How valuable would solutions be?
Third hour: Implementation assessment should answer the question: What will it take to succeed?

But here's the crucial part: Don't try to evaluate everything at once. Each workshop should focus on a specific practice area or function. This focused approach helps you identify opportunities you might miss in a broader analysis.

## DATA STRATEGY AS COMPETITIVE DIFFERENTIATION

As AI capabilities become commoditized, sustainable competitive advantage increasingly depends on data readiness rather than technology selection. Organizations with well-structured, semantically rich, and consistently maintained data assets extract significantly more value from AI investments than competitors using identical technology against unprepared data.

This creates what data strategists call "data network effects"—organizations with superior data infrastructure see compounding returns from AI investments, while those with poor data preparation experience diminishing returns regardless of technology spending. Consider two law firms implementing identical contract analysis AI systems:

**Firm A** has invested in semantic data modeling, consistent metadata standards, and intelligent data preparation. Their AI system immediately understands contract relationships, identifies subtle risk patterns, and provides contextual insights that enhance attorney decision-making.

**Firm B** deploys the same technology against fragmented document collections with inconsistent formatting and missing metadata. Their AI system struggles to provide reliable insights, requires extensive manual correction, and fails to deliver promised efficiency gains.

The difference isn't technological—it's foundational data management that determines AI success.

### Strategic Data Investment Priorities

Forward-thinking legal organizations recognize that data architecture represents a strategic asset requiring dedicated investment and expertise. Priority areas include:

- **Unified information architecture** that maintains data relationships across all systems while preserving existing workflow efficiencies.
- **Semantic relationship mapping** that captures how legal concepts, precedents, and strategies interconnect.
- **Automated data quality monitoring** that ensures consistency and reliability without manual overhead.
- **Contextual data enrichment** that preserves decision-making context and circumstances.
- **Privacy-preserving analytics** that enables sophisticated analysis while maintaining confidentiality requirements.

# BUILDING THE BUSINESS CASE

## Beyond ROI Calculations

Traditional return-on-investment (ROI) calculations remain an essential foundation for technology investment decisions, but successful AI implementations require a more comprehensive value framework. One legal department discovered this when their initial business case for an AI contract analysis tool focused solely on time savings. While these efficiency gains created a positive ROI, the broader value emerged in dimensions that traditional calculations often overlook.

This experience highlights an important principle: **Effective AI business cases bridge immediate financial returns with long-term value creation through improved client service.** The most compelling business cases demonstrate how initial efficiency gains directly enable enhanced client experiences that drive future profitability.

Consider developing a multidimensional value assessment that includes:

### *Quantifiable Financial Returns*

- Direct cost and time savings
- Resource allocation optimization
- Matter profitability improvements
- Billing realization enhancements

### *Client Experience Value*

- Faster response times
- More consistent and accurate deliverables
- Deeper analytical insights
- Greater transparency into processes and progress

### *Strategic Value Drivers*

- Competitive differentiation in service delivery
- Enhanced talent attraction and retention
- New service capabilities and offerings
- Risk reduction and quality improvements

The connection between these dimensions is crucial. For example, when document analysis time decreases by 60% (financial return), attorneys can provide faster turnaround times (client experience) while delivering more comprehensive analysis (strategic differentiation)—ultimately driving client retention and premium positioning that enhance long-term profitability.

When building your business case, articulate this value chain from efficiency to client experience to strategic advantage. This approach satisfies financial stakeholders' need for ROI while demonstrating how that ROI serves as a foundation for client-centered innovation rather than merely cost reduction.

## The Data Infrastructure ROI Model

Building comprehensive business cases for AI requires understanding how data infrastructure investments create compound value over time. Unlike traditional technology purchases with linear ROI calculations, data readiness investments generate expanding returns through multiple mechanisms:

- **Accelerated implementation:** Organizations with AI-ready data infrastructure can deploy new AI capabilities much faster than those requiring extensive data preparation for each initiative. This acceleration advantage compounds as AI technology continues advancing rapidly.
- **Cross-initiative leverage:** Well-structured data enables multiple AI applications from a single infrastructure investment. Document analysis capabilities that support contract review can simultaneously enable matter prediction, resource allocation, and knowledge management applications.
- **Quality amplification:** Superior data preparation dramatically improves AI accuracy and reliability, reducing manual correction time while increasing stakeholder confidence. Data quality improvements often create greater value than AI algorithm enhancements.
- **Innovation enablement:** Semantic data frameworks enable sophisticated analytics and insights that would be impossible with traditional data storage approaches. This includes predictive matter analytics, automated compliance monitoring, and strategic market intelligence.

When building business cases, demonstrate how initial data infrastructure investments serve as foundations for multiple future AI initiatives rather than single-use technology costs.

## Creating Compelling Cases

Leading organizations take a more comprehensive approach to AI business cases. One particularly effective framework examines value across four dimensions:

- **Efficiency value:** Direct cost and time savings
- **Risk value:** Reduced errors and enhanced compliance

- **Strategic value:** Competitive advantage and market positioning
- **Innovation value:** New service capabilities and client benefits

But don't stop at identifying value. Build cases that address specific stakeholder concerns. For partners, focus on profitability and market position. For associates, emphasize quality of work life and professional development. For clients, highlight service improvements and cost benefits.

### Making the Case Real

Smart organizations support their business cases with pilot projects and proof of concept. Before fully committing to any AI tool, run a structured pilot that:

- Tests the tool in real work situations.
- Measures actual results against projections.
- Identifies implementation challenges.
- Validates key assumptions.

This approach helps to build business cases based on real experience rather than vendor promises.

## MEASURING SUCCESS: METRICS AND KPIS FOR AI STRATEGY

Effective AI strategies require clear success metrics that go beyond traditional technology implementation measures. Leading legal organizations develop comprehensive measurement frameworks that evaluate progress across multiple dimensions.

We must emphasize the importance of tracking metrics beyond traditional ROI, including efficiency, quality, adoption, and innovation, to fully capture the impact of AI initiatives in legal practice.

A balanced scorecard approach for an AI strategy might track four categories of metrics:

#### *Efficiency Metrics Measure Operational Improvements*

- Time reduction for specific tasks
- Cost per matter or transaction
- Resource utilization rates
- Process cycle time reduction

### *Quality Metrics Evaluate Service Enhancement*

- Error reduction rates
- Consistency improvements
- Depth of analysis
- Client satisfaction scores

### *Adoption Metrics Track Organizational Uptake*

- User engagement rates
- Cross-practice utilization
- Frequency of use
- Proficiency development

### *Innovation Metrics Assess Strategic Advancement*

- New service capabilities
- Market differentiation
- Client acquisition impact
- Competitive positioning

Your metrics framework should maintain the focus on business outcomes rather than technology implementation. Balanced measurement prevents the common problem of achieving technical success but without achieving the desired business impact.

For each AI initiative, establish baseline measurements before implementation, set specific targets, and track progress. This measurement discipline will help achieve a high level of success.

Also, be willing to refine your metrics as implementations mature. While initial metrics might focus on adoption and efficiency, you should later evolve to measure improvements in quality and market differentiation.

## DATA-DRIVEN IMPLEMENTATION PLANNING

Successful AI strategy requires implementation planning that acknowledges data preparation as the critical path activity. Organizations that treat data readiness as a parallel activity rather than a prerequisite are likely to experience delays, quality issues, frustration, and disappointing results.

## PHASED DATA DEVELOPMENT APPROACH

### *Phase 1: Data Foundation Assessment and Architecture Design*

- Comprehensive data audit across all organizational systems
- Ontological relationship mapping for priority use cases

- Data quality and consistency analysis
- Privacy and security framework establishment
- Unified architecture design with integration specifications

***Phase 2: Core Infrastructure Implementation***

- Data preparation pipeline development
- Intelligent agent deployment for automated data processing
- Quality monitoring and governance system implementation
- Initial semantic model development and testing
- Integration with priority business systems

***Phase 3: AI-Ready Data Deployment***

- Full data tokenization implementation
- Advanced analytics capability activation
- Cross-system integration completion
- Performance monitoring and optimization
- Organizational data literacy development

***Phase 4: Continuous Evolution and Enhancement***

- Adaptive learning system activation
- Advanced semantic model deployment
- Cross-organizational knowledge sharing enablement
- Emerging technology integration preparation
- Strategic data capability expansion

This phased approach ensures that each AI initiative builds upon solid data foundations rather than requiring extensive preparation for individual implementations.

## SETTING REALISTIC GOALS AND TIMELINES

### Avoiding the Hype Trap

AI vendor presentations can make implementation seem deceptively simple. Keep in mind that the demos show you the destination but not the journey. Setting realistic goals requires understanding both what AI can achieve and what it takes to get there.

### Creating Achievable Plans

Successful organizations typically follow a staged approach to AI implementation. Starting with pilot programs and gradually expanding can be a good model for setting achievable goals and timelines. Iterative development and continuous learning are important to successful AI adoption.

One effective model divides implementation into four phases:

- **Foundation phase:** Building basic capabilities and addressing readiness gaps while testing solutions in controlled environments.
- **Pilot/validation phase:** Testing solutions in a limited, controlled environment to validate effectiveness, measure impact, and gather feedback before broader rollout. This phase is critical for risk mitigation and learning.
- **Expansion phase:** Rolling out successful pilots to broader use.
- **Optimization phase:** Refining, integrating, and enhancing AI solutions for maximum impact and sustainability.

Each phase has its own goals and success metrics. The key is making these goals specific and achievable while maintaining momentum toward larger objectives.

### Timeline Development

Smart organizations build timelines that reflect real-world challenges. We recommend creating what we call "accordion timelines"—plans that can expand or contract based on progress and learning.

The timeline development process considers:

- Team capacity and competing priorities.
- Training and adoption requirements.
- Technical integration needs.
- Change management activities.

Most importantly, you must allow ample time for learning and adjustment. With AI, the unexpected isn't just possible—it's probable.

## STRATEGIC VENDOR SELECTION AND MANAGEMENT

AI implementation requires careful vendor selection and ongoing management. Unlike traditional technology procurement, AI partnerships often involve significant co-development and evolution over time. Develop a comprehensive vendor strategy. Evaluate vendors on current capabilities and innovation capabilities. Consider questions such as:

- **Strategic alignment:** How well does the vendor's road map align with your strategic priorities? Vendors should demonstrate an understanding of legal-specific challenges and a clear vision for addressing them.

- **Deployment approach:** What implementation methodology does the vendor employ? The most successful implementations typically follow agile approaches with frequent iteration and adaptive planning rather than rigid waterfall methodologies.
- **Data practices:** How does the vendor handle data and confidentiality? Given the sensitive nature of legal information, vendors must demonstrate robust security practices, clear data policies, and appropriate confidentiality protections.
- **Partnership potential:** Can the vendor grow with your organization? The most valuable relationships involve co-development opportunities where vendors adapt solutions to your specific needs and incorporate your feedback into product evolution.

We have seen firms take this a step further with a structured vendor tiering process. Some have classified vendors into categories:

- **Strategic partners** receive significant investment and deep integration.
- **Solution providers** deliver specific capabilities with standard implementation.
- **Experimental vendors** undergo limited pilots to evaluate emerging technologies.

This approach helps to balance innovation with practical implementation. You can maintain relationships across all three tiers but concentrate resources on vendors that deliver the most value.

## ORGANIZATIONAL STRUCTURES FOR AI INNOVATION

How legal organizations structure their AI capabilities significantly impacts implementation success. Different structural approaches offer distinct advantages and challenges.

We have observed three primary organizational models for AI implementation in legal organizations:

- **Centralized innovation:** This model establishes a dedicated innovation team responsible for AI strategy, implementation, and management across the organization. This approach provides a center of excellence for all technology innovation. Advantages include specialized expertise, consistent implementation, and efficient resource utilization. Challenges include potential disconnection from practice needs and adoption resistance.

- **Distributed capability:** This model embeds AI specialists within practice groups or departments. We have seen this approach include "innovation ambassadors" within each practice area who combine legal expertise with technical knowledge. Advantages include close alignment with individual practice needs, stronger adoption, and practical implementation. Challenges include the risk of fragmentation, inconsistent standards, and resource duplication.
- **Hybrid structure:** Combining a central innovation function with embedded capabilities in practice groups has proven highly effective for some mid-size and large legal organizations, provided there is strong coordination and communication. A&O Shearman exemplifies this model: The firm maintains a centralized innovation team and technology incubator, while also rolling out advanced AI tools across specific legal practices. This approach enables the firm to balance specialized expertise, firm-wide strategy, and practical, domain-specific implementation, facilitating effective and scalable AI adoption.

Recent analyses confirm that hybrid models in the legal and compliance sectors leverage the strengths of both AI-driven automation and human legal expertise. AI algorithms handle large-scale data analysis, contract review, and regulatory research, while human professionals interpret AI-generated insights, make legal judgments, and ensure alignment with ethical and regulatory standards. Continuous feedback loops between technical and legal teams further optimize both AI performance and risk management.

The optimal organizational structure depends on organizational size, culture, and strategic objectives. Smaller organizations often succeed by leveraging external expertise rather than building internal capabilities, while global firms typically require more complex hybrid approaches.

Regardless of structure, successful organizations establish clear governance mechanisms that connect technical implementation with practice leadership. This governance should include:

- Executive sponsorship from practice leadership.
- Clear decision-making authorities for AI initiatives.
- Documented evaluation criteria for potential projects.
- Regular reporting on outcomes and impacts.
- Mechanisms for practice-driven prioritization.

# CHANGE MANAGEMENT CONSIDERATIONS

## The Human Side of AI

Technology implementation is relatively straightforward. Changing how people work is the real challenge. One firm learned this lesson the hard way when their AI document review tool sat largely unused despite proven benefits. The problem? They hadn't effectively addressed their attorneys' concerns about reliability and professional responsibility.

## Beyond Change Management: Cultural Transformation for AI Success

Successful AI implementation requires more than technical change management—it demands cultural transformation that reshapes how legal professionals think about their work. Organizations achieving the greatest success with AI focus on cultural evolution alongside technology implementation.

A large firm known for its "traditional" approach to legal practice (think typically slow to change) successfully implemented AI tools by focusing primarily on cultural alignment rather than technology enthusiasm. They positioned AI not as disruption but as an enhancement to continue exceptional legal services. This approach includes several key elements:

- **Values-based positioning:** It frames AI adoption in terms of a firm's existing values, such as excellence, client service, and intellectual rigor, rather than technology benefits alone. This positioning resonated with partners who might have resisted innovation for innovation's sake.
- **Practice-led governance:** It establishes an AI oversight group led by practicing attorneys rather than the technologists. This ensures that implementation decisions reflect practice realities and professional judgment.
- **Experiential learning:** Rather than traditional training, there are opportunities for attorneys to experience AI firsthand through well-designed proofs-of-concepts or pilot projects. This experiential approach can build authentic enthusiasm based on practical benefits.
- **Professional identity evolution:** It is important to address how AI might change professional identity, emphasizing that technology will enhance rather than diminish the lawyer's role. This directly confronts underlying anxieties that often drive resistance.

Cultural transformation is typically more challenging than technology implementation. But by shaping how attorneys think about AI's role in their practice, you can overcome resistance and create sustainable adoption and achievement of tangible value.

### Building Acceptance

Leading organizations approach AI change management systematically. One particularly effective framework addresses change across three levels:

1. Individual level: Helping each person understand how AI affects their work
2. Team level: Adapting team processes and workflows
3. Organizational level: Evolving culture and practices

But you should also go beyond frameworks to create specific programs that build acceptance and adoption. By establishing an "AI Champions" program, you can identify influential attorneys who are enthusiastic about AI and support them in becoming internal advocates and mentors.

### Managing Resistance

Recognize that resistance to AI is often rooted in legitimate concerns. One approach to resistance management is to create what we call "AI concern conversations"—regular forums where attorneys can raise concerns and work together to find solutions.

This process includes open discussion of concerns, collaborative solution development, regular progress reviews, and ongoing feedback collection. This approach helps to address resistance productively while building trust in AI adoption.

## NAVIGATING THE "MIDDLE MILE" OF AI IMPLEMENTATION

While most organizations focus on initial implementation challenges and long-term transformation, many AI initiatives falter in what we might call the "middle mile"—the period after successful pilots but before enterprise-wide integration.

This critical phase presents unique challenges:

## Scaling Beyond Early Adopters

Initial AI implementations often succeed with enthusiastic early adopters. The middle mile requires engaging more skeptical users who may have higher expectations and less tolerance for imperfection. Successful organizations address this through:

- Targeted adoption programs addressing specific user concerns.
- Enhanced training focused on practical application rather than technical capabilities.
- Peer success stories highlighting real-world benefits.
- Practice-specific adaptations that address unique workflow needs.

## Integration and Workflow Evolution

As AI usage expands, integration with existing systems becomes increasingly important. Organizations must move beyond standalone applications to create seamless workflows. This requires:

- Process redesign that fundamentally rethinks how work gets done.
- System integration connecting AI tools with document management, billing, and matter management.
- Standardized handoffs between human and AI components.
- Clear protocols for exception handling and escalation.

## Performance Monitoring and Improvement

The middle mile is where meaningful performance data becomes available, enabling systematic improvement. Leading organizations implement:

- Usage analytics tracking adoption patterns and identifying barriers.
- Quality monitoring systems measuring accuracy and consistency.
- Feedback mechanisms capturing user experiences and suggestions.
- Continuous improvement processes that systematically address identified issues.

Organizations that successfully navigate this middle mile emerge with AI capabilities that are deeply integrated into their practice rather than merely appended to existing processes.

## CONCLUSION

Developing an effective AI strategy isn't just about selecting technology, it's about creating a framework for transformation. Success requires careful attention to readiness, thoughtful prioritization, compelling business cases, realistic planning, and comprehensive change management.

Organizations that get this right will be positioned to leverage AI's benefits while managing its risks. The key is approaching AI strategy development systematically while remaining flexible enough to adapt as technology and needs evolve.

AI implementation in legal practice is not simply about technology adoption; it's about strategic transformation that aligns technology capabilities with organizational goals and professional values. The most successful organizations approach this transformation with discipline and vision, creating strategies that balance innovation with practical execution.

As you develop your AI strategy, remember that technology is merely an enabler. The true value comes from how it transforms your capabilities, enhances your service delivery, and strengthens your competitive position. By using the frameworks and approaches outlined in this chapter, you can create an AI strategy that delivers meaningful, sustainable value.

## ACTION ITEMS

1. **Assess Data Readiness**
    - Evaluate how effectively your current data infrastructure supports AI workloads across organizational silos.
    - Assess the availability of semantic models and ontologies that provide meaning to your data.
    - Assess data quality and completeness.
    - Assess existing frameworks for ensuring data compliance, privacy, and ethical use in AI applications.
    - Evaluate data preparation pipelines, automation capabilities, and data transformation processes.
    - Assess data sovereignty and security processes and controls.
2. **Assess Organizational AI Readiness**
    - Evaluate cultural, process, and skills readiness for AI adoption.
    - Identify readiness gaps and prepare improvement road map.
    - Assess governance capabilities for AI oversight.

3. **Identify and Prioritize AI Use Cases**
   - Conduct systematic use case identification across practice areas.
   - Apply impact vs. effort vs. risk analysis for prioritization.
   - Select lighthouse projects for initial implementation.
4. **Build Strategic Business Cases**
   - Develop multidimensional value assessments for priority AI initiatives.
   - Create ROI models incorporating efficiency, quality, and strategic benefits.
   - Design pilot programs to validate business case assumptions.
5. **Establish Strategic Success Metrics**
   - Define balanced scorecard approach measuring efficiency, quality, adoption, and innovation.
   - Create baseline measurements and target setting procedures.
   - Design measurement frameworks that evolve with AI maturity.
6. **Design Organizational Structure for AI Innovation**
   - Choose optimal organizational model (centralized, distributed, or hybrid).
   - Establish AI governance and decision-making authorities.
   - Create innovation ecosystems supporting continuous AI evolution.
7. **Develop Strategic Vendor Relationships**
   - Create vendor evaluation framework emphasizing strategic alignment.
   - Establish tiered vendor management approach (strategic partners vs. solution providers).
   - Design co-development and innovation partnership strategies.

CHAPTER 8

# AI Technology Selection and Implementation

## INTRODUCTION

*While traditional software operates on data, AI systems learn from data, making data quality, availability, and governance the primary determinants of AI success.*

Imagine spending six months and hundreds of thousands of dollars implementing an AI system, only to discover it can't integrate with your document management system. Or worse, finding out after deployment that it creates security vulnerabilities your IT team can't address. These aren't hypothetical scenarios. These are real stories from organizations that did their AI implementations without a thorough selection and implementation process.

The market for legal AI tools is expanding rapidly, with vendors promising everything from automated document review to predictive analytics. But here's the reality: Choosing and implementing the right AI technology for your organization is fundamentally different from selecting traditional legal software. With traditional software, you're evaluating fixed functionality based on defined features. With AI systems, you're assessing adaptable capabilities that will perform differently depending on your data, your specific use cases, and how the system evolves over time.

This fundamental difference makes AI selection more complex and consequential. You're not just buying a tool with predetermined outputs. You are selecting a system that will learn from your organization's data and evolve with your practice. Some capabilities may not exist at purchase but will develop as the system learns from your data. Conversely, impressive demo capabilities may underperform when applied to your specific documents and workflows if your data differs significantly from the vendor's training sets.

In this chapter, we explore how to navigate these complexities to make technology selections that set your organization up for success. We discuss how to evaluate AI capabilities rather than just features, how to integrate AI tools effectively with your existing systems, how to use pilot programs to validate real-world performance, and how to ensure your data infrastructure supports your AI initiatives. Most importantly, we focus on practical approaches that reflect the current reality of legal AI implementation.

## UNDERSTANDING THE AI TECHNOLOGY LANDSCAPE

Before evaluating specific AI solutions, you need to understand the landscape of AI technologies and how they apply to legal practice. This understanding helps you seek answers to important questions during the evaluation process.

As discussed in the earlier chapters of this book, the legal AI landscape includes several categories of technologies:

- **Machine learning (ML) systems** learn patterns from examples without explicit programming. In legal applications, supervised ML typically powers document classification, predictive coding in e-discovery, and contract analysis. These systems require substantial high-quality training data labeled by subject matter experts.
- **Natural language processing (NLP)** enables machines to understand, interpret, and generate human language. Legal-specific NLP powers contract analysis, document summarization, and legal research tools. The quality of NLP varies significantly based on training data relevance to legal language.
- **Large language models (LLMs)** represent the latest evolution in NLP, capable of sophisticated text generation and analysis across domains. While powerful, early versions of these general-purpose models lacked the specialized knowledge and precision required for high-stakes legal work without additional fine-tuning or retrieval augmentation. However, they have continued to improve at an exponential pace.
- **Expert systems** encode domain-specific rules and reasoning to automate decision-making in narrowly defined areas. These systems excel in compliance workflows, eligibility assessments, and structured legal analysis but require explicit rule creation rather than learning from data.

- **Hybrid systems** combine multiple AI approaches, such as ML-powered document analysis augmented by rule-based validation. Many sophisticated legal AI tools use hybrid approaches to balance flexibility with reliability.

Each technology type has distinct implications for data requirements, integration complexity, and governance needs. For example, supervised ML systems typically require more labeled training data but offer more predictable outputs than generative LLMs, which can be more flexible but unpredictable and less explainable, and potentially less precise for specialized legal tasks.

Unfortunately, legal organizations often select AI technologies that don't align with their actual use cases, leading to implementation failures. Understanding the underlying technologies helps legal organizations make more informed selection decisions.

## EVALUATING AI SOLUTIONS

### Beyond the Sales Pitch

If you've started looking at AI tools for your organization, you've probably sat through numerous vendor presentations. Most look impressive in demos. They promise revolutionary capabilities. They can seem easy to implement. But the distance between the demo and reality can be vast.

Consider this scenario: A large corporate legal department selects an AI contract analysis tool based primarily on impressive demonstrations and aggressive vendor promises. Six months into implementation, they discover the tool cannot handle their most common document formats without extensive pre-processing. The vendor's response? "That wasn't part of the demo scenario."

Analysts and buyers report that demo scenarios often reflect idealized conditions that don't match real-world deployments, so it is important to test with your actual documents and use cases.

### Building a Systematic Evaluation Process

To succeed, you must approach AI technology evaluation as a structured process, not a series of product demonstrations. You could use a structured approach and questions, such as what we outline in the "AI Technology Evaluation Framework" section that follows, to examine potential solutions across five key dimensions.

# AN AI TECHNOLOGY EVALUATION FRAMEWORK

## Threshold Issues

- **Technical capabilities:** This goes beyond reviewing feature lists to examine how the tool actually works. What types of AI does it use? How was it trained? What are its limitations? You should create specific test scenarios based on your actual needs rather than relying on vendor demo scenarios.
- **Data handling:** How does the tool handle data? Where is data stored? What rights does the vendor claim over uploaded content? What happens to data used for model training? You may need to ensure that your AI vendor's terms of service do not grant them rights to use your uploaded documents for model training, which could create serious client confidentiality issues.
- **Integration capabilities:** Can the tool work with your existing systems? What application programming interfaces (APIs) are available? What customization is possible? If you skip detailed integration analysis you may find yourself with powerful tools your organization can't use effectively.
- **Security and compliance:** What security measures are in place? How does the tool handle sensitive data? Can it meet your regulatory requirements? You should involve your security teams early in the evaluation process to assess these aspects.
- **Vendor stability:** What is the vendor's financial position? What is their track record? How do they handle support and updates? In today's rapidly evolving legal AI market, vendor stability is crucial, and you simply must ensure you have a realistic evaluation of any vendor you are considering.
- **Trust & standards alignment:** Ask vendors how they map to **NIST's Generative AI Profile** and whether they operate an **ISO/IEC 42001**–aligned AI management system. Request artifacts (risk register, evaluation results, update logs) you can audit during pilots.

## AI-Specific Evaluation Criteria

Evaluating AI solutions requires assessment criteria that go beyond traditional software evaluation. While factors like user interface, support, and cost remain important, AI solutions demand additional considerations.

## Training and Learning Capabilities

Understanding how an AI system learns is crucial for evaluation. Key questions include:

- **Training methodology:** How was the system initially trained? With what data? Does it use supervised learning requiring labeled examples, or can it learn from unstructured data?
- **Ongoing learning:** Does the system continue to learn from your organization's usage? If so, how is this learning governed and controlled? Can learning be paused or rolled back if necessary?
- **Training requirements:** What data volume is needed for effective customization? How much expert input is required for training? What is the time investment for initial and ongoing training?
- **Customization capabilities:** Can the system be fine-tuned for your specific needs? What level of technical expertise is required for customization? Can customization be performed by internal teams or does it require vendor involvement?

## Explainability and Transparency

AI systems differ significantly in their transparency. Assessment should include:

- **Output explanation:** Can the system explain how it reached specific conclusions? Does it provide confidence scores or alternative interpretations?
- **Model transparency:** How "black box" is the underlying model? Can you understand what factors influence its decisions?
- **Audit capability:** Can the system's decisions be reviewed and verified? Does it maintain appropriate audit trails?

As both scholars and courts have noted, explainability is particularly important for legal applications where decisions may need to be defended or explained to clients, courts, or regulators.

## Accuracy and Reliability Metrics

AI accuracy differs from traditional software correctness. Evaluation should consider:

- **Precision and recall:** What percentage of the system's positive identifications are correct? What percentage of actual positives does it identify?

- **Confidence indication:** Does the system communicate its confidence level appropriately? Can it recognize when it's operating outside its capabilities?
- **Edge case handling:** How does the system handle unusual or novel situations? Does it fail gracefully or produce misleading outputs?
- **Error correction:** How are mistakes identified and corrected? Does the system learn from corrections?

Understanding these metrics is essential for evaluating whether an AI tool meets professional responsibility requirements for competent representation.

### Adaptability and Evolution

Unlike traditional software with fixed functionality, AI systems evolve over time. Evaluation should address:

- **Version control:** How are model updates managed and deployed? Can previous versions be maintained if needed?
- **Performance stability:** Does the system maintain consistent performance as it evolves? How is drift monitored and managed?
- **Adaptation timeline:** How quickly does the system adapt to new requirements or data patterns? What processes govern adaptation?
- **Prompt/flow version control:** Treat prompts, tool-use flows, and guardrails like code—**pin versions and enable rollback**, so changes don't silently affect outcomes. (This becomes critical as systems take actions, not just generate text.)

Top-performing systems offer transparent update processes and performance stability measures.

## TESTING AI SYSTEM CAPABILITIES

Smart organizations recognize that AI tools have both capabilities and limitations. One innovative approach is to use customized capability testing scenarios. Develop specific use cases based on your actual needs and test tools against these scenarios rather than relying on vendor demonstrations. This testing process includes:

- **Base capability testing:** Can the tool perform basic functions as advertised?
- **Edge case testing:** How does it handle unusual or complex situations?
- **Error testing:** What happens when things go wrong?
- **Integration testing:** How well does it work with existing systems?

Go beyond technical testing to evaluate how well the tool fits your practice needs:

- **Workflow compatibility:** Does it match how your lawyers actually work?
- **Training requirements:** How much effort is needed to get people up to speed?
- **Support needs:** What ongoing support will be required?
- **Cost-benefit reality:** Do the benefits justify the total cost of ownership?

AI systems also demand additional testing methodologies:

## Benchmark Testing

Create standardized test datasets that represent your organization's actual documents and use cases. These datasets should include:

- **Representative samples:** Documents that reflect the typical range of materials the system will process.
- **Edge cases:** Unusual examples that test the system's boundaries.
- **Gold standard annotations:** Expert-validated correct answers for objective evaluation.

Compare multiple tools against these benchmarks to enable direct performance comparison. Maintain these datasets for ongoing evaluation as systems evolve.

## Challenge Testing

Develop specific challenge scenarios designed to test particular capabilities or potential weaknesses:

- **Adversarial testing:** Deliberately challenging inputs designed to identify failure points
- **Bias testing:** Scenarios designed to detect potential biases in system outputs
- **Stress testing:** High-volume or complex scenarios that test performance limits
- **Prompt-injection & tool-misuse tests:** Deliberately craft inputs that try to elicit off-policy actions or data leakage; verify the system resists and logs attempts.
- **Adversarial robustness checks:** Include corrupted/perturbed inputs to observe failure modes and recovery.

Document these challenges and use them consistently across evaluations to enable fair comparison. Challenge testing is a key component of responsible AI evaluation, particularly for systems used in decision-making contexts.

### Practical Workflow Testing

Rather than evaluating AI tools in isolation, test them within actual work processes:

- **Workflow integration:** How the system fits into existing processes
- **User experience:** How practitioners interact with the system
- **Practical efficiency:** Whether the system actually saves time in real-world use
- **Adoption factors:** What drives or hinders actual usage

These practical tests often reveal insights that technical evaluations miss. Reports indicate that a substantial number of AI implementations show strong performance in isolated testing but fail when integrated into actual workflows, highlighting the importance of practical testing.

### Iterative Validation

Unlike traditional software that either works or doesn't, AI systems exist on a spectrum of capability that improves with refinement:

- **Initial testing:** Baseline performance assessment
- **Refinement cycle:** Adjustments based on initial findings
- **Validation testing:** Re-testing after refinement
- **Iteration:** Continuing this cycle until performance meets requirements

This approach recognizes that most AI systems require tuning and adaptation to reach optimal performance. Iterative validation approaches are significantly more likely to lead to successful AI implementations than traditional one-time testing methods.

## MAKING THE RIGHT CHOICE

You should use a structured decision-making process for AI technology selection. One particularly effective approach uses a weighted scoring system that considers:

- **Must-have features:** Critical capabilities the tool must provide
- **Nice-to-have features:** Additional capabilities that add value
- **Integration requirements:** Ability to work with existing systems

- **Implementation effort:** Resources required for successful deployment
- **Total cost:** Including both direct costs and internal resource requirements

But don't just score features. Consider organizational fit:

- **Cultural compatibility:** Will your people actually use it?
- **Support requirements:** Can you or the vendor provide needed support?
- **Growth potential:** Can it scale with your needs?

## Technical Data Evaluation for AI System Selection

Building on the strategic data considerations from Chapter 7, AI system evaluation requires specific technical assessment of data compatibility:

### *Data Format and Processing Capabilities*

- Native support for legal document formats (PDF, DOC, email formats)
- Optical character recognition (OCR) accuracy for scanned documents and handwritten materials
- Metadata extraction capabilities from various file types
- Processing speed for large document collections

### *Integration Technical Requirements*

- API compatibility with existing document management systems
- Real-time versus batch processing capabilities
- Data transformation and mapping tools
- Error-handling and recovery mechanisms

### *Learning Algorithm Data Requirements*

- Minimum dataset sizes for effective training
- Data labeling and annotation requirements
- Transfer learning capabilities from pre-trained models
- Incremental learning and model update processes

Overall, developing a customized approach to evaluation and selection, rather than simply selecting technology based on recommendations, will lead to greater success.

# DATA AS THE FOUNDATION OF AI SUCCESS

While traditional types of software *operate* on data, AI systems *learn* from data, making data quality, availability, and governance the primary determinants of AI success. This fundamental difference transforms data from a resource that software uses into the foundation that shapes how AI systems develop and perform.

As we noted in the previous chapter on AI strategy, we can't emphasize enough that our review of many reports indicates that data quality is the strongest predictor of AI implementation success, with high-quality data correlating more strongly with success than any other factor including budget or technological sophistication.

## Building a Data Foundation for AI

If you are serious about AI implementation, you need robust data governance and management capabilities. These include:

- **Data inventory and mapping:** Comprehensive understanding of what data exists, where it resides, who owns it, and what restrictions apply to its use. This mapping should include both structured and unstructured data sources relevant to potential AI applications.
- **Data quality management:** Systematic processes for assessing, improving, and monitoring data quality. This includes deduplication, normalization, standardization, and verification procedures.
- **Data lineage tracking:** Systems that track data provenance and transformations, critical for understanding how data is processed before AI consumption.
- **Data classification and security:** Frameworks for categorizing data sensitivity and applying appropriate security controls, especially important for client-confidential information.
- **Data access and integration:** Technical capabilities that enable appropriate data access across systems while maintaining security and governance controls.

Here is the simple truth: Organizations with mature data management capabilities have significantly higher AI success rates. Law firms and legal departments, like other organizations, simply must train users on the importance of data governance as the leading way to ensure appropriate work product is stored in their data management systems.

## The Data Foundation

AI systems are only as good as the data they work with. For example, your AI research tool will produce inconsistent results if your document tagging is inconsistent. The tool might work perfectly but still not be able to make sense of poorly organized data.

One way to support data quality is to use a data quality framework to address:

- **Data standards:** Clear rules for data formatting and organization.
- **Quality controls:** Processes to maintain data quality.
- **Cleanup procedures:** Methods for addressing quality issues.
- **Monitoring systems:** Tools to track data quality over time.

You must recognize how AI requires different data management approaches than traditional systems to be effective. Take these differences into account by ensuring that you have appropriate processes for data preparation, data quality maintenance, access management that controls how data is used, and sufficient security to safeguard sensitive information.

## Integration with Existing Systems

### *The Integration Challenge*

Integration is often the make-or-break factor in AI implementation success. More than one legal department has learned this lesson the hard way when their new AI research tools couldn't effectively access their document management systems. A tool might work perfectly in isolation but provide limited value if it can't access the documents it needs to analyze.

AI integration presents unique challenges compared to traditional software. While conventional systems typically exchange structured data through well-defined interfaces, AI systems often need access to multiple data sources, may require ongoing learning capabilities, and can produce outputs that need specialized handling. These distinctions necessitate a different integration approach.

Deloitte's report, AI for In-House Legal 2025 Predictions, notes that the single biggest barrier to realizing value from use of AI will be user resistance to adoption, and calls for greater investment in training, shifting focus from implementing AI point solutions to integrating AI into existing business and legal workflows, and emphasis on data cleanup.[1] Many modern tools expose **action APIs** (for filing, ticketing, redlining); require **human-in-the-loop gates** and **least-privilege scopes** before enabling any action endpoints.

[1] Deloitte Legal, AI for In-house Legal: 2025 Predictions (2025), https://www.deloitte.com/global/en/services/legal/research/ai-inhouse-legal-2025-predictions.html.

### *Planning for Successful Integration*

Smart organizations approach integration planning systematically. We suggest that you create "integration maps" that show:

- **Data flows:** How information moves between systems.
- **Interface points:** Where systems need to connect.
- **Dependencies:** What systems rely on each other.
- **Security boundaries:** Where sensitive data needs protection.

We further recommend that you go beyond technical mapping and fully consider process integration to understand how AI tools fit into your work processes. You will want to consider the user experience as people interact with the systems, what training users will need, and how you will maintain the integrated systems.

While Chapter 7 discussed the strategic importance of data readiness, the technical reality during implementation is often more complex. You might discover that your existing data infrastructure requires significant technical remediation before AI systems can operate effectively:

- **Legacy system integration challenges:** AI systems require API-based data access that many legacy legal systems cannot provide without middleware development or system upgrades.
- **Real-time data processing requirements:** Unlike traditional batch-processing approaches, AI systems often require streaming data access and real-time processing capabilities that existing infrastructure may not support.
- **Metadata standardization at scale:** Implementing the semantic frameworks discussed in Chapter 7 requires technical solutions for automated metadata enhancement across millions of existing documents.
- **Performance and scalability constraints:** AI workloads create computational demands that may exceed current infrastructure capacity, requiring technical architecture planning beyond basic data preparation.

## Making Integration Work

Leading organizations recognize that successful integration requires both technical and operational components. You will want to apply an integration framework that addresses technical integration issues such as API connections and data exchange, authentication and access control, performance optimization, and error handling and recovery. Operational integration requires attention to process alignment, training and support, monitoring and maintenance, and continuous improvement activities.

We recommend a "business process first" approach to AI integration, with integration planning that starts with workflow mapping rather than technical specifications. And just a note about the resistance you are likely to find: We usually think about resistance to change as an obstacle that we must overcome. This sometimes leads to "orders" being issued that are circumvented or otherwise challenged. But in this process of integrating AI across the organization, in which you need the cooperation of many individuals and departments, it is better to think about resistance as a learning opportunity and a chance to develop additional champions for the changes that are underway. Ask those who own responsibility for systems that will be integrated what their concerns are and be prepared to address them. Show them how they will benefit from the integration and ensure them that training will be provided and issues they raise will be taken seriously. This is an opportunity to develop a team of supporters, so don't miss taking it.

## Data Preparation as the Critical Path

Most legal organizations discover that much of their AI implementation timeline involves data preparation, cleaning, and restructuring rather than AI system configuration. This reality transforms data preparation from a parallel activity into the critical path that determines implementation success.

## The Hidden Data Debt Challenge

Legal organizations typically carry substantial "data debt"—years of inconsistent data practices, incomplete metadata, and fragmented information architecture. This debt must be addressed before AI systems can generate reliable insights. Organizations that attempt to implement AI without first addressing data readiness often experience disappointing results, leading to the misconception that AI technology is overhyped rather than recognizing the underlying data preparation challenges.

## Incremental Data Transformation Strategy

Rather than attempting comprehensive data remediation before implementing AI systems, you can adopt incremental approaches that improve data quality while simultaneously deploying AI capabilities. Incremental approaches might look like this:

### *Phase 1: Foundation Assessment and Quick Wins*

- Comprehensive data audit across all systems
- Identification of highest-quality data sources for initial AI deployment
- Implementation of automated data quality monitoring
- Quick standardization projects for priority document types

### *Phase 2: Semantic Framework Development*

- Ontology design for priority practice areas
- Relationship mapping between key data entities
- Contextual metadata enhancement for core document types
- Integration planning for unified data access

### *Phase 3: Intelligent Automation Deployment*

- Implementation of automated data preparation pipelines
- Deployment of intelligent data agents for ongoing quality maintenance
- Advanced semantic processing for complex document relationships
- Cross-system data integration and tokenization

### *Phase 4: Advanced Analytics and Continuous Evolution*

- Full semantic data model deployment
- Predictive analytics capability activation
- Continuous learning system implementation
- Strategic data capability expansion

This phased approach enables organizations to see early AI value while building the data infrastructure necessary for advanced capabilities.

## Pilot Programs and Testing

### *The Power of Pilots*

Pilot programs can mean the difference between AI success and failure. Consider the example of one firm's experience: Rather than rolling out their AI contract analysis tool firm-wide, they started with a small pilot in their corporate practice. The pilot revealed several critical issues they could address before broader deployment, potentially saving millions in failed implementation costs.

The value of pilots is particularly pronounced with AI implementations because of their learning-based nature. Unlike traditional software where functionality is largely predetermined, AI capabilities evolve with exposure to your specific data and use patterns. This makes real-world testing essential for understanding actual performance. Organizations using formal pilot programs for AI implementations experience higher success rates than those moving directly to full deployment.

### *Designing Effective Pilots*

Leading organizations approach pilot programs systematically. An effective framework includes:

- **Scope definition:** Clearly defined boundaries and objectives.
- **Success metrics:** Specific measures for evaluation.
- **Timeline:** Realistic schedule with checkpoints.
- **Resource allocation:** Dedicated team and support.
- **Feedback mechanisms:** Ways to gather user input.

Pilot success requires active management. When done right, pilots are learning experiences, not just testing periods. Consider establishing regular check-ins and weekly meetings to discuss progress, ensuring issue tracking with systematic recording of problems and solutions, and structured gathering of user experiences and feedback.

## Governance and Oversight for AI Implementation

The adaptive nature of AI systems requires governance structures beyond traditional IT oversight. As systems learn and evolve, ongoing governance becomes essential to ensure they continue to meet organizational standards and requirements.

If you serve EU users or process EU data, confirm your vendor's roadmap for **EU AI Act** compliance (e.g., GPAI transparency, technical documentation, incident reporting) and build those checkpoints into your contracts.

### *Data-Specific Testing Protocols for AI Implementation*

Chapter 7 outlined the strategic importance of data quality. During implementation, this translates into specific testing requirements:

### *Data Compatibility Testing Creates Test Datasets That Represent Your Actual Data Challenges*

- Documents with inconsistent formatting and metadata
- Legacy files with missing or corrupted information
- Mixed document types from different practice areas
- Edge cases like partially redacted or annotated documents

### *Performance Testing Under Real Data Conditions*

- Processing speed with actual document volumes
- Accuracy degradation with poor-quality source data
- System behavior with incomplete or corrupted files
- Memory and computational resource requirements

### *Integration Testing with Existing Data Sources*

- Connectivity testing with document management systems
- Data synchronization and consistency validation
- Access control and security verification
- Backup and recovery process validation

## ESTABLISHING EFFECTIVE AI GOVERNANCE

Leading organizations establish dedicated governance structures for AI implementation:

- **AI ethics committees:** Cross-functional groups that evaluate AI use against ethical standards, typically including both technical experts and practicing attorneys
- **Technical review boards:** Specialized teams that assess the technical aspects of AI implementations, including security, data handling, and integration
- **Use case authorization:** Formal processes for approving specific AI applications, including risk assessment and mitigation planning
- **Model management:** Frameworks for overseeing model performance, updates, and potential drift over time

The American Bar Association's 2024 Formal Opinion 512 calls for governance over the use of AI, including requirements for managerial lawyers to establish clear policies regarding the law firm's permissible use of generative artificial intelligence (GAI), and supervisory lawyers to make reasonable efforts to ensure that the firm's lawyers and nonlawyers comply with their professional obligations when using GAI tools.[2]

[2] A.B.A. Standing Comm. on Ethics & Pro. Resp., Formal Op. 512, Generative Artificial Intelligence Tools (July 29, 2024), https://www.americanbar.org/content/dam/aba/administrative/professional_responsibility/ethics-opinions/aba-formal-opinion-512.pdf.

## Monitoring and Oversight

Unlike traditional software that remains relatively static between updates, AI systems require continuous monitoring:

- **Performance dashboards:** Real-time visibility into system performance and usage
- **Action logging and evidence packs:** For any feature that can take actions, require tamper-evident logs of who/what/when plus inputs, outputs, and linked source excerpts; review these alongside dashboards and alerts.
- **Alert systems:** Automated notification when metrics fall outside acceptable ranges
- **Regular auditing:** Scheduled comprehensive reviews of system behavior
- **Feedback channels:** Mechanisms for users to report concerns or issues

Continuous oversight is essential to identify potential problems before they impact client work. While some oversight of AI by AI is appropriate and timesaving, human oversight remains essential at this stage of AI development.

## Ethical and Responsible AI Use

When implementing AI need frameworks, you must establish ways to ensure responsible use, including:

- **Bias detection:** Processes for identifying and addressing potential biases.
- **Transparency requirements:** Standards for explainability based on use case risk.
- **Human oversight:** Clear roles and responsibilities for human supervision.
- **Intervention protocols:** Defined procedures for addressing concerns.

Integrate these elements into initial evaluations and ongoing management of AI. Schedule formal ethics reviews of AI systems, particularly those used for consequential decisions or client-facing applications. By maintaining these practices, you will go a long way toward establishing ethical consideration as a routine part of AI usage.

### *Vendor Oversight*

Most legal AI implementations involve third-party vendors, requiring specialized oversight that includes:

- **Performance monitoring:** Tracking vendor system performance against SLAs.

- **Security verification:** Ongoing assessment of security practices.
- **Data usage auditing**: Monitoring how vendors handle organization data.
- **Version control:** Managing the impact of vendor updates and changes.

Formalize oversight in vendor contracts, regularly review compliance, and enforced those terms. We recommend establishing a formal vendor management program specific to AI providers, including regular security assessments and performance reviews.

# SECURITY INFRASTRUCTURE

## The Security Imperative

AI introduces new security challenges that traditional security approaches may not adequately address. You don't want to find this out only when you discover that your AI tool is storing sensitive client data in ways your security tools can't monitor.

The security considerations for AI systems extend beyond traditional information security concerns. While standard security practices remain important, AI-specific challenges include:

- **Model security:** Protecting the AI models themselves from tampering or manipulation.
- **Training data protection:** Securing the data used to train and fine-tune models.
- **Inference security:** Ensuring the integrity of AI outputs and decisions.
- **Privacy preservation:** Protecting personal and confidential information throughout the AI life cycle.

These considerations require specialized security approaches that traditional tools may not provide. Organizations without AI-specific security controls will experience far more data breach incidents and other failures.

## Making Security Work

AI security requires both technical and operational measures. An effective approach includes:

### *Technical Controls*

- Encryption and access management
- Security monitoring and alerting

- Incident detection and response
- System hardening and protection
- **Agent/action audit trail.** Centralize immutable logs of all automated actions (including approvals and reversals), make them queryable via API, and align retention with matter and regulatory requirements.

### *Operational Controls*

- Security policies and procedures
- Training and awareness programs
- Audit and compliance processes
- Continuous improvement efforts

As many guides on AI cybersecurity state, integrated security approaches that combine technical controls with operational measures are significantly more effective for protecting AI systems than either approach alone.

## Data Security in AI-Ready Architectures

AI-ready data architectures require security approaches that protect not just stored information but also the semantic relationships and contextual metadata that enable AI insights. Traditional security models focused on perimeter defense and access control must evolve to address:

- **Semantic data protection:** Security frameworks must protect not just individual documents but also the relationship mappings and contextual enrichment that create value for AI systems. This includes securing knowledge graphs, ontology structures, and contextual metadata without disrupting AI functionality.
- **Tokenized data security:** In tokenized data environments, security controls must protect both the tokens themselves and the transformation processes that create them. This includes ensuring that tokenization preserves necessary context while anonymizing sensitive elements.
- **AI agent security:** Intelligent data agents require specialized security controls that monitor their data access patterns, processing activities, and learning behaviors. Security frameworks must ensure that automated data preparation maintains confidentiality while enabling the data integration necessary for AI effectiveness.
- **Continuous security monitoring:** AI-ready data architectures require continuous security monitoring that adapts to evolving data relationships

and AI capabilities. This includes anomaly detection for unusual data access patterns, automated compliance monitoring for data usage policies, and proactive threat detection for AI-specific attack vectors.

## CONCLUSION

To successfully select and implement AI technology, you must understand that AI fundamentally differs from traditional software. The most significant difference is that AI systems learn from and evolve with your data, making data quality, governance, and management the primary determinants of implementation success.

Effective AI selection requires evaluating not just current capabilities but also how well the system will learn from your specific data and adapt to your unique needs. This requires specialized evaluation approaches that often go beyond traditional software selection, including data-specific assessment, learning capability testing, and governance evaluation.

Organizations that succeed with AI implementation recognize that it's not a one-time event but a continuous process. They establish governance structures and teams that monitor system performance, manage evolution, and ensure responsible use. They invest in data preparation and quality, recognizing that even the most sophisticated AI technology will underperform with poor-quality data.

The most successful organizations approach AI implementation as a strategic journey rather than a tactical project. They build foundational capabilities in data management, establish appropriate governance frameworks, and develop specialized testing methodologies. If you apply a similarly comprehensive approach, you will leverage AI's transformative potential while managing its unique challenges.

As AI technology continues to evolve, the legal organizations that thrive will be those that focus on the organizational foundations that enable successful implementation: high-quality data, effective governance, and systematic evaluation processes.

## ACTION ITEMS

1. **Evaluate AI Technology Landscape**
    - Assess different AI technology types and their legal applications
    - Create technology evaluation framework for capabilities and limitations
    - Map technology options to identified use cases and requirements

2. **Conduct Systematic Solution Testing**
   - Design comprehensive testing protocols for AI system capabilities
   - Implement benchmark testing with organization-specific datasets
   - Conduct challenge testing and practical workflow validation
3. **Establish Data Foundation for AI Success**
   - Assess and improve data quality, accessibility, and governance
   - Implement data preparation and integration systems
   - Create data security and privacy frameworks for AI use
4. **Design System Integration Architecture**
   - Plan integration with existing legal technology infrastructure
   - Design data flows and interface specifications
   - Create unified user experience across integrated systems
5. **Implement Pilot Programs and Validation**
   - Execute structured pilot programs with defined success criteria
   - Validate AI performance in real-world legal workflows
   - Conduct iterative testing and refinement cycles
6. **Establish Implementation Governance**
   - Create oversight mechanisms for technology deployment
   - Implement monitoring systems for AI performance and usage
   - Design continuous improvement and optimization processes

CHAPTER 9

# Training Your People on AI

## INTRODUCTION

*Rather than merely managing resistance, you need to take steps to fundamentally reframe how your legal professionals conceptualize their relationship with technology.*

Wolters Kluwer's 2024 Future Ready Lawyer Survey Report notes the importance of training and skill development as AI grows in importance in law firms.

> There is an overwhelming consensus on the importance of GenAI training: 71% of survey participants say they are either already required to participate in formal training or will be required to do so within the next year.[1]

This shouldn't surprise anyone who's worked in legal technology adoption. You can have the most sophisticated AI tools available, but without properly trained people to use them, they could become expensive shelfware.

To illustrate this point, imagine investing in a powerful AI contract analysis tool. Your vendor provides basic operational training. Six months later, usage is minimal. Why? Because knowing how to operate the tool is different from understanding how to integrate it effectively into legal practice while maintaining professional standards.

This chapter explores how to develop the skills you and your team need for successful AI adoption. We examine technical and professional skills, identify

[1] Wolters Kluwer, 2024 Future Ready Lawyer Survey Report (2024), https://www.wolterskluwer.com/en/know/future-ready-lawyer-2024.

some effective training approaches, and discuss creating a learning culture that supports ongoing AI evolution.

## THE IMPERATIVE FOR EXPERIMENTATION IN LEGAL AI SKILL DEVELOPMENT

The unprecedented pace of AI advancement demands a fundamental shift in how legal organizations approach training and skill development. The traditional model of carefully researched programs with meticulously planned outcomes is no longer sufficient. Today's environment demands something different: structured experimentation and calculated risk-taking.

Unlike previous technologies that evolved incrementally, AI capabilities are expanding exponentially at breakneck speed. This means:

- What works today may be obsolete tomorrow.
- Best practices haven't been established yet—they're being created in real time.
- Organizations cannot wait for certainty before taking action.
- The greatest risk is not taking risks at all.

Law has traditionally been a risk-averse profession, valuing precedent and established practice. This cultural orientation served the profession well in a stable environment but becomes a liability in an era of rapid exponential change. Forward-thinking legal organizations are adopting what we call "disciplined experimentation"; structured approaches to trying new methods, learning from both successes and failures, and rapidly iterating.

This doesn't mean reckless adoption of unproven technologies. Rather, it means creating frameworks that enable:

- Rapid testing of new approaches in controlled environments.
- Systematic capture of lessons learned, especially from failures.
- Quick scaling of successful experiments.
- Continuous adjustment based on emerging insights.

Throughout this chapter, we emphasize not just the skills legal professionals need but also how organizations must approach skill development itself as an experimental discipline. The most successful training programs will be those designed not as fixed curricula but as adaptable frameworks that evolve as rapidly as the technologies they address.

# REQUIRED COMPETENCIES FOR LAWYERS

## Beyond Basic Technical Skills

While recent surveys consistently find that most lawyers recognize that AI will significantly impact their practice, far fewer feel confident in their ability to evaluate and appropriately use AI tools. Even though confidence has been improving over the past couple of years, the continuing gap between recognition and readiness presents both a challenge and an opportunity for law firms and legal departments.

There are multiple core competencies lawyers need for effective AI use. Here are a few:

- Understanding AI capabilities and limitations
- Ability to evaluate AI outputs critically
- Knowledge of ethical implications and professional obligations
- Skills in working effectively with technical teams

## Building a Competency Framework

To illustrate how these competencies work in practice, let's consider a hypothetical contract review scenario. It's not enough for a lawyer to know how to use an AI contract analysis tool. They need to also understand:

- What types of contracts does the tool handle well or poorly.
- How to spot potential AI errors or biases.
- When additional human review is needed.
- How to document AI use appropriately.
- What ethical obligations apply.

## A Structured Approach to Skill Development

Enterprises with structured approaches to AI training experience higher adoption rates than those with ad hoc training methods. Legal organizations are most successful with AI adoption when they develop skills across multiple levels:

- **Foundation level:** Basic understanding of AI concepts, capabilities, and limitations
- **Application level:** Practical skills in when and how to use AI tools effectively and ethically
- **Integration level:** Advanced capabilities in combining AI with expert legal judgment

## Role-Specific AI Competencies

Organizations with dedicated AI expertise centers generally realize higher successful adoption rates than those without such resources. These centers typically serve three key functions:

- Skill development and training
- Best practice development
- Technical support and guidance

The rapid evolution of AI demands that skill development be radically role-specific, going beyond traditional one-size-fits-all approaches. As AI capabilities change weekly rather than yearly, different roles within legal organizations must develop distinct, and constantly evolving, competency sets. The following frameworks should be treated not as static requirements but as starting points for continuous adaptation. The most successful programs tailor training to the following specific organizational roles.

### *For Associates and Staff Attorneys*

Associates need practical skills in using AI effectively while maintaining professional standards. Key competencies include:

- **Prompt engineering:** Ability to formulate effective queries and instructions that elicit useful AI responses.
- **Output validation:** Skills in critically evaluating AI-generated content for accuracy, completeness, and appropriateness.
- **Ethical usage:** Understanding when and how to use AI within ethical guidelines.
- **Documentation:** Proper recording of AI use for supervision and client transparency.

It is easy to understand that firms incorporating AI-specific skills into their associate training programs will experience higher satisfaction with technology adoption, not only by their associates but also by the partners who rely on them.

### *For Partners and Practice Leaders*

Partners need a strategic understanding of AI capabilities to guide client service and practice management. Key competencies include:

- **Strategic application:** Identifying high-value AI use cases within practice areas.

- **Risk management:** Understanding and mitigating potential AI risks.
- **Client communication:** Effectively discussing AI use with clients.
- **Supervision frameworks:** Creating appropriate oversight for AI-assisted work.
- **Experimentation leadership:** Ability to create environments where controlled experimentation with AI is encouraged and failures become valuable learning opportunities.
- **Rapid adaptation:** Skills in quickly adjusting practice strategies as AI capabilities evolve, without waiting for industry-wide consensus.

Practice groups with leaders who receive AI leadership training can be expected to achieve higher adoption rates than those without such training.

### *For Legal Technologists and Innovation Staff*

Support professionals need deeper technical understanding and integration capabilities. Key competencies include:

- **Technical evaluation:** Ability to assess AI capabilities and limitations.
- **Implementation planning:** Skills in designing effective AI workflows.
- **System integration:** Knowledge of how to connect AI tools with existing systems.
- **Training development:** Capability to create effective training materials.

Firms and legal departments will benefit from having support teams that can take on much of the technical work and training development needs.

### *For Knowledge Management (KM) Professionals*

KM staff require specialized skills in leveraging AI for knowledge capture and distribution:

- **Content optimization:** Preparing knowledge resources for AI consumption
- **Taxonomy development:** Creating effective classification systems for AI tools
- **Quality assurance:** Validating AI-generated knowledge resources
- **Training data management:** Curating high-quality examples for AI learning

We believe that organizations with KM teams trained specifically in AI data preparation will achieve higher effectiveness rates for their AI implementations than those without such specialized training.

# TRAINING PROGRAMS AND RESOURCES

## Designing Effective Training for Unprecedented Change

The pace of AI advancement renders traditional training approaches obsolete almost as quickly as they're developed. Today's legal organizations must build training systems characterized by adaptability, rapid iteration, and continuous evolution. We recommend that programs combine multiple learning approaches in proportions that can shift as needs evolve. For example:

- Formal instruction (20%)
- Hands-on practice (40%)
- Peer learning (25%)
- Self-directed experimentation (15%)

These percentages aren't fixed formulas but starting points for experimentation. You must constantly measure results and adjust your approach, perhaps dramatically, as both AI capabilities and learning needs evolve.

## Building Practical Skills

Effective legal AI training programs should address three key dimensions:

1. The technical dimension (understanding how AI works)
2. The practical dimension (applying AI to legal work)
3. The ethical dimension (maintaining professional standards with AI)

To illustrate this principle, consider scenarios like these during training and discuss your responses:

Scenario 1: An AI tool suggests an unusual contract clause. How should lawyers evaluate its appropriateness?

Scenario 2: AI analysis misses a key provision. What review protocols would catch this?

Scenario 3: A client questions AI use. How should lawyers explain their approach?

Including such discussions in training contributes to the development of clearer communications, identification of needed policies, and other improvements to your AI governance overall.

### Creating Safe-to-Fail Environments

Traditional legal training minimizes risk and error, but AI skill development requires a fundamentally different approach. Consider creating what innovation experts call "safe-to-fail environments"—spaces where attorneys can experiment with AI tools, make mistakes, and learn without client or reputational risk.

Effective safe-to-fail environments include:

- **Sandboxed practice areas:** Designated environments using anonymized or synthetic data where attorneys can experiment with AI approaches.
- **Failure capture systems:** Mechanisms for documenting and sharing lessons from unsuccessful AI applications.
- **Graduated risk exposure:** Structured progression from low-stakes experiments to more consequential applications.
- **Rapid feedback loops:** Immediate evaluation of experimental approaches to accelerate learning cycles.

These environments recognize that in rapidly evolving domains, controlled failure often teaches more than safe success. Organizations that systematically learn from AI experiments—including unsuccessful ones—develop institutional capabilities that no training manual can provide.

## MEASURING TRAINING EFFECTIVENESS: BEYOND COMPLETION METRICS

Traditional training programs often measure success by completion rates, but effective AI skill development requires more sophisticated measurement approaches. In an era of exponential change, measurement itself must become dynamic and forward-looking. Traditional lagging indicators, like completion rates or satisfaction scores, must be supplemented with leading indicators that predict future adaptability. Organizations at the forefront of AI adoption are measuring not just what their people have learned but also their capacity to learn, unlearn, and relearn as AI capabilities evolve.

### Multidimensional Measurement Framework

If you establish a comprehensive training measurement framework, you are more likely to report successful AI adoption than those tracking only completion metrics. An effective measurement framework should examine multiple dimensions. For example:

- **Knowledge acquisition:** Measured through assessment tests and practical demonstrations
- **Behavioral change:** Tracked through tool usage patterns and workflow integration
- **Performance impact:** Evaluated through efficiency and quality metrics
- **Client value:** Assessed through service delivery improvements and client feedback
- **Adaptation speed:** Measuring how quickly professionals can pivot to new AI approaches and capabilities as they emerge

This multidimensional approach provides a more complete picture of training effectiveness than simple participation metrics.

In an era of exponential change, measurement itself must become dynamic and forward-looking. Traditional lagging indicators (like completion rates or satisfaction scores) must be supplemented with leading indicators that predict future adaptability.

## Progressive Competency Assessment

We recommend a competency growth measurement approach that includes tracking development across multiple skill levels:

- **Awareness:** Understanding of basic AI concepts and applications
- **Literacy:** Ability to use AI tools with appropriate oversight
- **Proficiency:** Capabilities to apply AI tools to standard legal work
- **Mastery:** Skills extending AI use for complex situations
- **Leadership:** Ability to guide others and develop new applications

You should include self-assessment and objective evaluation through practical challenges to gain a more accurate picture of actual capability development.

## Return on Learning Investment

A recent Thompson Reuters Institute paper asserts that "AI should not be viewed merely as a means to reduce human input but rather as a tool to elevate legal service delivery. This, in turn, will make lawyers more effective, insightful, and responsive to client needs, ultimately unlocking additional value."[2] The authors argue that AI adoption can and should be looked at through the lens of "revenue leakage." They say, "By starting with a leakage analysis that covers both revenue and time, law firms can then prioritize AI investments in those areas that will drive the most financial value while best improving client outcomes."[3]

Recognizing the potential for such bottom-line benefits, some legal organizations apply ROI methodologies to their AI training investments. This can include:

1. **Baseline measurement:** Pre-training efficiency metrics for specific tasks.
2. **Post-training tracking:** Same metrics measured at 30, 60, and 90 days.
3. **Time savings calculation:** Quantified efficiency improvements.
4. **Quality assessment:** Review of work product quality before and after training.
5. **Cost-benefit analysis:** Comparison of training investment with quantified benefits.

If you use this approach to measure the results of your AI training investments, you can make a compelling case for comprehensive AI skill development.

## INTEGRATING ETHICS INTO AI TRAINING

Effective AI training must address ethical considerations alongside technical skills. We believe that programs integrating ethics throughout training will achieve higher compliance with professional responsibility standards than those treating ethics as a separate module.

### Ethics-First Approach

The ABA's 2024 Formal Opinion 512 on generative AI, states that supervisory lawyers must ensure that subordinates are trained in the ethical and practical use of GAI tools. We believe that ethical considerations are best addressed through establishment of:

[2] Thomson Reuters Inst., The AI Driven Future of Legal Efficiency (2025), https://www.thomsonreuters.com/en-us/posts/wp-content/uploads/sites/20/2025/04/The-AI-driven-future_2025.pdf.

[3] *Id.*

1. **An ethical framework foundation:** Beginning all training with professional responsibility principles.
2. **Scenario-based learning:** Using ethical dilemmas as the context for teaching technical skills.
3. **Decision trees:** Developing structured approaches to common ethical questions.
4. **Documentation practices:** Training on proper recording of AI use and supervision.
5. **Ethics champions:** Identifying attorneys to provide guidance on complex issues.

Organizations that implement this approach should expect better ethical compliance and higher user confidence and adoption rates.

## Building Ethical Muscles Through Practice

We embrace recommendations for what some call "ethical muscle building," specifically in the context of AI training. This involves regular exercises that strengthen professionals' ability to identify and address ethical issues. These might include:

- **Ethics sprints:** Short, focused exercises applying ethical principles to specific scenarios.
- **Red team challenges:** Sessions where teams deliberately try to identify ethical risks in proposed AI uses.
- **Decision simulations:** Realistic scenarios requiring ethical judgment about AI applications.
- **Reflection practices:** Structured approaches to evaluate past decisions and improve future choices.

This approach acknowledges that ethical judgment improves with practice and deliberate development, not just knowledge of rules.

## Ethics Documentation and Communication

Training on the documentation and communication of AI use has become an important component of comprehensive AI ethics training. Programs should include instruction on:

- **Disclosure templates:** Standardized approaches for explaining AI use to clients.

- **Court notification guidelines:** Protocols for disclosing AI use in litigation contexts.
- **Internal documentation:** Structured approaches to recording AI use for supervision.
- **Client communication scenarios:** Practice explaining AI use and its benefits to clients.

The ability to clearly articulate how and why AI is being used builds client trust and demonstrates commitment to appropriate technology use.

## PREPARING FOR CLIENT CONVERSATIONS ABOUT AI

As clients become more sophisticated about AI, lawyers need specific skills for effectively discussing AI use. Leading firms are developing training specifically focused on client communication aspects of AI adoption.

### A Client Conversation Framework

Effective client communication about AI use has become a key differentiator for legal organizations. We expect it to become table stakes. Lawyers will need to be trained on:

- **Value articulation:** Clearly explaining how AI enhances service delivery.
- **Transparency practices:** Appropriately disclosing when and how AI is used.
- **Comparison techniques:** Contrasting AI-assisted and traditional approaches.
- **Limitation acknowledgment:** Honestly addressing AI constraints and oversight.
- **Responsibility clarification:** Maintaining clear attorney responsibility.

Remember, you are not just explaining AI technology. You are assuring clients that they can reasonably expect sound professional judgment and accountability.

### Client-Specific Customization

Client attitudes toward AI use in legal services vary dramatically, requiring lawyers to adapt their approaches based on client perspectives. Expect to deal with a variety of client views:

- **AI-enthusiastic clients:** Define how to discuss responsible boundaries with technology-forward clients
- **AI-cautious clients:** Establish techniques for explaining safeguards and oversight
- **AI-prohibitive clients:** Set protocols for respecting client restrictions while maintaining service quality
- **Client policy navigation:** Ensure your team understands and complies with client-specific AI policies

Many corporate legal departments now have specific policies regarding outside counsel's use of AI, making customization of your communication approach increasingly important. Review of client AI policies as each matter is initiated should be routine, just like conflict checking.

### Demonstrating Value Through Metrics

Corporate clients expect their outside counsel to provide metrics demonstrating the value of AI use rather than general claims about efficiency. Effective training programs prepare lawyers to discuss:

- **Efficiency metrics:** Quantified time savings for specific tasks
- **Quality comparisons:** Measurable improvements in consistency or thoroughness
- **Risk reduction:** Specific risk factors that are addressed through AI tools
- **Cost implications:** Transparent discussion of how AI affects service costs

This grows in importance as chief legal officers send less work to outside counsel, because their in-house legal staff can accomplish more for less as they adopt AI tools.

## MANAGING RESISTANCE TO CHANGE

### Understanding Resistance Sources

There are four primary sources of resistance to AI adoption in legal organizations:

1. Professional identity concerns
2. Quality control fears
3. Job security worries
4. Ethical uncertainties

Many lawyers express some level of concern about AI's impact on their practice, with the most common concerns centered on professional responsibility implications.

## Effective Resistance Management

Rather than merely managing resistance, you need to take steps to fundamentally reframe how your legal professionals conceptualize their relationship with technology. This goes beyond persuasion to building what organizational theorists call "adaptive capability," that is, the institutional capacity to embrace continuous technological evolution.

This capability develops through several key approaches:

- **Immersive experiences:** Hands-on exposure that demonstrates AI's potential to enhance rather than threaten professional judgment
- **Success narratives:** Compelling stories of how early adopters have leveraged AI to do their best professional work
- **Professional identity evolution:** Explicit discussions about how legal identity can incorporate technological fluency while preserving core professional values
- **Risk-taking incentives:** Reward systems that recognize and value technological experimentation, even when it doesn't immediately succeed

The most successful organizations don't just overcome resistance—they transform it into curiosity, engagement, and, ultimately, leadership. They recognize that in today's environment, technological adaptability isn't just another skill but a fundamental professional capability.

We believe that, for some lawyers, one way to address resistance to AI is to focus on the benefits and the opportunities. We endorse the following view in the article titled *How Lawyers Can Stand Out and Add Value in the Age of AI*:[4]

> Will artificial intelligence replace humans in the workplace? Will lawyers become obsolete? It can be tough to not get caught up in the AI media hype. It's not strictly hyperbole, after all; with the advent of generative AI tools, the legal profession is at the cusp of a radical transformation.
>
> . . . But they should never stop pitching the unique value they bring to employers as seasoned problem solvers, risk advisors, and strategic thinkers.

[4] Haylee Harrison, *How Lawyers Can Stand Out and Add Value in the Age of AI*, Major, Lindsey & Africa (June 4, 2024), https://www.mlaglobal.com/en/insights/articles/how-lawyers-can-stand-out-and-add-value-in-the-age-of-ai.

# CREATING A LEARNING CULTURE

## Building Sustainable Learning

In the age of exponential AI advancement, creating a robust learning culture isn't optional—it's essential for survival and success. Law firms and legal departments that foster continuous learning consistently outperform those with static approaches. The difference isn't marginal; it's transformative.

To build this culture, you must implement several key elements:

- **Continuous learning infrastructure:** Establish regular, structured learning opportunities such as weekly technology updates, monthly deep dives, quarterly skill refreshes. These should become as routine as client meetings. This isn't about occasional training but weaving learning into the fabric of daily practice.
- **Cross-functional knowledge networks:** Create systems where knowledge flows freely between practice groups, technologists, and business professionals. When a litigator discovers an effective AI application, corporate attorneys should learn about it immediately, not months later.
- **Protected innovation time:** Carve out dedicated time, even just a few hours weekly, for experimentation with emerging AI tools. The firms leading in AI adoption aren't just using technology, they're actively exploring its boundaries.
- **Recognition and incentive alignment:** Reward learning, experimentation, and innovation as core professional activities, not peripheral nice-to-haves. Consider how compensation, advancement, and recognition systems can enable or stifle continuous adaptation.

## Allocating Resources for Future Readiness

A commitment to thriving in the age of AI requires tangible resource allocation. While specific percentages will vary by organization, forward-thinking legal entities are making substantial investments:

- Dedicating significant professional time to skill development and technology exploration
- Allocating meaningful portions of IT and innovation budgets to learning infrastructure
- Investing in both formal training programs and informal learning opportunities

- Building partnerships with technology providers, academic institutions, and client organizations to stay at the leading edge

This investment isn't a drag on profitability. Rather, it's becoming a driver of competitive advantage. As AI continues to commoditize routine legal work, the ability to continuously learn, adapt, and innovate will increasingly differentiate leading organizations from those that merely survive.

The firms that recognize this shift aren't just preparing for the future—they're actively creating it. They understand that in an era of exponential change, learning isn't just another professional obligation; it's the foundation upon which all other professional capabilities rest.

## CONCLUSION

Effective training and skill development are crucial for successful AI adoption in legal practice. Organizations must build comprehensive programs addressing both technical and professional skills, while creating cultures that support continuous learning and adaptation.

The most successful training approaches recognize that AI competency development differs from traditional technology training. It requires integration of technical skills with ethical considerations, role-specific customization, practical application in real work contexts, and sophisticated measurement of effectiveness.

Leading organizations are moving beyond traditional training models to create comprehensive skill development ecosystems including formal instruction, hands-on practice, peer learning, and continuous reinforcement. They integrate ethics throughout training rather than treating it as a separate consideration, and they prepare attorneys for the crucial client conversations that accompany AI adoption and use.

As AI capabilities evolve, organizations must create sustainable learning cultures that support ongoing AI development. This requires not just initial training but also continuous refreshment, structured knowledge sharing, and recognition of skill development as a core professional responsibility.

To thrive in the AI era, you must invest not only in technology but also in the human capabilities that enable its effective use. By developing comprehensive training programs aligned with practice needs and professional values, you can harness AI's benefits while maintaining the highest standards of practice.

## ACTION ITEMS

1. **Assess AI Competency Requirements**
   - Define role-specific AI competencies for attorneys, paralegals, and support staff
   - Conduct skills gap analysis against current capabilities
   - Create competency development road maps for different roles
2. **Design Comprehensive Training Programs**
   - Develop layered training approach combining formal instruction, hands-on practice, and peer learning
   - Create role-specific curricula addressing technical, practical, and ethical dimensions
   - Build scenario-based training using real legal practice examples
3. **Establish Safe-to-Fail Learning Environments**
   - Create sandboxed practice areas for AI experimentation without client risk
   - Design failure capture systems that document and share learning from unsuccessful AI applications
   - Implement graduated risk exposure from low-stakes experiments to consequential applications
4. **Integrate Ethics Throughout AI Training**
   - Embed professional responsibility considerations into all AI training modules
   - Create ethical decision-making frameworks specific to AI use in legal practice
   - Develop bias recognition and mitigation training capabilities
5. **Implement Training Effectiveness Measurement**
   - Design multidimensional measurement beyond completion metrics
   - Track behavioral change, performance impact, and client value outcomes
   - Create progressive competency assessment systems
6. **Build Sustainable Learning Culture**
   - Establish continuous learning infrastructure and protected innovation time
   - Create AI champions networks and peer-mentoring programs
   - Align recognition and advancement with AI expertise development

CHAPTER 10

# Creating AI Policies and Governance

## INTRODUCTION

*You must recognize that AI governance shouldn't exist in isolation but should integrate with broader enterprise risk management (ERM) frameworks.*

AI governance emerged as a top priority in 2024, as legal departments and law firms rapidly adopted generative AI but faced challenges in implementation. According to Wolters Kluwer's 2024 Future Ready Lawyer Survey, 76% of legal professionals in corporate legal departments and 68% in law firms use generative AI at least once a week, with about one-third using it daily. However, many legal professionals report significant challenges, including integrating generative AI with existing systems and processes, as well as concerns about using the technology ethically and effectively. This indicates a lack of well-established governance.

A gap between AI adoption and governance creates significant risks. To illustrate, consider this scenario: Your attorneys are using various AI tools for everything from legal research to document review, each making individual decisions about appropriate use. Without clear policies and governance structures, how do you ensure consistent standards, maintain quality control, and protect client interests?

# THE POLICY DEVELOPMENT CHALLENGE

## Beyond Traditional Technology Policies

Many law firms and legal departments are developing and deploying technology policies to address AI's unique challenges. The process is evolutionary. Traditional policies typically focus on security, acceptable use, and data protection. However, AI requires additional policy considerations around professional responsibility implications, quality control, and oversight requirements; client disclosure and consent; model training and data usage; and bias monitoring and mitigation.

To demonstrate how traditional policies fall short, consider this hypothetical example. A litigation team uses an AI tool to analyze deposition transcripts. Traditional IT policies might cover data security and confidentiality, but they don't address crucial questions like: What level of attorney review is required for AI analysis? How should potential AI biases be identified and addressed? When should AI use be disclosed to clients or courts? How should AI-assisted work be documented?

The data governance frameworks discussed in Chapters 7 and 8 become essential policy components because AI governance cannot be separated from data governance. Organizations attempting to create AI policies without addressing underlying data management—data quality standards, access controls, lineage tracking, and semantic classification—discover that their AI governance lacks enforceable boundaries and measurable compliance indicators.

## Current and Developing Guidance

Prior to AI becoming broadly recognized as a transformative force in legal practice, the American Bar Association's Formal Opinion 498 (issued March 2021) emphasized that lawyers' duties of competence included understanding the benefits and risks of relevant technology. This opinion provided guidance on the ethical obligations of lawyers engaging in virtual law practice. The ABA's Formal Opinion 512, issued in 2024, added detail about the supervisory obligations when AI is being used.

The legal profession's oversight bodies, in the U.S. and elsewhere, are continuing to provide guidance for AI use. Some state bar associations also have issued AI-specific guidance. These cover things like attorney oversight of AI tools, client disclosure requirements, quality control protocols, documentation standards, confidentiality obligations when using AI, duty of competence in AI tool selection, and requirements for supervising AI use.

But law firms and legal departments must also consider broader legislative and policy developments about AI governance across a range of jurisdictions, and not only rely on guidance issued for the legal profession. The International Association of Privacy Professionals (IAPP) has established a Global AI Law and Policy Tracker that can assist in keeping up with these developments.[1]

## *Example of an AI Governance Framework*

Many law firms have developed AI governance frameworks, but all are works in progress. Some firms have shared their approaches in surveys or research reports. Some address both immediate governance needs and anticipate evolving requirements.

What is clear is that effective AI governance requires more than policies. It demands integrated processes and systems, and cultural alignment. Your governance framework must be flexible enough to evolve with rapidly improving technology while maintaining core principles and professional standards.

We believe that AI governance frameworks should include but not be limited to the following four components:

1. **Tiered policy architecture:** Rather than a monolithic AI policy, adopt a three-tiered structure:
   - Core principles (ethical foundations)
   - Operational guidelines (practical standards)
   - Tool-specific protocols (requirements for specific AI applications)
2. **Distributed governance model:** To balance oversight with innovation with the following oversight groups:
   - A global AI ethics committee (approves standards and evaluates emerging issues)
   - Implementation teams (adapt standards to local requirements)
   - Practice group AI champions (provides guidance and feedback)
3. **Dynamic risk management:** Changes with improving AI capabilities and implementation maturity:
   - Initial phase: Intensive oversight with comprehensive review
   - Established phase: Risk-based reviews validation
   - Mature phase: Exception-based review with automated monitoring

[1] IAPP, Global AI Law and Policy Tracker, https://iapp.org/resources/article/global-ai-legislation-tracker/ (last updated May 2025).

4. **Continuous learning program:** To ensure governance evolves with both technology and practice needs:
   - Quarterly policy reviews based on implementation experience
   - Structured feedback collection from users and clients
   - Regular environmental scanning for emerging issues and regulations

A framework's effectiveness will be enhanced by its integration with existing practice policies and processes. It should not operate as a separate compliance exercise. AI governance should not be something separate from how you practice law. It should be an integral component of a professional practice.

# KEY POLICY COMPONENTS

## Core Policy Requirements

Many legal organizations struggle with AI governance because they approach policy development as a checklist rather than an integrated system designed for their specific organization. Effective AI governance requires policies that work together to address four essential areas: (1) use guidelines, (2) oversight requirements, (3) documentation standards, and (4) risk management protocols.

Let's examine why each of these components matters and how they work together. AI use guidelines form the foundation of AI governance, providing clear direction about when and how AI tools can be used in legal practice. However, these guidelines must go beyond permitted/prohibited lists. They also need to help attorneys understand the context for AI use and make informed decisions about AI applications in their practice.

For example, a policy shouldn't just state that AI can be used for document review. It should outline the types of matters where AI review is appropriate, the level of complexity or risk that requires additional oversight, and the factors attorneys should consider when deciding whether to employ AI tools. (In the future, it may become more practical to define the contexts where using AI would be considered inappropriate.)

Oversight requirements should then build on these guidelines, creating frameworks for meaningful attorney supervision. The challenge here isn't just ensuring work gets reviewed. It's establishing processes that maintain professional standards, while leveraging AI's capabilities efficiently. This would likely include different levels of review based on matter complexity, clear protocols for validating AI outputs, and specific requirements for documenting oversight activities.

Documentation standards play a crucial role in both risk management and quality control. The key is finding the right balance between creating an adequate audit trail and avoiding unnecessary administrative burden. These standards should answer practical questions like: What aspects of AI use need to be documented? How should validation and review be recorded? What level of detail is required for different types of matters? How long should documentation be retained?

### *Data governance integration*

AI use guidelines must incorporate the data readiness standards outlined in Chapters 7 and 8, including requirements for data quality validation before AI processing, semantic classification requirements for different AI applications, and lineage tracking for audit and compliance purposes. Without these data governance foundations, AI policies lack the technical infrastructure necessary for consistent enforcement.

Risk management protocols tie these components together into a coherent system. They should provide clear guidance for identifying potential risks in AI use, assessing impact and likelihood, implementing appropriate controls, monitoring and reporting issues, and responding to problems when they arise.

The effectiveness of these protocols depends heavily on how well they integrate with existing risk management systems while addressing AI-specific challenges.

## Client-Facing Governance Policies

While internal governance policies address how organizations use AI, some legal organizations develop structured approaches to client-facing AI policies. These policies address how the organization communicates about AI use, manages client expectations, and respects client preferences. More and more legal departments have specific requirements regarding how their outside counsel use and disclose AI in their matters. This creates both a necessity and opportunity for law firms to develop thoughtful client-facing policies.

## Disclosure Protocols

Your framework should include structured disclosure protocols that vary based on both matter type and AI application. For example:

- **Standard disclosure:** Basic information provided for routine AI use in all matters
- **Enhanced disclosure:** More detailed information for novel applications or **sensitive matters**
- **Client-specific disclosure:** Customized approaches for clients with specific AI policies

Regardless of whether you use these specific categories, the key point is your disclosure framework must recognize that different clients and different matters require different approaches.

A systematic approach for understanding and respecting client preferences will be beneficial:

- **Client AI preference assessment:** Structured process for documenting client requirements
- **Preference implementation system:** Operational processes ensuring preferences are followed
- **Compliance validation:** Regular reviews confirming adherence to client guidelines

We also encourage the development of structured methods for communicating AI value to clients. For example:

- **Value metrics:** Specific measurements of efficiency, quality, or risk reduction
- **Comparison approaches:** Clear methods for contrasting AI-assisted and traditional methods
- **ROI calculations:** Frameworks for demonstrating client value from AI use

Your clients will want to understand the tangible benefits of AI use. Your framework should help attorneys articulate the benefits in terms that are meaningful to their clients.

Your system also should include gathering client feedback on AI use. For example:

- **Structured surveys:** Assessments of client satisfaction with AI-related aspects of legal services
- **Feedback integration:** Routines for incorporating client input into your governance processes
- **Continuous improvement:** Processes for adapting or adding client approaches based on feedback

This client-facing framework will complement your internal governance, enabling an approach that supports professional obligations and client expectations.

# QUALITY CONTROL AND OVERSIGHT

Quality control in AI governance requires a systematic approach that addresses three critical stages of AI:

- Input governance or control
- Throughput governance or process control
- Output governance or validation

Understanding how these stages interconnect is crucial for effective governance.

## Input Control

Input control focuses on data quality and appropriateness, essentially ensuring that what goes into AI systems will support reliable outputs. This involves more than just checking data accuracy. Legal organizations must consider a variety of issues. Input control is the foundational stage of AI governance, and is particularly critical in legal contexts where precision, confidentiality, and integrity of information are paramount. At this stage, legal organizations ensure the accuracy, quality, and ethical sourcing of data used to train and guide AI systems. Data quality issues, such as completeness and consistency, are just the starting point. Input control also requires careful consideration of potential biases in training data, appropriateness of data sources for specific legal tasks, and compliance with client confidentiality requirements.

For example, an AI tool used for contract analysis must be trained on legally compliant, well-structured, and representative contracts to avoid embedding biases or inaccuracies that could lead to flawed outputs. Law firms and legal departments must implement stringent data vetting and preprocessing measures, checking for confidentiality, verifying relevance, and eliminating potential sources of bias, ensuring that AI decisions align with professional standards and ethical obligations.

## Process Control

In the next stage, process control involves overseeing and managing the internal operations of AI systems throughout their active use within legal workflows. In the context of law practice, this means continuously monitoring and managing how AI systems process data, make predictions, or generate outputs. Effective process control includes auditing algorithmic behavior, ensuring transparency and interpretability, and maintaining accountability throughout the AI life cycle. For example, legal teams deploying AI-driven document review must regularly assess how the system identifies relevant clauses, flags risks, and provides legal summaries. Lawyers need clearly defined processes for routine checks, documentation of AI-generated work, and systematic oversight to ensure compliance with professional obligations and emerging regulations.

Process control represents perhaps the most complex aspect of AI quality management. It's not enough to simply monitor whether people are following procedures. Organizations need to understand how AI tools are being integrated into legal work processes and whether that integration maintains professional standards. Key considerations include:

- Real-time monitoring of AI tool usage.
- Integration with legal workflows.
- Adherence to ethical guidelines
- Documentation of decision-making
- Validation of intermediate results.

Organizations with strong process controls will have higher success rates in AI adoption compared to those focusing solely on input and output controls.

## Output Validation

Output validation serves as the critical gatekeeping phase, where results generated by AI systems are rigorously evaluated before being relied upon or delivered to clients. In the legal profession, output validation is essential for maintaining trust, ensuring accuracy, and upholding ethical standards of practice. Lawyers must possess the competencies required to critically assess AI-generated content, including contract language, litigation strategies, or regulatory compliance reports. Output validation requires clear frameworks for human oversight—experienced legal professionals who can apply nuanced judgment, contextual understanding, and ethical considerations to ensure AI outputs are correct, reliable, and appropriate for client use. Robust output validation practices not only protect law firms from potential liability and ethical pitfalls but also reinforce client and judicial confidence in the responsible use of advanced technologies.

Output validation completes the quality control triangle. Effective validation requires a nuanced understanding of both AI capabilities and legal professional standards. Determining what constitutes appropriate validation varies by context. Document review might require statistical sampling and error rate analysis, while legal research applications might need structured protocols for verifying that AI-suggested authorities are current and accurately applied.

## AI MODEL RISK MANAGEMENT

As legal organizations increasingly rely on AI tools with complex underlying models, leading organizations are developing specialized governance approaches for model risk management. These approaches address the unique challenges of evaluating and monitoring AI models that may evolve.

Traditional technology risk approaches are insufficient for AI systems. The reason is that AI models can continuously learn and adapt. As such, you need a risk management framework that addresses several critical dimensions:

### Model Inventory and Classification

The foundation of the risk approach must be a comprehensive inventory of all AI models used in your practice. You might include the following elements:

- **Impact potential:** How significantly the model could affect client matters
- **Learning characteristics:** Whether and how the model learns from firm data
- **Transparency level:** How explainable the model's operations and outputs are
- **Validation requirements:** What testing and verification the model requires
- **Data integration requirements**: How extensively the model requires access to organizational data and whether it processes data according to the governance standards established in your enterprise data framework (Models requiring broad data access or complex data integration present higher governance risks and require enhanced oversight protocols.)

This classification determines appropriate governance, with more rigorous requirements for high-impact, learning-enabled, or less transparent models.

### Model Validation Protocols

For each model class, you should establish specific validation requirements:

- **Initial validation:** Comprehensive testing before approval for use
- **Periodic re-validation:** Scheduled reassessment based on risk classification

- **Trigger-based validation:** Events that require immediate reassessment
- **Validation documentation:** Standard methods for recording validation results

Model validation isn't a one-time event but an ongoing process. Your risk management protocols should seek to ensure that models maintain appropriate performance as they learn and change.

## Model Drift Monitoring

A key element in any AI risk management program is systematic monitoring for model drift. This includes changes in model performance or behavior over time. You'll want to include:

- **Performance metrics:** Key indicators monitored for unexpected changes.
- **Drift detection:** Statistical approaches for identifying significant shifts.
- **Alert thresholds:** Defined boundaries triggering investigation.
- **Response protocols:** Standard procedures when drift is detected.

Model drift represents a significant risk for AI governance. As such, your monitoring systems should provide early warnings if and when models start to behave differently than you expected.

## Explainability Requirements

Explainability in artificial intelligence refers to the capacity of AI systems to provide clear, understandable justifications for their outputs and decisions. In the legal profession, explainability is particularly crucial due to the ethical, professional, and regulatory obligations that attorneys must uphold. You cannot rely solely on opaque or "black-box" AI systems; you must understand how AI-derived outcomes are reached to confidently defend those outcomes in legal settings and ensure compliance with professional standards. Explainability fosters transparency and accountability, allowing you to effectively validate AI recommendations; justify your legal strategies to clients, courts, and regulators; and mitigate risks associated with potential AI biases or inaccuracies. Consequently, prioritizing explainability in legal AI implementations helps maintain trust and uphold ethical practice, and ensures that you and your team remain fully responsible and capable stewards of your professional judgment.

Your framework should establish explainability standards scaled to risk level:

- **Documentation standards:** Required model documentation varying by risk class
- **Explanation capabilities:** Required ability to explain specific outputs
- **Audit trails:** Records connecting inputs, processing, and outputs
- **Human oversight:** Requirements for human review and interpretation

Your explainability framework should integrate with your broader AI governance and address the specific requirements of model risk management. Your models are the engines driving AI capabilities. Without effective model governance, AI governance remains incomplete because explainability is essential for maintaining professional judgment and responsibility.

## Methods for Ensuring Explainability

Ensuring explainability in AI used within legal practice requires a combination of technical, procedural, and organizational strategies. One foundational method is the use of interpretable models such as decision trees, rule-based systems, or linear regression. These model types offer transparency by design. While these models may not be suitable for all tasks, especially complex ones like natural language processing, they provide clear insight into how their decisions are made, which is often sufficient for tasks like legal classification or document triage.

For more complex AI systems, particularly those involving machine learning or deep learning, explainability can be enhanced through post hoc interpretability tools. Techniques such as LIME (Local Interpretable Model-agnostic Explanations) and SHAP (SHapley Additive exPlanations) allow practitioners to analyze which inputs had the greatest influence on a particular output. In a legal context, these tools can help an attorney understand why an AI system flagged a clause as risky or recommended a particular litigation strategy, thereby enabling meaningful review and informed oversight.

Additionally, implementing model documentation and audit trails is essential. Legal teams should require that all AI systems used in practice maintain logs of inputs, outputs, decision pathways, and any model changes over time. These records are critical for both internal accountability and external review—such as responding to client inquiries or regulatory audits. They also support the principle of human-in-the-loop oversight, where attorneys or legal professionals retain final responsibility for interpreting and applying AI outputs within ethical and professional boundaries.

Cross-disciplinary collaboration plays a key role in ensuring explainability. Involving legal experts, data scientists, and governance professionals in the design and deployment of AI systems helps ensure that explainability is embedded from the outset. This includes aligning AI behavior with legal reasoning, ensuring the system supports rather than replaces human judgment, and facilitating transparency in both language and logic. These methods, when applied consistently, enable law firms and legal departments to use AI responsibly while maintaining the trust, clarity, and accountability essential to the profession.

## IMPLEMENTATION STRATEGIES

### Building Effective Frameworks

Successful AI policy implementation requires a carefully phased approach. Rather than attempting a "big bang" rollout, we recommend you follow a structured sequential implementation path. For example:

**Phase 1: Foundation building:** This initial phase focuses on establishing core policies and processes. Success requires extensive stakeholder engagement to ensure policies address real-world needs while remaining practical to implement. Key activities include:

- Policy development and review.
- Stakeholder consultation.
- Initial training development.
- Pilot testing of procedures.

**Phase 2: Controlled rollout:** Once foundation elements are in place organizations can begin a controlled implementation focusing on:

- Phased deployment by practice area or matter type.
- Intensive monitoring and support.
- Regular feedback collection.
- Quick response to issues.

The key during this phase is maintaining balance between pushing adoption forward and ensuring adequate support and oversight are maintained.

**Phase 3: Expansion and refinement:** As experience grows, organizations can begin expanding AI use while refining their governance approaches based on actual implementation experience. This phase typically involves:

- Broader deployment across practice areas.
- Integration with standard workflows.
- Policy refinement based on implementation learnings.
- Enhanced monitoring and measurement governance structure optimization.

## Integrating AI Governance with Enterprise Risk Management

You must recognize that AI governance shouldn't exist in isolation but should integrate with broader enterprise risk management (ERM) frameworks. This integration ensures AI risks are appropriately prioritized, resourced, and managed alongside other organizational risks.

A comprehensive approach for integrating AI governance with your enterprise risk management can avoid duplication, inefficiencies, and potential gaps. Treating AI governance as separate from your overall risk management can potentially lead to unnecessary complexity, conflicts, and potential blind spots. Integration should strengthen your AI governance and your broader enterprise risk management.

## Unified Risk Assessment

Rather than treating AI risks as a separate category, integrate AI considerations into your enterprise risk assessment processes:

- **Risk identification:** AI risks are identified alongside other operational risks
- **Risk evaluation:** Common methodology for assessing likelihood and impact
- **Risk prioritization:** Unified approach to determining resource allocation
- **Risk ownership:** Clear assignment of responsibility within existing structures

A unified assessment can help ensure that AI risks receive appropriate attention within your overall risk landscape. It may prevent inadequate addressing of significant AI risks or over playing lower-priority risks.

Data governance risks represent a critical intersection between AI and enterprise risk management. Organizations with mature data governance frameworks—including the semantic models and intelligent classification systems described in earlier chapters—can more accurately assess and manage AI risks because they understand their data exposure and can implement appropriate controls. This data governance foundation enables more precise risk assessment and more effective control implementation.

## Coordinated Control Framework

You should seek to align AI controls with broader organizational controls:

- **Integrated policies:** AI policies that align with and reference broader policies
- **Consistent control language:** Common terminology across control frameworks
- **Complementary controls:** Controls designed to work together without duplication
- **Control rationalization:** Regular review to eliminate redundant requirements

Your team needs and wants a coherent framework rather than competing requirements. Proper coordination should seek to prevent policy proliferation that can lead to confusion.

## Combined Monitoring and Reporting

Your monitoring systems should incorporate AI indicators into your broader dashboards:

- **Unified dashboards:** Integrated views of key risk indicators
- **Coordinated reporting:** Aligned reporting cycles and formats
- **Consolidated analysis:** Holistic assessment of interrelated risks
- **Comprehensive response:** Coordinated approach to cross-cutting issues

Integrated monitoring helps identify how AI risks interact with other risks. This can be very valuable for complex issues spanning technology, client service, and professional matters.

## Shared Governance Structures

Perhaps most importantly, align your governance structures:

- **Overlapping membership:** Key individuals serve on both AI and ERM committees
- **Coordinated meeting schedules:** Aligned timing to facilitate information flow
- **Joint risk assessments:** Combined evaluation of interconnected risks
- **Unified escalation paths:** Clear routes for raising issues needing attention

An integrated approach will yield tangible benefits, including lower governance overhead, improved risk visibility, and more consistent application of controls.

Plus, integration can help avoid lawyers viewing AI governance as a compliance burden and instead seeing it as a natural component of your risk management approach.

Effective AI governance requires structures that balance oversight with innovation. Simply creating a technology committee isn't sufficient. Organizations need a multilayered governance approach that addresses strategic, operational, and tactical needs.

At the strategic level, organizations need a formal body responsible for AI governance. Typically, this takes the form of an AI governance committee that includes:

- Senior attorneys who understand both practice needs and professional obligations.
- IT leadership with deep understanding of technical implications.
- Risk management professionals who can assess potential issues.
- Ethics advisors who can address professional responsibility concerns.

This committee shouldn't operate as a distant oversight body. Instead, successful organizations integrate committee members into regular practice operations through structured touch points and feedback loops.

Day-to-day governance requires dedicated operational management. Successful organizations establish clear roles and responsibilities for AI oversight, regular monitoring and reporting processes, structured escalation procedures, and ongoing training and support systems. The key is creating operational processes that provide adequate oversight without creating unnecessary bureaucracy that might stifle innovation or efficiency.

Effective operational support networks typically include:

- Practice group champions who understand both the technology and practical applications.
- Technical support resources for tool-specific issues.
- Subject matter experts for complex questions.
- Documentation and training resources.

## GOVERNANCE TECHNOLOGY: TOOLS FOR EFFECTIVE AI OVERSIGHT

As AI governance requirements grow more complex, legal organizations are implementing specialized technology tools to support effective oversight without creating an unmanageable administrative burden. These technologies automate routine aspects of governance while providing enhanced visibility into AI use across the organization.

Manual governance processes couldn't scale with expanding AI use. Effective governance requires real-time visibility and deep analytic capabilities that manual processes simply can't deliver at scale. A purpose-built, technology-enabled approach ensures comprehensive oversight in an efficient manner

## AI Inventory Management

An automated system for tracking all AI models and applications might include:

- **Automated discovery:** Identification of new AI tools as they're deployed.
- **Classification engine:** Automated risk categorization based on defined criteria.
- **Approval workflow:** Streamlined processes for governance review.
- **Documentation repository:** Centralized storage of all governance artifacts.

## Policy Automation

Systems that make policies accessible and actionable:

- **Policy navigator:** Interactive tool helping users find relevant requirements
- **Decision support:** Guided workflows for common governance questions
- **Automated validation:** Systems checking for policy compliance
- **Exception management:** Structured processes for handling unique situations

## Usage Monitoring

Tools providing visibility into actual AI use patterns:

- **Usage analytics:** Data on tool utilization across practices and matters
- **Pattern recognition:** Identification of unusual or potentially problematic use
- **Threshold alerting:** Notification when usage exceeds defined parameters
- **Trend analysis:** Insights into evolving use patterns requiring attention

It has been said that "You can't govern what you can't see." Monitoring tools provide the visibility essential for effective oversight.

### Compliance Dashboard

Integrated views providing comprehensive governance insights:

- **Status visualization:** Clear presentation of key governance metrics
- **Exception highlighting:** Visual identification of areas needing attention
- **Trend tracking:** Visualization of changing patterns over time
- **Drill-down capabilities:** Ability to investigate specific areas of concern

Dashboards can help to transform governance data into actionable insights. They can help focus your attention where it's most needed.

### Documentation Automation

Tools streamlining the documentation of governance activities:

- **Template generation:** Automated creation of standardized documentation
- **Workflow integration:** Documentation embedded in normal work processes
- **Audit trail creation:** Automatic capture of key governance actions
- **Evidence collection:** Systematic gathering of compliance verification
- **Data lineage integration:** Automated connection to data governance systems that track how information flows through AI processing, enabling comprehensive audit trails.

An integrated suite of purpose-built technology tools can improve governance effectiveness and reduce administrative overhead. It can help maintain comprehensive oversight while focusing attorney time on professional judgment rather than administrative matters.

## INTERNATIONAL DIMENSIONS OF AI GOVERNANCE

For global legal organizations, AI governance must address divergent international regulatory requirements. Leading organizations are developing sophisticated approaches to navigate this complex landscape while maintaining consistent professional standards. We suggest implementing a globally coordinated, locally adapted governance framework that maintains consistent standards while respecting significant regional variations in both regulation and client expectations. Large international firms have taken this approach. You need to address several key dimensions:

## Regulatory Monitoring System

The foundation is a comprehensive system for tracking evolving requirements:

- **Global coverage:** Monitoring across all jurisdictions where you operate
- **Regulatory classification:** Categorization of requirements by type and impact
- **Impact assessment:** Analysis of how changes affect your current operations
- **Update triggering:** Automated notification of relevant stakeholders

You are best served by identifying relevant developments before they impact your practice.

## Layered Policy Architecture

Use a tiered approach to balance consistency with local adaptation, including:

- **Global principles:** Consistent standards applied across all jurisdictions
- **Regional frameworks:** Adaptations addressing major regulatory variations
- **Local implementations:** Specific protocols for jurisdiction-unique requirements

This will provide the flexibility essential for global operations.

## Cross-Border Matter Management

Develop specialized approaches for matters spanning multiple jurisdictions:

- **Jurisdiction mapping:** Identification of all relevant regulatory regimes
- **Requirements analysis:** Assessment of potentially conflicting obligations
- **Governance reconciliation:** Resolution of conflicting requirements
- **Documentation protocol:** Standardized recording of cross-border decisions

## Regional Centers of Excellence

To maintain expertise across diverse requirements, you may want to establish a center of excellence that includes:

- **Regional AI governance experts:** Specialists in local regulatory environments.
- **A knowledge sharing network:** Systems for exchanging insights across regions.

- **Escalation pathways:** Structured routes for addressing complex questions.
- **Harmonization working groups:** Teams focused on reconciling approaches.

A framework like this will add value as jurisdictions adopt increasingly divergent approaches to AI regulation.

## DEVELOPING EFFECTIVE POLICIES

Creating effective AI policies requires careful attention to both content and communication.

Scope and applicability policies need clear boundaries about what they cover and who must follow them. This includes: Which AI tools and applications are covered? Who needs to comply with the policies? When do policies apply to specific situations? How do policies relate to existing procedures?

Rather than creating rigid rules, effective policies provide frameworks for decision-making. For example, instead of simply stating when AI can or cannot be used, policies should help attorneys understand how to evaluate AI use in different contexts. The key is finding the right balance between providing clear direction and maintaining flexibility to address novel situations.

Guidance in policy development and management, such as that provided by the OCEG Policy Management Capability Model, offers detailed steps that are relevant for any AI governance plan.[2]

## CONCLUSION

Policy development and governance for AI in legal practice requires a delicate balance. Too little governance creates unacceptable risks, too much stifles innovation and adoption. The key to success lies in creating frameworks that protect professional standards and client interests while enabling the benefits AI can bring to legal practice.

Organizations succeeding with AI governance share several common characteristics:

- Clear policies that provide guidance rather than just rules
- Governance structures that balance oversight with innovation

---

[2] OCEG, https://www.oceg.org/grc-standards/#policy-management-capability-model (last visited Oct. 2, 2025).

- Strong support systems that help users navigate AI use effectively
- Regular review and updates to address emerging challenges

Effective AI governance isn't just about compliance; it's also about enabling responsible innovation. Leading organizations are moving beyond checkbox approaches to create integrated governance frameworks that align with broader risk management, address specific AI challenges, and adapt to evolving regulatory requirements.

Perhaps most importantly, successful governance frameworks recognize that AI presents both unique challenges and unprecedented opportunities. The organizations that thrive will be those that develop governance approaches that protect professional values while enabling the transformative benefits AI can bring to legal practice.

As AI capabilities continue to evolve, governance frameworks must evolve as well. Organizations need to build flexibility into their approaches while maintaining core principles that protect professional standards and client interests.

## ACTION ITEMS

1. **Develop AI Governance Framework**
    - Create tiered policy architecture with core principles, operational guidelines, and tool-specific protocols
    - Establish distributed governance model with ethics committee, implementation teams, and practice champions
    - Design dynamic risk management that evolves with AI maturity
2. **Create Comprehensive Policy Components**
    - Develop AI use guidelines addressing when, how, and under what circumstances AI can be used
    - Establish oversight requirements with appropriate supervision levels
    - Create documentation standards and risk management protocols
3. **Implement Quality Control Systems**
    - Design input control processes ensuring data quality and appropriateness
    - Establish process control mechanisms for ongoing AI system monitoring
    - Create output validation frameworks with appropriate human oversight

4. **Establish AI Model Risk Management**
   - Create model inventory and classification system based on impact and risk
   - Implement model validation protocols and drift monitoring systems
   - Establish explainability requirements scaled to risk level
5. **Build Client-Facing Governance Policies**
   - Develop disclosure protocols varying by matter type and AI application
   - Create client preference assessment and implementation systems
   - Establish value demonstration and feedback collection mechanisms
6. **Integrate with Enterprise Risk Management**
   - Align AI governance with broader organizational risk frameworks
   - Create unified risk assessment and coordinated control systems
   - Establish shared governance structures and combined monitoring

CHAPTER 11

# Preparing Your Workforce for the AI Future

## INTRODUCTION

*AI will fundamentally reshape the legal workforce.*

Various surveys and reports indicate over 80% of law firms plan to increase AI investment over the next year, yet few have comprehensive workforce plans to address how AI will impact their teams. A significant gap between technology adoption and workforce planning could create significant risks for legal organizations. The risks are highlighted by the findings of the 2025 Clio Legal Trends report,[1] which include:

- AI adoption is rapidly increasing—93% of mid-size firms reporting using AI in their practices.
- Hourly work is at risk—74% of hourly work could be automated by generative AI.
- The work that's most exposed to AI automation includes documenting and recording information, getting information, and analyzing data or information, all of which make up 66% of hourly work.

To illustrate the challenge, consider a scenario occurring in many firms: A practice group implements an AI contract analysis tool, expecting immediate efficiency gains. Instead, they face resistance from experienced paralegals who see

[1] Clio, *2025 Legal Trends Report for Mid-Sized Law Firms* (2025), https://www.clio.com/resources/legal-trends/.

the tool as a threat to their roles, while attorneys struggle to leverage the AI capabilities without proper paralegal support. The result? Underutilized technology and frustrated staff.

This chapter explores how to develop workforce strategies that align with AI adoption, addressing the opportunities and challenges AI presents for different roles within legal organizations. We examine how AI is transforming traditional legal roles, identify new skills and competencies required, explore emerging organizational structures, and provide practical guidance for implementing effective workforce transitions.

## A Cautious Perspective

Not every lawyer sees AI as a transformative force for good. Some view it as a distraction—or worse, a threat to the profession. While we believe that the overall trend toward increased use of AI is inevitable in the legal profession, we respect the fact that, as we write this in 2025, not everyone is currently enthused about this direction. Have you heard comments like these?

> *Law is built on precedent, human judgment, and deep expertise—none of which AI can replicate.*
>
> *The push to integrate AI into legal work is driven more by vendors looking to sell software than by genuine client needs.*
>
> *AI tools can generate impressive-looking outputs, but they lack the depth of understanding required in legal reasoning. And let's be honest: The more we automate, the less training young associates and paralegals receive in foundational skills.*
>
> *If we replace early-stage legal work with AI, we are not just jeopardizing jobs, we're undermining the development of the next generation of lawyers. A legal career isn't about efficiency; it's about mastery.*
>
> *AI can be a useful tool, but relying on it too much will create a generation of lawyers who can't think critically or argue persuasively. I wouldn't advise any associate to build their career around AI. Instead, focus on building real legal expertise—because when AI-generated mistakes start causing malpractice suits, it won't be the software taking the blame; it'll be the lawyer who trusted it.*

As you develop new workforce structures and expectations about increasing the use of AI, you will encounter resistance like this, and you will need to be ready to respond.

# THE CHANGING LANDSCAPE OF LEGAL ROLES

## Impact Assessment: How AI Transforms Legal Work

The integration of AI into legal practice doesn't just change how work gets done, it fundamentally reshapes roles across the organization. Some successful organizations are taking a nuanced approach to role evolution rather than viewing AI simply as a replacement for human work. We agree with this approach.

For attorneys, AI is creating both opportunities and obligations. We see several key shifts: increased focus on strategic analysis rather than routine research, new obligations regarding AI oversight and validation, enhanced need for technology competence, and growing emphasis on data-driven decision-making.

Support roles are experiencing even more dramatic transformation. Paralegals, often assumed to be most vulnerable to AI displacement, are instead evolving into crucial intermediaries between AI tools and legal practice. Rather than being replaced, their responsibilities are shifting from routine document review to analysis and quality control, AI tool operation and output validation, enhanced client communication, and new responsibilities in compliance and risk management.

Legal secretaries and administrative staff are similarly seeing role redefinition, with decreased focus on document production and increased emphasis on project coordination, client communication, and technology support. This evolution requires all legal professionals to develop new skills while leveraging their existing knowledge in more sophisticated ways.

A hypothetical case study. This story provides an instructive example of a workforce transformation alongside AI implementation. Rather than viewing AI adoption as primarily a technology initiative, the firm approached it as a comprehensive workforce transformation project.

According to the global managing partner in our hypothetical case study, "We recognized early that our success with AI would depend less on the technology itself and more on how effectively we helped our people evolve alongside it. This meant reimagining roles, developing new skills, and creating career paths that embraced technological change."

The firm began with a comprehensive workforce assessment inventorying relevant skills. But they also mapped how work flowed through the organization, identifying where AI could enhance human capabilities rather than replace tasks currently done by people. This assessment revealed that their paralegal workforce represented the greatest opportunity and the greatest challenge in their AI transformation.

Their paralegals had deep knowledge of documents, clients, and processes. But many saw AI as a threat rather than an opportunity. The firm needed to transform negative perceptions while helping people to develop new capabilities. Their approach included several key elements:

First, they created a paralegal evolution program that explicitly addressing how roles would change with AI. Rather than diminishing the paralegal role, they elevated it to include AI oversight, quality control, and client-facing responsibilities. This included creating new titles like legal technology specialist and AI application manager, recognizing the value of these new and important roles.

Second, they developed tiered training that matched their phased AI implementation. Initial training focused on general AI literacy and tool basics. As implementation progressed, training evolved to include advanced features, quality control protocols, and strategic application within specific practice areas.

Third, they established a shadow program where paralegals worked alongside the technology implementation team during AI deployment. This gave paralegals direct input into how tools were configured and integrated into workflows, while building both technical knowledge and ownership of the new processes.

Perhaps most importantly, they revised their compensation and promotion structures to reward AI expertise and innovation. Paralegals who developed advanced capabilities in AI oversight and implementation could advance along new career paths with corresponding compensation increases.

The results were impressive: Most of their paralegals successfully transitioned to enhanced roles, productivity metrics improved significantly across AI-enabled practice areas, and paralegal retention increased significantly during a period when competitors were seeing high turnover in these roles.

The key in this hypothetical story is approaching AI implementation as workforce transformation rather than just a technology implementation. By focusing on how people's work changed alongside the technology, the firm achieved good adoption, more effective implementation, and better overall results.

# ESSENTIAL SKILLS AND COMPETENCIES

## The New Skill Landscape

Legal organizations need to develop three distinct skill layers: technical proficiency, analytic capabilities, and strategic integration. Technical proficiency is a foundational requirement. Contrary to common assumptions, technical proficiency does not mean coding or data science, it means understanding how AI tools work in legal practice. For paralegals, this means mastering AI-powered platforms for document review, research, and analysis. For attorneys, it means understanding AI capabilities and limitations well enough to make informed decisions about tool use and oversight.

Analytic capabilities become more important as routine tasks become automated. Paralegals need strong analytical skills, as they will spend significant time analyzing AI outputs and identifying potential issues. This represents a big shift from traditional paralegal activities.

Strategic integration skills may be the most crucial development area. Legal professionals need to understand how to integrate AI capabilities into legal practice effectively. This isn't just about operating tools. It's about reimagining how work gets done.

Effective workforce planning for AI implementation begins with a comprehensive understanding of current capabilities and future requirements. Some firms have developed structured skills assessments. The assessment frameworks typically examine distinct skill dimensions for each role in the organization.

Technical readiness assesses fundamental capabilities needed to work effectively with AI tools. Rather than focusing on only advanced technical skills, include assessment of comfort with technology, adaptability to new tools, and basic digital literacy.

Regarding analytic capabilities, evaluate skills in critical thinking, pattern recognition, and logical analysis. These are capabilities essential for effective oversight of AI systems. Paralegals with strong analytical skills may excel in AI validation roles, even when they have limited technology experience.

Regarding change readiness, you should examine adaptability, learning agility, and comfort with ambiguity. These attributes are very valuable during a technological transformation. People with strong change readiness capabilities often become informal leaders during implementation, helping others navigate the transition.

Assessments typically include a combination of methods including skills inventories, scenario-based evaluations, and manager assessments to build a comprehensive picture of current capabilities. This multi-method approach provides deeper insights than simple self-assessments or manager ratings alone.

After mapping current capabilities, a well-designed assessment framework will enable the identification of gaps relative to future requirements. Then you can define the skills needed for effective AI use in each role to create a clear target for development efforts.

Next, evaluate the gaps between current and required skills, and classify them by importance and development difficulty. This classification helps you to prioritize training investments and identify where role adjustments might be needed. The analysis then informs targeted development plans that address specific needs rather than providing generic training. For some roles, the skill gaps might be better addressed through role redesign rather than individual development.

Organizations implementing this approach, targeting development efforts precisely where they're needed most, should achieve significantly better AI adoption with less disruption.

## ORGANIZATIONAL STRUCTURE AND ROLE EVOLUTION

As AI transforms legal work, new specialized roles are emerging to bridge technology and practice. These new roles go beyond simply adding technology responsibilities to existing positions. In some cases, they represent fundamentally new functions within legal organizations.

### Legal AI Specialists

Legal AI specialists combine legal knowledge with specialized AI expertise, focusing specifically on optimizing AI applications for legal work. They typically handle tool evaluation, implementation planning, and ongoing optimization of AI systems. Most come from legal backgrounds, often paralegals or attorneys with technology aptitude, rather than pure technology backgrounds, as their value comes from understanding both the technology and legal practice.

### AI Validation Analysts

AI validation analysts focus specifically on quality control and risk management for AI outputs. Their role involves designing validation protocols, conducting systematic reviews of AI-generated work, and documenting compliance with professional standards. This role has proven particularly valuable in litigation and regulatory practices where AI outputs require rigorous verification.

## AI Ethics and Governance Officers

AI ethics and governance officers oversee the responsible use of AI across an organization. They develop and implement AI governance frameworks, monitor compliance with ethical guidelines, and address emerging risks. This role typically operates at a senior level, often reporting directly to executive leadership.

## Legal Data Specialists

Some organizations are creating specialized roles that combine legal and data science expertise. These professionals help organizations leverage data to enhance AI effectiveness. They develop data strategies, oversee data preparation and quality improvement, and create analytics that complement AI capabilities.

Most importantly, these new roles aren't isolated technology functions—they're integrated into practice operations. Successful organizations position these roles as practice resources rather than separate technology functions, ensuring they remain connected to real-world legal work while bringing specialized expertise to AI implementation.

## Team Structures and Models

Integrated teams combine traditional legal roles with new positions specifically focused on AI integration. Hub and spoke or "service center" models represent an effective approach. In this structure, central AI expertise teams support multiple practice groups. This model can be particularly effective in larger organizations where specialized AI expertise can be shared across geographies.

Some organizations are creating flexible hybrid structures that adjust based on matter type and AI involvement. This might mean having core teams of AI-proficient staff who can be deployed as needed while maintaining traditional staffing for matters where AI use is limited.

## Paralegal Transformation

Perhaps no role illustrates the impact of AI on legal workforce planning better than paralegals. Far from being displaced by AI, paralegals are evolving into crucial technology intermediaries. Paralegals with AI oversight skills can command higher salaries, reflecting the enhanced value these capabilities bring.

Compensation alignment ensures that enhanced responsibilities are reflected in paralegal remuneration. Some organizations have implemented skills-based compensation components that recognize specific AI capabilities alongside traditional factors like experience and legal subject expertise.

Career path development creates advancement opportunities specifically tied to AI expertise. New positions provide growth opportunities that don't require management responsibilities, while some paralegals are moving into dedicated technology roles while maintaining their connection to legal practice.

The transformation can yield significant benefits for both paralegals and the organization, including increased satisfaction, improved retention rates, and enhanced client service capabilities.

Most importantly, effective transformation programs shift perceptions of AI from threat to opportunity. This perception shift accelerates adoption while improving implementation quality.

The key insight from successful transformations is that effective paralegal evolution requires addressing both practical skills and professional identity. By helping paralegals understand how AI can enhance their professional contributions, organizations can create a workforce that embraces rather than resists technological change.

## CAREER PATHS AND COMPENSATION

The impact of AI on legal career paths requires careful consideration. Some legal organizations are creating new career pathways that specifically recognize AI expertise. For paralegals, this often means creating specialized tracks that focus on AI tool management and optimization, quality control and validation, training and support, and compliance and risk management. For attorneys, career paths increasingly include expectations about AI governance responsibilities, technology leadership, innovation contributions, and cross-functional collaboration.

The most successful organizations are developing clear competency models that define advancement requirements at each career stage, creating transparent paths for professional growth. These models typically include both technical proficiency and strategic application skills, ensuring that career advancement rewards the ability to leverage AI effectively in practice contexts.

Traditional legal compensation models often don't adequately account for AI-related skills and responsibilities. Some organizations are adapting their compensation structures to recognize AI expertise and certification, reward innovation in the use of AI, and account for productivity improvements driven by AI. Some are also recognizing the value of continuous education and learning around AI.

The metrics used to evaluate performance are also evolving. Organizations are increasingly incorporating AI-related metrics into personnel performance evaluations. These might include effective use of AI tools, innovation in AI applications, training and mentoring contributions, and quality control effectiveness.

Successful organizations will strike a balance between rewarding technical proficiency and recognizing the application of that proficiency to legal practice. Rather than compensating for technology skills in isolation, they reward the effective integration of those skills into client service and practice efficiency.

# IMPLEMENTATION STRATEGIES

## Setting Realistic Expectations

The rapid evolution of AI capabilities can create unrealistic expectations about efficiency gains and role changes. Smart organizations are taking a measured approach to managing expectations. Firms successful in integrating AI typically communicate clear timelines and expectations for adopting AI, set realistic targets, define role changes, and provide regular progress updates.

AI transformation is a journey rather than an event or destination. Organizations that set appropriate expectations about the benefits and challenges of AI adoption will tend to experience less resistance and achieve better results.

## Training Program Development

Effective training programs evolve alongside AI capabilities. As stated earlier, organizations must create layered approaches that begin with basic AI literacy and progress through advanced application. As discussed in more detail in Chapter 9, successful AI training programs typically include several key components:

- **Foundational training** introduces basic AI concepts, capabilities, and limitations. This training focuses on building general understanding rather than specific tool skills.
- **Tool-specific training** addresses the operational aspects of particular AI applications. This training teaches specific functionality and highlights appropriate use cases and limitations.

- **Application training** bridges the gap between tool operation and legal practice. This training focuses on integrating AI capabilities into specific practice contexts.
- **Oversight training** prepares supervisors to effectively manage AI-assisted work. This training emphasizes quality control, risk management, and ethical considerations.

By developing comprehensive training pathways that address both technical skills and practice integration, organizations can build the capabilities needed for effective AI adoption while maintaining professional standards.

## Feedback and Support Mechanisms

Continuous feedback becomes crucial during periods of technological transformation. Organizations need to understand how AI adoption affects their workforce in real time.

Successful organizations will implement structured feedback mechanisms, including regular check-ins, anonymous surveys, and focus groups. These mechanisms help identify issues before they become significant problems while highlighting successful approaches that can be shared across practice groups.

Equally important are robust support systems that help staff navigate the challenges of AI adoption. These systems might include technical help desks, peer mentoring programs, and resource libraries. By providing accessible support, organizations build confidence and accelerate adoption.

## Change Management

Clear, consistent communication becomes crucial during periods of technological change. Organizations need to help staff understand how AI will affect their roles while addressing concerns about job security and skill requirements. Successful organizations will develop comprehensive communication strategies that explain the rationale for AI adoption and how it fits into broader organizational strategy. This helps staff understand why changes are necessary and how they support long-term success.

Communication strategies should address concerns about job security directly, explaining how roles will evolve. This transparency helps reduce anxiety and resistance to change. Sharing success stories and practical examples of where, why, and how AI enhances human capabilities also proves valuable. Concrete examples can help make abstract concepts more relatable and less threatening.

Even with excellent communication, you should expect resistance to AI adoption. The key is addressing this resistance openly, honestly, and constructively rather than dismissing it. Resistance often highlights legitimate concerns that need to be addressed. By listening to concerns and involving staff in developing and deploying AI solutions, organizations can build support for change and improve adoption.

## Emerging Skill Requirements

As AI capabilities continue to advance, you will need to anticipate future skill requirements. Data literacy is becoming increasingly crucial as AI tools enable more sophisticated analytics. Legal professionals need to understand how to interpret and apply these insights effectively.

Ethical AI use will require a deeper understanding of bias, fairness, and transparency issues in data analyses. This goes beyond current professional responsibility requirements and requires specific knowledge about AI ethics and governance issues, including emerging regulations and guidance.

Strategic integration skills will become even more important as AI capabilities expand. You must think creatively about how to combine human and machine capabilities effectively. Remember, we are just in the early stages of AI in the legal profession, and the capabilities of AI are expanding and improving exponentially.

By anticipating the emerging skill requirements, legal organizations can begin to build new capabilities before they become critical, positioning themselves for continued success as AI technology evolves.

The rapid pace of AI evolution requires building flexibility into workforce planning. Organizations need structures that can adapt as AI capabilities and requirements change. This might mean creating more fluid role definitions, developing cross-training programs, and maintaining a mix of permanent and flexible staffing arrangements.

Organizations that effectively navigate technological change develop the ability to respond to evolving technology without major disruption. This capacity includes several key components:

- **Innovation culture** fosters environments where experimentation is encouraged and learning from failure is valued. This means moving beyond traditional legal culture's risk-averse tendencies to embrace controlled innovation.

- **Cross-functional collaboration** breaks down traditional departmental silos. Successful organizations actively encourage collaboration among the legal, IT, and operations teams, fostering a shared approach to technology adoption.
- **Knowledge transfer mechanisms** ensure that expertise is shared across the organization. This goes beyond formal training to include mentoring programs, communities of practice, and regular knowledge-sharing sessions.

By building these capabilities, you will create workforces that can adapt continuously to technological change rather than requiring disruptive transformation with each new advancement.

## PREDICTION ON AI'S NET EFFECT ON THE LEGAL WORKFORCE

AI will fundamentally reshape the legal workforce. While we have emphasized the transformational potential, there will be significant ramifications and likely transitional effects that must be considered.

- **Reduction of routine roles:** AI will likely lead to a decrease in demand for entry-level associates and traditional paralegals, as AI-powered legal research, contract analysis, and document review reduce the need for junior professionals performing repetitive tasks. Some firms are indicating they may reduce their associate hiring by 20–30%.
- **Emergence of hybrid roles:** New positions like AI specialists, legal data analysts, and AI compliance officers will emerge. These roles will require legal professionals to blend traditional expertise with AI oversight and analytics skills.
- **Increased demand for strategic and high-value legal work:** While some legal support roles will shrink, AI will create opportunities for lawyers who can navigate AI governance, ethical AI usage, and litigation related to AI-driven errors.
- **Rise of the "lean law firm" model:** Many firms will operate with smaller, more specialized teams, using AI to handle administrative and research-heavy tasks. Firms that embrace AI effectively will be able to service more clients with fewer billable hours, leading to lower overhead costs and reduced hiring.

- **Net effect:** The legal workforce will likely be smaller overall, but the demand for AI-competent legal professionals will increase. Rather than mass job losses, we will see a realignment of roles, with firms prioritizing professionals who can leverage AI effectively rather than those performing routine tasks.

## CONCLUSION

Successful AI implementation requires thoughtful workforce planning addressing current and future needs. Organizations must help their people develop new skills while creating structures that support ongoing evolution. Most importantly, they need to recognize that AI implementation is as much about people as it is about technology.

The organizations that thrive during this transformation will be those that approach workforce planning with the same strategic focus they apply to technology implementation. They'll develop comprehensive skill development programs, create new career paths that recognize technology expertise, and build cultures that embrace rather than resist change.

Perhaps most importantly, they'll recognize that the true potential of AI comes not from replacing human capabilities but from enhancing them. By focusing on how technology and people can work together more effectively, these organizations will create workforces that leverage AI's strengths while maintaining the human judgment, creativity, and relationship skills that remain essential to legal practice.

As you develop your workforce strategy, remember that success lies not in how effectively you implement the technology itself, but in how well you help your people evolve alongside it. By focusing on this human dimension of AI adoption, you'll build not just a more technologically capable organization, but a more resilient, adaptable, and effective one.

## ACTION ITEMS

1. **Assess AI Impact on Workforce**
   - Evaluate how AI will transform roles across attorneys, paralegals, and support staff
   - Identify positions at risk, emerging roles, and evolving skill requirements
   - Create workforce transformation road map addressing both opportunities and challenges

2. **Develop Role-Specific Competencies**
   - Define AI competency frameworks for different legal roles and experience levels
   - Create skills assessment tools and identify capability gaps
   - Design competency progression pathways from basic literacy to advanced expertise
3. **Design New Organizational Structures**
   - Create hybrid roles bridging legal expertise with AI specialization
   - Establish AI specialist positions and technology integration teams
   - Develop reporting structures that support AI-enhanced legal delivery
4. **Implement Career Development Programs**
   - Create AI-focused career pathways and advancement opportunities
   - Design compensation structures recognizing AI expertise and innovation
   - Establish mentoring and cross-training programs for role transitions
5. **Manage Workforce Transition**
   - Develop change management strategies addressing resistance and concerns
   - Create retraining programs for evolving roles, especially paralegals
   - Implement support systems for staff adapting to AI-enhanced workflows
6. **Plan for Future Workforce Evolution**
   - Anticipate continued AI advancement impact on legal workforce needs
   - Create flexible staffing models adapting to changing technology capabilities
   - Build organizational capacity for continuous workforce adaptation

# CHAPTER 12
# Communicating with Clients About AI

## INTRODUCTION

*Organizations that maintain open dialogue about successes and challenges with AI will develop stronger client relationships.*

The integration of artificial intelligence into legal practice represents both a transformative opportunity and a significant communication challenge. Most corporate legal departments now expect their outside counsel to effectively use AI tools, yet few report being satisfied with how law firms communicate about their AI use. This gap between expectations and reality creates significant risks for client relationships.

The challenge isn't just about using AI effectively. It's also about building and maintaining client trust in an era where AI use raises novel questions about everything from confidentiality to billing practices. Legal organizations must develop thoughtful approaches to discussing AI use with clients while ensuring their communications maintain transparency and build confidence.

Perhaps lawyers and regulators are more concerned than their clients. As recent Clio research on legal trends indicated, clients aren't worried about AI. Clio reported in 2024 that 70% of clients were either agnostic or would prefer to work with firms that use AI.[1] As AI becomes more commonplace, more clients are likely to expect that law firms have access to the ease and efficiency that AI provides.

[1] Clio, *Legal Trends Report* (2024), https://www.clio.com/resources/legal-trends/2024-report.

# COMMUNICATING AI USE TO CLIENTS

## Setting the Right Tone

The way organizations initially discuss AI use with clients often sets the tone for the entire relationship. We believe that clients will respond most positively when legal organizations present AI as a tool for enhancing service rather than simply reducing costs.

For example, when discussing AI-powered document review, focus first on how the technology improves accuracy and consistency, with efficiency gains presented as an additional benefit rather than the primary outcome. This approach helps clients understand that AI adoption aims to enhance service quality rather than simply reduce bills.

As Richard Tromans, founder of Artificial Lawyer, notes on his website devoted to legal tech and AI news and views: "If bringing in genAI tools—or any tool—helps to sustain or increase value in the eyes of the client then you're on the right track. . . . Everything else is subordinate to that."[2] Clients don't want to hear about how AI makes your life easier—they want to know how it makes their legal outcomes better. It's simple: Law firms that frame AI use in terms of client benefits rather than internal efficiencies receive more positive reactions from clients.

## Transparency in Practice

We believe that lawyers are most successful with client communication about AI when they integrate it into their regular client discussions and documents rather than treating it as a separate topic. They make AI use part of their standard engagement letters and matter planning discussions, ensuring clients understand how technology will support their legal work from the outset.

This transparency extends to discussing both benefits and limitations. You can help clients understand what AI can and cannot do, setting realistic expectations while building confidence in your thoughtful approach to technology adoption. If you proactively address potential limitations, you will face fewer client concerns about AI use later in engagements.

---

[2] https://www.artificiallawyer.com/2025/03/11/what-is-ai-for-we-need-to-think-about-end-goals/.

## LEGAL AND ETHICAL DISCLOSURE REQUIREMENTS

The emerging consensus around AI disclosure reflects both ethical and legal considerations. The ABA Model Rules of Professional Conduct, particularly Rules 1.1 (Competence), 1.4 (Communication), and 1.5 (Fees), have implications for how attorneys disclose AI use to clients.[3] The American Bar Association's Formal Opinion 512[4] directly addresses the ethical and legal considerations for attorneys disclosing AI use to clients, specifically referencing the ABA Model Rules of Professional Conduct:

- **Rule 1.1 (Competence):** Lawyers are required to provide competent representation, which now includes understanding "the benefits and risks associated" with technologies like AI used in legal services.
- **Rule 1.4 (Communication):** Lawyers must "reasonably consult" with the client about the means by which the client's objectives are to be accomplished, which can include disclosing the use of AI when it is relevant to case outcomes, fees, or client inquiries.
- **Rule 1.5 (Fees):** Fees must be reasonable and transparent, and the use of AI may affect what is considered reasonable or how fees are communicated and justified to clients. Lawyers may charge for the time using AI tools and for reviewing results, but normally may not charge for time learning how to use the tools.
- **Rule 1.6 (Confidentiality of Information)** Lawyers must ensure confidentiality related to client representation and information when using AI tools.

Several state bar associations also have issued formal ethics opinions addressing AI disclosure requirements. The New York State Bar Association's 2024 Task Force on Artificial Intelligence report is the authoritative document recommending

---

[3] Model Rules of Pro. Conduct (A.B.A. 2023), https://www.americanbar.org/groups/professional_responsibility/publications/model_rules_of_professional_conduct/.

[4] A.B.A. Standing Comm. on Ethics & Pro. Resp., Formal Op. 512, Ethical Obligations of Lawyers Using Generative Artificial Intelligence (GAI) Tools in the Practice of Law (July 29, 2024), https://www.americanbar.org/content/dam/aba/administrative/professional_responsibility/ethics-opinions/aba-formal-opinion-512.pdf.

that attorneys disclose to clients when AI tools are employed in their cases, especially for tasks traditionally performed by attorneys.[5]

Earlier, the California State Bar issued guidance saying that attorneys should consider disclosure to clients about their intent to use generative AI, particularly when it could impact representation, but it does not establish a strict requirement to disclose AI use unless specific circumstances (such as confidentiality, fees, or significant impact on representation) warrant it. The guidance states: "The lawyer should consider disclosure to their client that they intend to use generative AI in the representation, including how the technology will be used, and the benefits and risks of such use."[6] It also notes that a fee agreement should explain the basis for fees associated with the use of generative AI and that hourly fees may not be charged for time saved by using generative AI. Finally, the guidance does note that lawyers should review any client instructions or guidelines regarding the use of AI.

These are only a few examples of guidance and rules promulgated so far, and more will be developed soon. You should review any rules of conduct for lawyers in other countries where you may be involved in client representation to ensure compliance.

Beyond ethical requirements, contractual obligations with clients may also dictate disclosure practices. Many corporate clients now include specific provisions about technology use in outside counsel guidelines, with some explicitly requiring notification or approval for AI use in certain contexts.

## PRICING AND VALUE PROPOSITION

### Evolving Fee Structures

The integration of AI into legal practice requires rethinking traditional billing approaches. Leading law firms are actively rethinking traditional billing approaches in response to AI adoption. They are developing new frameworks for fee structures that address AI-driven efficiencies and emphasize the need to ensure clients understand and appreciate the value they receive, not just cost reductions. You need to develop a client-centered approach to AI adoption and

---

[5] N.Y. State Bar Ass'n Task Force on Artificial Intelligence, Report and Recommendations of the Task Force on Artificial Intelligence (Apr. 8, 2024), https://nysba.org/app/uploads/2022/03/2024-April-Report-and-Recommendations-of-the-Task-Force-on-Artificial-Intelligence.pdf.

[6] State Bar of California, Generative AI Practical Guidance (Nov. 16, 2023), https://www.calbar.ca.gov/Portals/0/documents/ethics/Generative-AI-Practical-Guidance.pdf.

pricing, aligning AI deployment with both profitability and enhanced client value.

Some organizations are moving toward hybrid models that combine traditional hourly billing for attorney analysis and strategy with fixed fees for AI-assisted document review or research. Others are developing value-based pricing models that focus on outcomes rather than inputs. The key is ensuring clients understand how AI use affects service delivery and pricing.

## Examples of Billing Structures

Here are some examples of new billing structures to consider:

### *For Litigation Practices*

#### Value-Based Fee Structures

Fees tied to litigation stages (pleadings, discovery, trial preparation) rather than hours

Success fees or contingent components based on case outcomes

Risk-sharing arrangements where fees adjust based on case complexity discovered during AI-powered document review

#### Hybrid Models

Base fee for AI-assisted work plus premium hourly rates for strategic work requiring judgment

Technology access fees covering AI tools with discounted hourly rates for human oversight

#### Subscription-Based Services

Monthly retainers covering routine litigation needs with predictable budgets

Tiered access to different levels of AI-assisted service

### *For Corporate Transaction Practices*

#### Fixed-Fee Deal Structures

Fee bands based on transaction value rather than documentation time

Milestone-based payments tied to transaction stages

Complexity multipliers determining base fees

#### AI-Specific Fee Components

Separate fees for AI-driven due diligence vs. strategic negotiation

Value pricing for AI-assisted contract drafting and review

Premium fees for expedited AI-driven closings

### *For Regulatory Counseling*

#### Outcome-Based Pricing

Fees tied to regulatory approvals or compliance achievements
Risk-premium pricing for high-stakes regulatory matters
Subscription models for ongoing compliance monitoring

#### Knowledge Product Pricing

Packaging AI-generated compliance materials as products rather than services
Licensing fees for firm-developed regulatory AI tools
Tier-based pricing for different levels of regulatory intelligence

## Implementation Challenges

The transition from billable hours will require client education to demonstrate how there is value being delivered beyond time spent on matters. It will also demand new attorney evaluation metrics beyond billable hour targets, with compensation structures that reward efficiency and client satisfaction. Perhaps most challenging, you will need to build data-driven insight into matter cost analyses, relying on pricing specialists who understand the matter at hand and how AI will contribute.

## The Transition Period

Most firms will likely adopt hybrid approaches during the transition from purely hourly billing. They will maintain billable hours for complex, judgment-intensive work while introducing alternative fee arrangements for routine, AI-automatable tasks. Then they will gradually shift toward value-based metrics as client relationships adapt. The most successful firms will be those that can articulate how AI enhances rather than replaces the judgment, strategy, and advocacy that clients truly value.

## Demonstrating Value Beyond Cost Savings

Clients increasingly value how AI enhances service quality and outcomes. Organizations should focus on demonstrating multiple dimensions of value.

Quality enhancement represents a primary concern for clients. You should be able to provide clear and specific examples of how AI improves work product quality. For instance, you might demonstrate how AI-powered contract review catches issues that traditional review might miss, or how AI research tools ensure more comprehensive legal analysis.

Risk reduction becomes increasingly important as clients better understand AI's capabilities. Organizations that effectively communicate about AI help clients understand how technology reduces risk through more comprehensive analysis and consistent application of legal standards. This might include sharing examples of how AI tools identified potential issues in similar matters or helped ensure regulatory compliance.

Strategic insights often provide the most compelling value proposition. Advanced AI tools can provide insights that inform legal strategy. For example, litigation analytics can help clients better understand their positions and make more informed decisions about case strategy. Organizations that effectively communicate these strategic benefits often find clients more receptive to AI use.

### Impact on the Bottom Line

The shift from billable hours to value-based models in the AI era will likely create both short-term disruption and long-term opportunity for law firm finances. We believe that firms that quickly optimize their talent mix, invest strategically in AI, and develop value-based pricing expertise will likely see profit increases within five years, while those that cling to billable hour models while competitors offer fixed fees will face significant revenue declines in affected practice areas.

The most profound financial impact may be the breakdown of the traditional law firm pyramid structure, with its broad base of billable junior lawyers. We believe that successful firms will evolve toward diamond-shaped organizations with fewer junior lawyers, more senior specialists, and dedicated technology roles—potentially delivering higher profits despite lower gross revenues.

## MANAGING CLIENT EXPECTATIONS

### Initial Engagement Discussions

AI is widely used to automate and streamline the legal intake process. Organizations are using AI tools for efficiency, document automation, data extraction, client communication (e.g., chatbots), and workflow management. Incorporating discussions about AI in initial client intake processes can help clients understand how AI will support their legal work, what oversight mechanisms exist, and how quality control is maintained. These early discussions should cover specific aspects of AI use that might affect the client relationship. For example, organizations might explain how AI tools analyze documents, what security measures protect client data, and how attorney oversight ensures work quality. This transparency helps build trust while setting realistic expectations about AI's role in legal service delivery.

## Ongoing Communication

The relationship between legal service providers and clients continues to evolve as AI capabilities expand. You should maintain regular dialogue with clients about AI use, updating them on new capabilities and adjusting approaches based on client feedback.

This ongoing communication might include regular briefings on new AI tools, discussions of potential applications, and reviews of how AI has benefited specific matters. The key is maintaining transparency while demonstrating continuous improvement in how AI supports client service.

## Successful Client Communication Approaches

### *Proactive Transparency*

We recommend developing and sharing formal protocols regarding your use of AI. A comprehensive approach includes:

- A dedicated section in engagement letters outlining how AI might be used during representation.
- Matter-specific AI use plans that detail which tools might be employed for different aspects of client work.
- Regular client briefings on AI capabilities and limitations.
- Discussion of how AI might use client data.
- Clear documentation of human oversight mechanisms for all AI-generated work.

This approach can significantly reduce client concerns about AI use while creating opportunities to demonstrate how technology enhances service delivery. Transparency about AI use can transform potentially difficult conversations into opportunities to demonstrate technology prowess and commitment to improving client service.

### *Client Education*

Focus on client education. Develop a simple visual tool that helps clients understand:

- Which legal tasks can be enhanced with AI.
- What specific AI tools the firm employs.

- How human oversight ensures quality.
- Where the greatest efficiency gains occur.
- How these capabilities translate to client value.

Your clients will appreciate knowing that you use AI, and, even more so, understanding how it enhances their representation. A visual approach can make complex technology easier to understand and demonstrate a commitment to transparent communication.

### *Handling Client Concerns*

Develop clear, thoughtful responses to questions about:

- **Data security and confidentiality:** Clients want to understand how their information is protected when AI tools are used. Organizations need to explain their security measures, data-handling practices, and compliance with confidentiality obligations.
- **Quality control and oversight:** Clients often question how organizations ensure AI-assisted work maintains professional standards. Smart organizations explain their oversight processes, validation procedures, and quality control mechanisms.
- **Cost and billing practices:** Questions about how AI use affects billing require careful explanation. Organizations need to help clients understand their pricing models and how AI use influences overall cost structures.

### *Building Trust Through Transparency*

Trust builds through consistent demonstration of responsible AI use. Organizations that maintain open dialogue about successes and challenges with AI will develop stronger client relationships. This might include sharing lessons learned from AI implementation or discussing how the organization addresses potential limitations in AI tools.

# THE ROLE OF CLIENT FEEDBACK IN AI IMPLEMENTATION

## Structured Feedback Mechanisms

Some organizations are implementing structured feedback mechanisms specifically focused on AI use. We believe that formally soliciting client feedback about AI-assisted services will improve client satisfaction scores and lead to more effective technology implementations.

These feedback mechanisms might include:

- Post-matter surveys with specific questions about AI use
- Regular client advisory board meetings focused on technology
- Structured interviews with key client stakeholders
- Analytics tracking satisfaction with AI-enhanced deliverables

### Adapting to Client Preferences

Client preferences regarding AI use vary significantly across industries, organization sizes, and individual relationships. You should expect substantial variation in client comfort with different AI applications. Most clients will be comfortable with AI-assisted legal research, accept AI-enhanced document review, and support AI-powered contract analysis. But expect fewer to be comfortable with AI drafting significant portions of legal documents or providing deep strategic analysis and planning.

Smart organizations adapt their AI use and communication based on these preferences. This might mean using different approaches for different clients or adjusting AI use overall based on client feedback. Organizations experiencing the greatest success with AI aren't necessarily those using the most advanced technology. They are the ones most attuned to their clients' comfort levels and preferences.

## TRAINING LEGAL PROFESSIONALS IN CLIENT COMMUNICATION

### Communication Skills Development

Effective communication about AI requires skills that some legal professionals may not naturally possess. Organizations investing in communication training specifically focused on technology will experience higher client satisfaction ratings about use of AI than those that don't. Such training should help attorneys and staff:

- Explain complex technology in accessible terms.
- Address common client concerns about AI.
- Demonstrate the value of AI-enhanced service.
- Navigate difficult conversations about technology limitations.
- Adapt communication to different client preferences.

### Building Organization-Wide Capabilities

Beyond individual skills, successful organizations develop consistent, organization-wide approaches to technology communication. This might include:

- Standardized language for engagement letters.
- Talking points for common client questions.
- Case studies demonstrating successful AI implementation
- Clear guidelines on disclosure requirements..
- Frameworks for discussing value proposition.

The key is ensuring all client-facing professionals can communicate effectively about AI use, even if they aren't directly involved in technology implementation.

## FUTURE CONSIDERATIONS

### Evolving Client Expectations

As AI capabilities continue to evolve, client expectations will likely shift as well. The trends that organizations should prepare for include growing sophistication in how clients evaluate AI use in legal practice, increasing expectations for data-driven insights and predictive analytics, and greater demand for transparency in how AI supports legal work. You must stay ahead of these evolving expectations while maintaining your focus on delivering high-quality legal services.

### Innovation and Client Service

The future of client service will almost certainly involve increasingly sophisticated AI applications. Innovative organizations are already planning for this future by developing new service models that leverage emerging AI capabilities, creating ways to deliver value through AI-enhanced services, and building flexible frameworks that can adapt to changing client needs.

## REGULATORY HORIZON: INCREASED OVERSIGHT TO PROTECT CLIENTS

### Emerging Regulatory Framework

The regulatory landscape surrounding AI use in legal practice is rapidly evolving. The European Union's AI Act established a comprehensive framework for regulating AI across industries, with specific implications for legal services providers.

While the United States currently lacks comprehensive federal AI regulation, several state initiatives and professional guidelines are more advanced. Legal organizations should monitor developments in several key regulatory areas:

- Disclosure requirements regarding AI use
- Data protection and privacy regulations
- Professional responsibility standards
- Consumer protection frameworks
- Industry-specific compliance requirements

The American Bar Association's formation of an AI Task Force demonstrated the profession's recognition that more specific guidance was needed.[7] The ABA AI Task Force remains active as of this writing and is expected to continue its work, with ongoing research, events, and forthcoming recommendations. As of October 3, 2025, the task force notes that its 2025 report is coming soon. Organizations that proactively develop and implement frameworks that reflect consideration of emerging regulatory concerns and professional guidance will be better positioned to manage the risks while gaining value from AI investments.

## Preparing for Compliance

Forward-thinking legal organizations are already developing comprehensive practices that will support future regulatory compliance. These include:

- Detailed records of AI use in client matters.
- Documentation of human oversight mechanisms.
- Clear audit trails for AI-assisted work.
- Validation procedures for AI outputs.
- Client disclosure protocols.

The law firms and legal departments that treat compliance as an opportunity rather than a burden will thrive, while those that fail to proactively structure AI governance will fall behind in the not too distant future.

[7] Am. Bar Ass'n, Task Force on Law and Artificial Intelligence, https://www.americanbar.org/groups/centers_commissions/center-for-innovation/artificial-intelligence/ (last visited Oct. 20. 2025).

# CONCLUSION

Effective client communication about AI use requires balancing transparency with practical value demonstration. Organizations that succeed in this area typically focus on helping clients understand both the benefits and limitations of AI while maintaining clear focus on how technology enhances service delivery.

Success requires commitment to ongoing dialogue with clients, adaptation to evolving expectations, and continuous refinement of communication approaches. As AI capabilities grow more sophisticated, so too must the ways legal organizations discuss technology with their clients.

The most successful organizations view AI communication not as a compliance burden but as an opportunity to demonstrate their commitment to innovation, quality, and client service. By thoughtfully addressing client concerns while clearly articulating value, these organizations transform AI adoption from a potential challenge into a significant competitive advantage.

# ACTION ITEMS

1. **Develop AI Disclosure and Communication Framework**
    - Create clear protocols for when and how to disclose AI use to clients
    - Design materiality assessment frameworks for determining disclosure requirements
    - Establish transparent communication approaches that build rather than undermine client trust
2. **Create Client Value Demonstration Systems**
    - Develop metrics and case studies showing how AI enhances service quality and outcomes
    - Design value communication frameworks emphasizing client benefits beyond cost savings
    - Create ROI demonstrations and comparative analyses for AI-enhanced versus traditional services
3. **Implement Client Preference Management**
    - Establish systems for assessing and documenting client AI preferences and restrictions
    - Create client-specific adaptation procedures respecting individual comfort levels and policies
    - Design consent procedures for AI processing of sensitive client information

4. **Build Client Education and Engagement Programs**
   - Create educational materials explaining AI capabilities, limitations, and safeguards
   - Design client briefing programs on AI benefits and implementation approaches
   - Establish regular communication about AI developments and their impact on service delivery
5. **Establish Client Feedback and Adaptation Systems**
   - Create structured feedback mechanisms specifically focused on AI-enhanced services
   - Design client satisfaction monitoring for AI applications and outcomes
   - Implement adaptive service delivery based on client input and preferences
6. **Train Legal Professionals in AI Client Communication**
   - Develop communication skills training for discussing AI use with clients
   - Create talking points and response frameworks for common client concerns
   - Establish protocols for handling client objections and customizing AI approaches

CHAPTER 13

# Using AI for Project Management and Budgeting

## INTRODUCTION

*AI's ability to support strategic decision-making about matter management will become more advanced over the next few years.*

"We need a detailed budget for the expected life of this litigation." Few phrases create more anxiety for law firm partners. Historically, creating accurate legal budgets has been more art than science, relying heavily on individual experience and often faulty assumptions, despite increasing client pressure for budget predictability.

AI is changing this equation. AI tools are transforming how legal organizations approach project management and budgeting by analyzing historical matter data, identifying cost patterns, and providing real-time tracking capabilities. This transformation couldn't come at a better time for law firms and legal departments. The stakes are high. Budget management has become an important metric for clients evaluating outside counsel. For legal organizations seeking competitive advantage, effective AI-powered budget management represents not just a technological upgrade but also a critical business imperative.

## TRADITIONAL BUDGETING CHALLENGES

Creating accurate legal budgets has always been challenging. Every matter is unique, unexpected issues arise, and scope changes are common. Partners have traditionally relied on experience and intuition, often reviewing similar matters and making educated guesses about required resources and timelines. This approach has significant limitations and suffers from several persistent challenges:

- **Limited data analysis:** Traditional methods rely on easily remembered examples rather than comprehensive data analysis.
- **Inconsistent variables:** Different partners consider different variables when creating budgets, leading to inconsistency across the organization.
- **Static projections:** Once created, traditional budgets struggle to adapt to changing circumstances.
- **Delayed variance detection:** Budget issues often aren't identified until significant overruns have occurred.

Traditional legal budgeting resembles weather forecasting before modern meteorology—heavily dependent on pattern recognition and individual experience, with predictable inconsistency in results.

## AI'S IMPACT ON BUDGET DEVELOPMENT

### Data-Driven Foundations

Modern AI systems transform budgeting by analyzing vast amounts of historical data to identify patterns and relationships that humans might miss. Using AI for budget development should be expected to show significantly higher accuracy rates than using traditional methods alone.

For example, some firms have discovered through AI analysis that the complexity of corporate structure, not just deal size, was a strong predictor of M&A due diligence costs. This insight allowed them to create more accurate budgets by incorporating structural complexity metrics into their calculations.

The value of AI in legal budgeting will come from analyzing more data and being able to identify non-obvious correlations that human experts would not be able to spot. An experienced lawyer might sense that corporate complexity can affect due diligence costs, but AI will quantify this relationship.

While AI can build better budgets based on analysis of past expenditures on similar matters, even this may be misleading at first, given that the use of AI in performance of the work to be done will also change the budget. Therefore, estimating a budget based solely on past "billable hour" matters will only go so far. Adjustments will have to be made as the time-saving contribution of AI and changes in methods of billing are taken into account.

### Comprehensive Variable Analysis

AI systems can simultaneously analyze multiple variables affecting matter costs. Several key factors these systems can typically consider include:

- **Matter complexity:** AI tools can assess complexity based on multiple factors, including document volume, number of parties, jurisdictional requirements, and legal issues involved.
- **Resource requirements:** Systems analyze historical staffing patterns to predict resource needs across different matter phases.
- **Timeline impacts:** AI can model how different timeline scenarios affect overall costs and resource requirements.
- **Client-specific factors:** Systems learn from client-specific historical data to account for unique client characteristics and requirements.

### Building Better Budgets

The process of creating AI-assisted budgets differs significantly from traditional approaches. Organizations can build budgets from granular data analysis, rather than starting with a partner's estimate and adjusting based on gut feel. When developing a litigation budget, for instance, AI tools might:

- Analyze similar past matters, considering variables like jurisdiction, claim type, and opposing counsel.
- Calculate likely discovery costs based on document volume predictions.
- Predict staffing needs across different phases.
- Suggest contingency amounts based on historical variance patterns.

Legal organizations implementing AI-powered budgeting report significant accuracy improvements compared to traditional methods. There are a growing number of consulting and AI firms focused on helping law firms define budgets with predictive analytics and machine learning applications.

## REAL-TIME BUDGET TRACKING AND MANAGEMENT

### Active Monitoring

Traditional budget tracking often identifies issues too late for a meaningful correction. The importance of early detection of budget issues, proactive management, and client communication is widely appreciated. Anything that legal project managers can do to keep matters on track and manage client expectations is helpful. Early identification of budget issues is crucial for avoiding write-offs and client dissatisfaction.

AI systems provide real-time monitoring and early warning capabilities. Organizations using AI-powered budget tracking identify problems earlier than those using traditional methods. AI solutions allow legal and finance teams to spot potential overruns and risks while matters are still in progress, rather than waiting for end-of-month or post-invoice reports.

### Predictive Analytics

Modern AI systems don't just track current spending; they predict future patterns based on current activities. For example, an AI system might notice that document review takes 20% longer than projected and automatically calculate the likely impact on the overall budget and timeline.

The power of this capability becomes clear in practice. One global law firm reported that their AI system identified a potential budget overrun in a major litigation by noticing that the ratio of potentially relevant documents to total documents was significantly higher than historical patterns suggested. This early warning allowed them to discuss the issue with their client and adjust the budget.

## CLIENT COMMUNICATION AND REPORTING

### Enhanced Transparency

AI tools enable unprecedented budget transparency with clients. Rather than providing simple budget-to-actual comparisons, now organizations can offer sophisticated insights into budget status and projections. Clients value understanding not just where their matter stands, but why it might be tracking differently than expected.

Transparency fundamentally changes client relationships. When lawyers can provide data-driven explanations for budget variances rather than generalizations, difficult conversations can turn into collaborative problem solving. Clients experience higher satisfaction with firms that provide this level of transparency.

### Real-Time Reporting

Modern AI systems generate customized reports that help clients understand budget status in context. These reports typically include:

- Current spending against budget broken down by phase.
- Projected costs through completion.
- Key factors influencing any variances.
- Early warnings about potential issues.
- Recommended adjustments.

Most importantly, these reports can be generated in real time, allowing for informed discussions about the budget implications of strategic decisions. You should be aware that large corporate clients may soon (if they aren't already) require firms to use the client's budget management systems so that they can track status in real time and compare how the firms they use manage ongoing matters. This may require integration of your firm's budget system with a number of clients' systems, which will rely upon having well-organized quality data.

## ADAPTATION STRATEGIES

When budget variances occur, AI systems help organizations understand why and recommend adjustment strategies. Organizations using AI for budget management are more likely to successfully address budget issues before they become significant problems. The key lies in the system's ability to:

- Identify the root causes of variances.
- Model the impact of different adjustment strategies.
- Recommend optimal approaches based on matter specifics.
- Track the effectiveness of implemented changes.

AI's ability to support strategic decision-making about matter management will become more advanced over the next few years. For instance, when deciding whether to file an additional motion or pursue a particular discovery strategy, AI systems will be able to provide detailed cost-benefit analysis based on historical data and current matter patterns. The most sophisticated AI systems will model the implications of legal decisions and help attorneys make informed choices about how to allocate resources across different options.

## IMPLEMENTATION GUIDANCE

Successful implementation of AI budgeting tools requires careful preparation. Several critical success factors include:

- **Data quality:** Organizations must ensure their historical data is accurate and properly categorized. This often requires significant initial investment but is crucial for AI system accuracy.
- **Process integration:** AI budgeting tools need to integrate seamlessly with existing workflows. The goal should be to enhance, not complicate, the budgeting process.
- **Training and support:** Users need thorough training not just in tool operation but in understanding and utilizing AI-generated insights.

We recommend that you take a phased approach to implementation, beginning with straightforward matters where good historical data exists. This allows you to validate AI predictions and build confidence in the system. Then, gradually expand to more complex matters, continuously refining models and processes based on experience. Eventually, you can optimize your use and focus on maximizing value through advanced features and integrations.

## AI-POWERED BUDGET ANALYSIS FOR CORPORATE LEGAL DEPARTMENTS

Historically, corporate legal departments struggle to effectively compare costs across similar matters handled by different law firms. Without sophisticated analysis tools, many departments rely on basic metrics like average hourly rates or total matter costs, missing deeper insights about efficiency and value.

AI is transforming this landscape. Departments using AI-powered analytics gain better insights into outside counsel performance and an improved ability to predict future costs.

Consider a corporate legal department managing multiple employment litigation matters across different jurisdictions. Traditionally, comparing costs between similar cases has been challenging due to the number of variables involved. AI systems can now analyze multiple factors simultaneously to provide meaningful comparisons, and this ability will sharpen over time:

- **Matter characteristics:** The system might identify truly comparable matters by analyzing factors like jurisdiction, claim type, company division involved, and complexity indicators.

- **Staffing patterns:** AI might compare how different firms staff similar matters, identifying which approaches deliver the best results most efficiently.
- **Phase timing and costs:** The system might analyze how different firms manage similar phases of litigation, identifying which firms move matters through phases most efficiently.

The power of AI in cost analysis becomes clear when examining specific applications. If you can show a firm exactly how their approach differs from others, backed by detailed data rather than general impressions, it creates a much more productive conversation about process improvement.

AI systems will also help corporate legal departments become more sophisticated consumers of legal services by providing:

- **Budget validation:** When receiving proposed budgets from outside counsel, AI can compare them against similar historical matters to assess reasonableness.
- **Cost projection:** Systems can predict likely total costs based on matter characteristics and early phase expenses.
- **Risk assessment:** AI can identify factors that historically led to budget overruns, helping departments proactively address potential issues.

The ability to truly compare and manage budgets across the firms your organization employs will be dependent on having clean, high quality data. Taking the first step to ensure data is being provided in a consistent manner will drive success in this endeavor.

## AI IN RESOURCE ALLOCATION AND STAFFING

AI tools are increasingly helping legal organizations optimize staffing decisions based on matter characteristics and budget constraints. Organizations using AI for resource allocation can achieve higher matter profitability compared to those using traditional staffing approaches. These systems analyze various factors to recommend optimal team compositions:

- **Matter complexity:** Matching attorney expertise levels to matter complexity
- **Historical performance:** Identifying which attorney combinations have produced the best results on similar matters

- **Budget constraints:** Optimizing staffing mix to meet budget targets while maintaining quality
- **Availability:** Considering current workloads and scheduling constraints

AI systems can also help optimize the sequencing and timing of work to improve efficiency. For instance, in analyzing historical data these systems can identify optimal approaches to common legal tasks. This will give attorneys the ability to identify and replicate the most effective workflows across similar matters.

As AI tools mature, you will be able to use them not just to track what tasks cost but also to understand and optimize how they should be performed.

## CONTRACTUAL FRAMEWORKS FOR AI-ENABLED BUDGET MANAGEMENT

### Engagement Letter Provisions

As AI becomes increasingly central to legal project management, you now need to address its use in client engagement letters. Several key provisions to develop for your engagement letters include:

- **Technology use disclosure:** Clear statements about how AI will be used in matter management and budgeting.
- **Data usage permissions:** Specifications regarding how client data will be used in AI systems, including anonymization requirements and limitations on use for system training.
- **Budget update mechanisms:** Formal processes for budget revisions based on AI-identified variances and changing circumstances.
- **Reporting commitments:** Specific commitments regarding the frequency and detail of AI-generated budget reports.

You should standardize these clauses across all of your engagement letters, but recognize that clients may have their own requirements demanding some alterations to your preferred phrasing. As such, you should have a process in place to consider, approve, and record any alterations.

### Outside Counsel Guidelines

Corporate legal departments are increasingly incorporating AI-specific provisions into their outside counsel guidelines. These include specific requirements related to budgeting technology and reporting. These guidelines typically address:

- **Required budget detail:** Specifications for the level of granularity in initial budgets.
- **Update frequency:** Requirements for how often budgets must be reviewed and updated.
- **Variance reporting:** Thresholds for when variances must be reported and explained.
- **Technology compatibility:** Requirements for compatibility with the client's budget tracking systems.

If you are outside counsel, you should consider all of your client guidelines and compare them to identify where you can standardize your approach to compliance. AI can be used in this process. You may find that you will benefit from broadly standardizing your own actions even if you are providing more to some clients than they request.

If you are inside counsel developing such guidelines, you should look to models provided by inhouse counsel organizations or encourage the development of such models to encourage a standard approach.

## Sample Contract Clauses

Effective contract clauses addressing AI use in legal project management balance clarity with flexibility. These may include clauses specifically addressing security and confidentiality concerns but may also address where and how your counsel may use AI in delivery of services. Consider clauses like these as examples:

**Budget Development and Monitoring**

"Law Firm shall utilize its AI-enabled budget development system to create a detailed budget for this matter within 14 days of engagement. This budget shall include phase-level detail with associated timelines and resource requirements. Both parties agree to review this budget monthly, with Law Firm providing AI-generated variance analysis for any phase exceeding 15% of projected cost or timeline."

**Data Security and Confidentiality**

"Law Firm warrants that all AI systems used for matter management and budgeting comply with industry-standard security protocols. Client data utilized by these systems shall be anonymized where feasible and shall not be used to train AI systems without Client's explicit written consent. Law Firm shall provide, upon request, documentation of its AI security protocols and data handling practices."

**Continuous Improvement Commitment**

"Law Firm commits to ongoing refinement of its AI budget models based on matter experience. Law Firm shall provide quarterly updates on model accuracy and improvements, including analysis of budget-to-actual variances and steps taken to enhance future accuracy."

# ETHICAL CONSIDERATIONS IN AI-POWERED PROJECT MANAGEMENT

## Transparency Obligations

As AI plays an increasingly significant role in legal project management, important ethical questions arise regarding disclosure and transparency. The ABA Model Rules of Professional Conduct, particularly Rules 1.4 (Communication) and 1.5 (Fees), have implications for how attorneys disclose AI use in budgeting and matter management.[1]

A growing consensus suggests that attorneys should disclose material AI use in matter management, particularly when it significantly impacts how services are delivered or billed. Clients need to know what they're paying for, how those services are being delivered, and the role technology plays in that delivery.

## Competence Requirements

ABA Model Rule 1.1 requires attorneys to provide competent representation, including understanding "the benefits and risks associated with relevant technology." For AI-powered project management, this means attorneys must understand both the capabilities and limitations of their systems.

Bar associations are increasingly interpreting this competence requirement to include understanding how AI systems develop budgets and project plans, not just passively accepting their outputs. This interpretation creates an obligation for attorneys to maintain sufficient technical knowledge to evaluate AI-generated recommendations critically.

## Supervision Responsibilities

ABA Model Rule 5.3 addresses attorney responsibilities regarding nonlawyer assistance. As AI plays a larger role in project management, questions may arise

---

[1] Model Rules of Pro. Conduct (A.B.A. 2023), https://www.americanbar.org/groups/professional_responsibility/publications/model_rules_of_professional_conduct/.

about appropriate supervision and oversight. In July 2024, the American Bar Association issued ABA Formal Opinion 512, addressing the use of generative-AI tools. The opinion requires that attorneys maintain meaningful oversight of AI systems, including regular validation of their outputs and clear processes for handling potential errors or biases.

Notably, this formal opinion only addresses the use of generative AI and particularly focuses on use in direct legal tasks such as legal research, drafting of documents, contract and document review, and due diligence. It does not address the use of AI in legal matter management, budgeting, or other business-related uses. We expect the ABA to issue additional guidance to address these uses of AI as such use matures and expands.

## Future Considerations

Several emerging capabilities that will further enhance legal project management and budgeting include:

- **Advanced natural language processing:** Improved ability to extract budget-relevant information from unstructured data like emails and documents.
- **Automated scenario planning:** Enhanced capabilities for modeling different strategic approaches and their budget implications.
- **Integrated resource optimization:** Better alignment of staffing decisions with budget optimization.

We are not suggesting that every law firm and corporate legal department will or should jump into using these and other emerging AI tools, but we do suggest that you keep track of what is coming, what might be useful in your practice, and what your peers are doing in this rapidly changing environment.

The regulatory landscape surrounding AI use in legal practice continues to evolve. You should monitor developments in areas like:

- Data privacy regulations affecting how client information can be used in AI systems.
- Potential disclosure requirements regarding how AI influences legal service delivery.
- Emerging standards for algorithm transparency and explainability.

Regulatory frameworks will almost certainly increasingly require legal organizations to demonstrate both the effectiveness and fairness of their AI systems, including those used for project management and budgeting.

The future of AI-powered project management lies in deeper integration with other legal technologies. Several promising integration paths include:

- **Document analysis integration:** Connecting document analysis AI with project management systems to automatically identify scope changes and budget implications based on document content.
- **Outcome prediction linkage:** Integrating outcome prediction tools with budget systems to better align resource allocation with case value and risk.
- **Client collaboration platforms:** Developing integrated platforms where clients can interact directly with project data and simulations, enabling more collaborative decision-making.

## CONCLUSION

AI is transforming legal project management and budgeting from an educated guessing game into a data-driven discipline. By enabling more accurate budgets, providing early warning of potential issues, and supporting strategic decision-making, these technologies help legal organizations meet growing client demands for predictability and transparency.

Success requires thoughtful implementation that combines technological capabilities with human judgment and client communication. Organizations that effectively integrate AI into their project management approaches can expect to see significant improvements in budget accuracy, client satisfaction, and overall matter profitability.

We believe the law firms and legal departments that thrive in the coming decade will be those that most effectively combine AI capabilities with human expertise to deliver predictable, transparent, and valuable legal services.

## ACTION ITEMS

1. **Implement AI-Enhanced Budget Development**
    - Deploy AI systems that analyze historical matter data to create more accurate budgets
    - Establish data-driven budget development processes incorporating multiple variables and patterns
    - Create budget validation and benchmarking systems using AI analytics

2. **Establish Real-Time Budget Tracking and Management**
   - Implement AI-powered monitoring systems providing early warning of budget variances
   - Create predictive analytics that forecast budget performance based on current activities
   - Design automated budget adjustment and optimization recommendations
3. **Enhance Client Communication and Reporting**
   - Develop AI-generated budget reports providing detailed insights and explanations
   - Create real-time budget transparency systems allowing client access to current status
   - Establish proactive communication protocols for budget changes and recommendations
4. **Optimize Resource Allocation and Staffing**
   - Use AI to analyze optimal staffing patterns and resource allocation across matters
   - Implement intelligent workload distribution and capacity planning systems
   - Create AI-assisted project sequencing and timing optimization
5. **Develop Contractual Frameworks for AI-Enabled Budgeting**
   - Update engagement letters and outside counsel guidelines to address AI use in project management
   - Create contractual provisions for AI-enhanced budget development and reporting
   - Establish liability and responsibility frameworks for AI-assisted budget management
6. **Build Ethical and Professional Compliance Systems**
   - Ensure AI budgeting tools comply with professional responsibility requirements
   - Create transparency and disclosure protocols for AI use in budget development
   - Establish validation and oversight procedures maintaining attorney accountability

# CHAPTER 14
# International AI Considerations

## INTRODUCTION

*Different regions are likely to continue developing distinct and possibly conflicting approaches to AI regulation.*

Picture this scenario: Your firm's AI-powered document review system, which has been working brilliantly for U.S. matters, suddenly creates significant regulatory exposure when used for a European client. Or consider this situation: Your successful AI implementation strategy, which transformed your Tokyo office, faces unexpected resistance in your New York branch. While hypothetical, these scenarios illustrate the very real challenges legal organizations face as they navigate AI adoption across international boundaries.

Many law firms and legal departments operating internationally report significant challenges in maintaining consistent AI practices across jurisdictions. The complexity isn't just technical—it's a multifaceted challenge involving regulatory compliance, cultural adaptation, and operational consistency.

For law firm leaders and general counsel, the international dimensions of AI adoption create a unique set of challenges that go far beyond domestic implementation. You're not just managing AI adoption—you're orchestrating it across a complex web of regulatory requirements, cultural expectations, and technological infrastructures.

The real test of AI implementation success will be creating systems that can adapt to the varied traditions, regulatory environments, and professional expectations in different countries.

## Cross-Border Data Protection Requirements

The regulatory landscape for AI use in legal practice has become increasingly complex, with different regions adopting distinct approaches to data protection and AI governance. The European Union's AI Act establishes stringent requirements for AI systems used in legal applications. Meanwhile, China's Personal Information Protection Law (PIPL) imposes strict data localization requirements that can significantly impact how international law firms deploy AI tools. New laws and regulations are coming on a regular basis.

To understand the complexity, consider this hypothetical scenario: An international law firm implements an AI-powered contract analysis system across its global offices. The system works perfectly for U.S. operations, but when the London office begins using it for a matter involving EU data, they discover their data transfer mechanisms don't meet GDPR requirements. Meanwhile, their Hong Kong office can't use the system for mainland China matters due to PIPL restrictions. The firm must now navigate three distinct regulatory frameworks while maintaining operational efficiency.

## Navigating Regulatory Divergence

The key challenge for legal organizations lies in understanding how different regulatory approaches impact AI deployment. Significant regulatory differences emerge in three areas:

- **Data transfer mechanisms:** Regions have fundamentally different approaches to cross-border data flows, from the EU's strict adequacy requirements to China's data localization mandates.
- **Algorithmic transparency:** Some jurisdictions (particularly in the EU) require significant transparency about how AI algorithms function, while others focus more on outcomes than processes.
- **Human oversight requirements:** Professional responsibility rules vary widely regarding the level of human supervision required for AI tools in legal practice.

We expect these conflicts in regulations to expand in the absence of any global standards, and you must be sure to establish strong regulatory mapping to understand how requirements interact in cross-border matters.

## Creating a Data Sovereignty Framework

Smart organizations are developing comprehensive approaches to managing cross-border data protection. Consider how a hypothetical global law firm might structure their approach:

First, they create a detailed data sovereignty framework that maps jurisdictional requirements. This includes not just current regulations but also monitoring systems for regulatory changes. They might discover, for instance, that while their AI contract review system can process documents in any jurisdiction, data from EU clients must remain within EU borders, while Chinese client data requires separate infrastructure entirely.

Next, they establish appropriate transfer mechanisms for each jurisdiction. For EU data, this means implementing Standard Contractual Clauses and conducting transfer impact assessments. For Asia-Pacific regions, they might need separate instances of their AI tools in each jurisdiction. The key is creating systems flexible enough to adapt to regional requirements while maintaining consistent service delivery.

Documentation becomes crucial in this context. You need to maintain comprehensive audit trails showing not just compliance but also the reasoning behind compliance decisions. This might include regular assessments of your AI tools against evolving regulatory requirements, documented data flow maps showing how information moves between jurisdictions, and detailed records of your compliance measures.

# REGIONAL REGULATORY OVERVIEW

Understanding regional variations in AI regulation is essential for effective international practice.

## European Union

The EU has adopted the most comprehensive regulatory approach to AI through the AI Act, which creates a risk-based framework for AI oversight. For legal applications, key requirements include:

- Transparency obligations regarding AI use in legal services.
- Documentation requirements for high-risk AI applications.
- Human oversight mandates for any AI used in legal decision-making.
- Strong data protection standards under both GDPR and the AI Act.

The EU considers AI governance to be a matter of individual rights protection that ensures AI systems are used only with meaningful human oversight.

Under the EU AI Act, legal tools are not per se 'high-risk'; classification depends on Annex III use cases (e.g., justice functions). Key dates: prohibitions/ AI-literacy (Feb 2, 2025), GPAI duties (Aug 2, 2025), most high-risk obligations (Aug 2, 2026; some to Aug 2, 2027).

## United States

The U.S. has adopted a more sectoral approach, with a patchwork of regulations at the federal and state levels. Key considerations include:

- Professional responsibility requirements from ABA Model Rules and state bar associations.
- Federal agency guidance on AI use in regulated industries.
- Emerging frameworks for AI governance in federal government use.

In the U.S., expect a patchwork: NYC's LL 144 governs automated employment tools; Colorado's AI Act (SB 24-205) takes effect June 30, 2026. California's 2024 SB 1047 was vetoed. The U.S. approach seems to prioritize innovation while still addressing certain potential harms. While this approach may create flexibility, it also adds complexity and risk.

## United Kingdom

United Kingdom has adopted a principles-based, regulator-led regime (no single AI statute). Government responses in 2025 reaffirm a pro-innovation approach, with targeted measures for powerful models under consultation.

## Asia-Pacific Region

The Asia-Pacific region presents perhaps the most varied regulatory landscape, with approaches ranging from China's comprehensive regulatory framework to more limited interventions in other jurisdictions:

- China's approach emphasizes data sovereignty and security, with strict requirements for AI systems handling Chinese data.
- Japan has adopted a more principles-based approach focused on ethics and human-centric AI. **Japan** updated its **AI Guidelines for Business** to v 1.01 (Mar 28, 2025).
- Singapore has developed a governance framework that provides detailed guidance while maintaining flexibility. **Singapore** published a **Model AI Governance Framework for Generative AI** (2024).

- Australia, thus far, has focused primarily on guidance rather than binding regulation. **Australia** advanced a **national AI assurance framework** for government in 2024/2025.

China now operates three cross-border data transfer tracks (security assessment, standard contract, certification), with 2024 easing measures and 2025 certification rules effective Jan 1, 2026; plan for jurisdiction-specific instances or carefully structured transfers. The diversity of approaches in the Asia-Pacific region reflects different cultural and political priorities. You need to understand these variations to operate across multiple countries in the region.

## AI GOVERNANCE ACROSS JURISDICTIONS

The challenge of managing AI governance across jurisdictions extends beyond data protection. Different regions have fundamentally different approaches to AI regulation, professional responsibility requirements, and ethical standards. You must understand these variations to have an effective international practice.

### Addressing Varying Requirements

Consider how requirements might vary across regions. In a hypothetical scenario, your global law firm's AI research tool might need different configurations and oversight depending on location.

In the U.S., the focus might be on ensuring appropriate attorney supervision and validation of AI outputs. You might implement a system where AI-generated research must be verified against traditional legal databases before being used in client work.

For EU operations, the same tool might require additional documentation of the AI's decision-making process to meet explainability requirements. You might need to implement systems that track and document how the AI reaches its conclusions.

In Asia, where some jurisdictions have stricter requirements about data sovereignty, you might need to create entirely separate instances of AI tools, each trained only on jurisdiction-specific data.

These variations create significant operational challenges. How do you maintain consistent quality when oversight requirements differ by region? How do you ensure efficient operations while meeting varying regulatory requirements? These are questions your AI governance team must address and resolve.

## Adaptive Governance Frameworks

Some international organizations develop adaptive governance frameworks. Here's how such a framework might work in practice:

- At the global level, you establish core principles that apply everywhere. These might include basic standards for AI oversight, minimum requirements for data protection, and fundamental quality control processes.
- At the regional level, you add specific requirements based on local regulations and professional standards. For instance, EU operations might have additional documentation requirements, while Asia-Pacific operations might need specific data localization protocols.
- At the local level, you implement specific procedures that address individual office or jurisdiction requirements. This might include special review processes, specific client communication protocols, or unique documentation requirements.

The key to making this work is finding the right balance between global consistency and local adaptation. Too much standardization creates compliance risks; too much variation creates operational inefficiency.

## Professional Responsibility Considerations

Professional responsibility requirements regarding AI use vary significantly across jurisdictions.

1. **Disclosure requirements:** Jurisdictions differ on whether and how you must disclose AI use to clients and courts. Disclosure obligations in the U.S. are court- and context-specific: some judges and courts require certifications or policies; many bars (e.g., ABA Formal Opinion 512) emphasize competence, confidentiality, and verification rather than blanket disclosure.
2. **Supervision standards:** Requirements for human oversight of AI tools vary widely, from general competence requirements to specific review protocols.
3. **Confidentiality implications:** Different bar associations have reached varying conclusions about whether using third-party AI tools creates a disclosure requirement to a third party and what protections are necessary.

International legal organizations must navigate varying standards while maintaining consistent ethical practice. It is essential to institute approaches that maintain professional integrity across jurisdictional boundaries.

# INTERNATIONAL CLIENT SERVICE DELIVERY

Perhaps the most nuanced challenge in international AI adoption involves managing varying client expectations and cultural attitudes toward AI use in legal services. These variations can significantly impact how organizations approach both implementation and communication about AI use.

## Cultural Expectations and AI Acceptance

Consider this hypothetical situation: Your global law firm implements an AI-powered due diligence system. Your U.S. clients generally focus on efficiency gains and cost savings, asking detailed questions about accuracy rates and time savings. Your German clients, while interested in efficiency, place greater emphasis on data protection and algorithmic transparency, requiring detailed explanations of how the AI makes decisions. Your Japanese clients express more concern about maintaining traditional client relationships and want assurance that senior attorneys remain deeply involved in the process.

These varying expectations require thoughtful adaptation of both service delivery and communication strategies. A one-size-fits-all approach simply won't work. Organizations need to develop what we might call "culturally adaptive AI frameworks" that maintain consistent core capabilities while adjusting implementation and communication based on regional expectations.

## Adapting Communication Strategies

For U.S. clients, communications might emphasize quantitative benefits—time saved, cost reduced, accuracy improved. The focus would be on demonstrating how AI brings efficiency and enhances service delivery while maintaining professional standards. Highlight how AI enhances human expertise rather than replacing it.

For EU clients, the emphasis might shift to transparency and control. Communications would detail data protection measures, explain AI decision-making processes, and emphasize human oversight mechanisms. Emphasize compliance with regional regulations.

For Asia-Pacific clients, the focus might be on how AI supports rather than replaces traditional legal service relationships. Communications would emphasize how AI tools free senior attorneys to focus on strategic advice and client relationships. Discuss respect for local legal traditions and ensure the continuation of personal service.

Clients aren't just buying technical capabilities. They want relationships and professional services that align with their values and needs. International firms need communication strategies that fit the cultures and priorities of their clients.

## TECHNICAL IMPLEMENTATION CHALLENGES

The technical challenges of international AI deployment often surprise organizations that have successfully implemented AI tools domestically. These challenges go far beyond simple issues of infrastructure and connectivity.

### Legal Tradition and Language Barriers

Consider this scenario: Your law firm implements an AI contract analysis system that works brilliantly in English but struggles with the nuances of civil law contracts in French and German. The system's accuracy drops significantly when analyzing documents under different legal traditions, creating quality control challenges and requiring extensive human review.

Or consider this situation: Your legal department implements an AI research tool that works perfectly in common law jurisdictions but struggles to properly analyze civil law sources, missing important doctrinal writings that carry significant weight in civil law systems.

These scenarios illustrate how technical challenges often intertwine with substantive legal issues in international contexts. Organizations need to consider language and legal system variations. AI tools trained primarily on English-language common law materials may struggle with other legal traditions. Organizations need to carefully evaluate tool performance across different legal systems and languages. This might mean maintaining separate training datasets for different jurisdictions or implementing additional validation protocols for cross-border matters.

### Infrastructure and Deployment Challenges

Technical infrastructure variations create additional implementation challenges. Organizations may face several infrastructure barriers:

- **Technical infrastructure:** Different regions often have varying technical capabilities and restrictions. Organizations might need to implement multiple instances of their AI tools, each configured for specific regional requirements. This could include separate data centers for different jurisdictions, specialized encryption for certain regions, or modified user interfaces for different languages.

- **Support and maintenance:** Technical support becomes more complex in international operations. Organizations need to consider time zone differences, language barriers, and varying technical capabilities across regions. This might require building regional support teams or implementing follow-the-sun support models.
- **Integration challenges:** Different regions often use different technology platforms, creating integration challenges. Organizations might need to develop custom integrations for each region or maintain multiple versions of their AI tools to ensure compatibility with local systems.

### Training Data and Model Localization

Perhaps the most fundamental technical challenge involves developing appropriate training data for different jurisdictions. AI systems require jurisdiction-specific training to function effectively, particularly for:

- Local legal language and terminology.
- Jurisdiction-specific document formats and conventions.
- Region-specific legal concepts and principles.
- Local regulatory requirements and standards.

Unlike some AI business applications, legal AI cannot just be translated. It must be retrained on jurisdiction-specific data.

## MANAGING INTERNATIONAL OUTSIDE COUNSEL RELATIONSHIPS

For in-house legal departments, managing AI use across international outside counsel relationships creates unique challenges. Consider this scenario: Your legal department has implemented strict guidelines about AI use for document review in your U.S. matters, including specific requirements for tool selection, oversight, and quality control. But what happens when you need to manage a multi-jurisdictional matter involving law firms in five different countries, each with different AI capabilities and regulatory constraints?

Maintaining consistent AI standards across international outside counsel relationships isn't easy. The challenges go beyond simple technology alignment to include fundamental questions about service delivery, cost allocation, and risk management.

## Varying Capabilities and Standards

Consider how this plays out in practice. Your U.S. law firm might have sophisticated AI tools for document review and due diligence, while your German counsel has strict limitations on AI use due to data protection requirements, and your Japanese counsel still prefers traditional manual review methods. How do you maintain consistent quality and efficiency across these varying approaches?

Smart legal departments are developing adaptive outside counsel guidelines that establish core requirements while allowing for regional variation. Such guidelines typically address:

- **Standard requirements:** Establishing baseline expectations for AI use, including minimum oversight requirements, quality control standards, and documentation protocols.
- **Regional variations:** Acknowledging and accommodating jurisdiction-specific constraints while maintaining consistent overall standards.
- **Integration protocols:** Defining how work product from different firms using different AI tools should be integrated and validated.

## Cost Management and Billing

The variation in AI capabilities across firms creates significant challenges for cost management. Consider this hypothetical situation: A major litigation involves document review across multiple jurisdictions. Your U.S. firm uses AI tools that significantly reduce review time, while firms in other jurisdictions perform more traditional review. How do you manage these cost differentials while maintaining fairness and efficiency?

You might create jurisdiction-specific billing guidelines that account for varying levels of AI adoption, develop hybrid fee arrangements that balance efficiency incentives with regional constraints, and implement monitoring systems that track efficiency across different review approaches. Some legal departments are moving beyond cost comparisons to value-based assessments to account for regional variations, using AI tools to assist in this evaluation.

## Outside Counsel Management Frameworks

Some emerging practices for managing AI in the use of international outside counsel include:

1. **Tiered guidelines:** Multi-level guidelines with global baseline requirements and regional adaptations.

2. **Capability mapping:** Comprehensive inventories of outside counsel AI capabilities across jurisdictions to inform matter staffing and management.
3. **Outcome-based metrics:** Focused on results and quality, allowing firms in different regions to achieve similar outcomes through different means.
4. **Technical integration standards:** Clear standards for how work from different firms using different AI tools should be combined and validated.

# ETHICAL AND SOCIAL IMPACT CONSIDERATIONS

The ethical implications of AI use in legal practice take on additional dimensions in international contexts. Different societies have varying perspectives on fundamental questions about algorithmic decision-making, automation impacts, and appropriate governance models.

## Cross-Cultural Ethics and Values

There are significant variations in how different societies approach AI ethics questions:

- Western jurisdictions typically emphasize individual rights, transparency, and explainability.
- East Asian approaches often place greater emphasis on social harmony and collective outcomes.
- Middle Eastern perspectives frequently incorporate religious and cultural values into ethical frameworks.

Organizations operating internationally need to understand these varying perspectives and consider how to address them in communications.

### *Employment and Social Impact Variations*

Concerns about AI's impact on legal employment vary significantly across jurisdictions:

- In jurisdictions with stronger employment protections (like many EU countries), concerns about job displacement tend to be more prominent.
- In regions with growing legal sectors (like parts of Asia), the focus shifts more toward skills development and transition.
- In markets with lawyer shortages (like many developing economies), AI is often viewed primarily as an access enhancer.

Organizations using AI across borders need to be sensitive to local and regional concerns.

## Responsible AI Implementation

Some organizations are developing cross-cultural frameworks for responsible AI implementation that respect these variations while maintaining consistent ethical standards. Key components of such frameworks might include:

- **Cultural impact assessment:** How AI implementation might be perceived in different cultural contexts.
- **Inclusive governance:** Ensuring regional perspectives are incorporated into AI governance structures.
- **Adaptable ethics frameworks:** Ethical guidelines that maintain core principles while accommodating regional variations.
- **Stakeholder engagement:** Mechanisms for ongoing dialogue with affected parties across different regions.

However you develop your own approach, be sure to use your global team members who can contribute to understanding the local and regional points of view.

### *Learning from Global Implementation Experience*

Organizations that have successfully navigated international AI implementation offer valuable lessons.

## Hypothetical Case Study: Global Financial Institution

A major multinational bank implemented an AI-powered contract analysis system across its multi-country legal department. Their approach included:

- **Phased regional deployment:** Rather than simultaneous global implementation, they began with regions having similar legal systems and data protection frameworks.
- **Federated technical architecture:** They created a core system with region-specific instances, each configured for local requirements.
- **Tiered governance framework:** Their governance model included global baseline requirements with regional adaptations.
- **Continuous cross-regional learning:** They established formal mechanisms for sharing implementation lessons across regions.

The firm initially tried to force consistency everywhere, but faced significant resistance. They changed to a model that respected regional differences, but maintained core standards.

## Hypothetical Case Study: International Law Firm

A global law firm with offices in 25 countries implemented an AI-powered legal research system following a balanced approach:

1. **Regional champion model:** They identified key partners in each region to lead implementation, ensuring adaptation to local needs.
2. **Technical customization:** They worked with their vendor to develop jurisdiction-specific models trained on local legal materials.
3. **Graduated oversight requirements:** They created oversight frameworks tailored to each jurisdiction's professional responsibility requirements.

The key was balancing global consistency with local relevance. Rather than forcing one approach everywhere, they focused on consistent outcomes but allowed implementation to reflect local and regional realities.

## Key Success Patterns

Across successful implementations, several patterns emerge:

- **Respect for regional differences:** Successful organizations acknowledge and accommodate regional variations rather than forcing rigid standardization.
- **Federated approaches:** They implement federated technical and governance models that maintain core standards while allowing regional adaptation.
- **Continuous learning:** They create mechanisms for sharing implementation lessons across regions, allowing the organization to improve continuously.
- **Outcome focus:** They emphasize consistent outcomes rather than identical processes, giving regional operations flexibility in how they achieve results.

# FUTURE CONSIDERATIONS

The international landscape for legal AI use continues to evolve rapidly. Organizations need to prepare for several emerging trends:

## Regulatory Evolution and Divergence

Different regions are likely to continue developing distinct and possibly conflicting approaches to AI regulation. The EU's AI Act sets one standard, while other regions develop different frameworks. Organizations will need increasingly sophisticated approaches to managing these varying requirements.

We could be seeing a period of regulatory divergence instead of convergence. You should prepare for global AI governance becoming more complex, not simpler. Several potential regulatory developments include:

- **Increasing regulatory specificity:** As AI becomes more established in legal practice, regulators will develop more specific requirements for different applications.
- **Growing focus on outcomes:** Regulatory approaches will likely shift from general principles toward specific outcome requirements and testing protocols.
- **Emerging accountability frameworks:** New approaches to establishing responsibility for AI outputs will develop, potentially with significant jurisdictional variations.

## Technological Evolution

New AI capabilities will create both opportunities and challenges for international practice. Organizations will need to evaluate how these capabilities fit within different regulatory frameworks and cultural expectations.

Consider how these trends might affect future operations. Your firm or department might need to separate AI implementation strategies for different regions, each aligned with local regulations and expectations. You would also look at creating sophisticated monitoring systems to track regulatory changes across jurisdictions and adjust operations accordingly. To make this work, you would need to build flexible technical infrastructures that can adapt to varying requirements while maintaining consistent service delivery.

# CONCLUSION

Successfully managing AI adoption across international boundaries requires organizations to think beyond domestic implementation considerations. You need to develop approaches that can adapt to varying regulatory requirements, cultural expectations, and technical challenges while maintaining consistent professional standards.

The organizations that will thrive are those that:

- Build flexible frameworks that can adapt to regional variations.
- Maintain strong governance while accommodating local requirements.
- Develop culturally sensitive communication approaches.
- Create robust technical infrastructures that support international operations.

Most importantly, you must recognize that international AI adoption isn't just about managing complexity—it's about leveraging it to create competitive advantages in an increasingly global legal market. The firms that will win in the global AI-enabled legal market will be those that adapt to varied legal environments, regulatory frameworks, and client expectations.

## ACTION ITEMS

1. **Map Cross-Border Regulatory Requirements**
   - Conduct comprehensive analysis of AI regulations across all operational jurisdictions
   - Create regulatory compliance matrix addressing conflicting requirements and data sovereignty issues
   - Establish monitoring systems for evolving international AI regulations and guidance
2. **Develop International AI Governance Framework**
   - Design adaptive governance that balances global consistency with local regulatory compliance
   - Create tiered policy architecture with global principles, regional frameworks, and local implementations
   - Establish cross-jurisdictional decision-making and coordination mechanisms
3. **Implement Data Sovereignty and Transfer Controls**
   - Create data localization strategies addressing varying international data protection requirements
   - Establish secure cross-border data transfer mechanisms complying with GDPR, PIPL, and other frameworks
   - Design jurisdiction-specific data-handling protocols and technical safeguards

4. **Address Cultural and Client Expectation Variations**
    - Develop culturally adaptive AI communication strategies for international clients
    - Create region-specific service delivery approaches respecting local professional and cultural norms
    - Establish client preference systems accommodating varying international attitudes toward AI
5. **Manage International Outside Counsel Relationships**
    - Create AI capability assessment and management frameworks for global outside counsel networks
    - Develop consistent AI standards while accommodating regional constraints and capabilities
    - Establish integration protocols for AI-enhanced work across multiple jurisdictions
6. **Build Technical Infrastructure for International Operations**
    - Design federated technical architecture supporting regional AI requirements
    - Create language and legal tradition adaptations for AI tools and training data
    - Establish jurisdiction-specific AI deployment and support systems

# CHAPTER 15

# Next-Generation AI and Beyond

## INTRODUCTION

*The legal profession stands at the threshold of its "Kurzweilian moment"—a period where technological advancement will occur at a pace and scale that defies conventional planning.*

Picture this scenario: Your organization has successfully implemented current-generation AI tools across several practice areas. The systems are working well, adoption is strong, and you're seeing real benefits. Then a partner asks: "What's next? What should we be preparing for?" It's a crucial question that every legal organization needs to consider, not just for incremental improvement but for the revolutionary changes on the horizon.

The pace of technological change in legal practice continues to accelerate exponentially, not linearly. According to various surveys and reports, over 80% of legal organizations expect significant technology changes in the next three years, with AI evolution leading these changes. Yet surveys reveal that less than 30% have specific plans for adapting to these emerging technologies. While a preparation gap like this would threaten to create a new digital divide between forward-looking firms and those caught unprepared, we believe the gap will close very soon. Even looking at surveys conducted in late 2024 and comparing them to those in Q2 of 2025, we see tremendous movement and greater understanding that this shift is happening, whether we are ready for it or not.

Computer scientist and futurist Ray Kurzweil, known for his remarkably accurate technological predictions, observed more than 20 years ago that "We won't experience 100 years of progress in the 21st century, it will be more like 20,000 years of progress at today's rate."[1] For legal practice, this means preparing not just for incremental improvements but for fundamental transformations in how legal work is conceived, executed, and delivered.

This chapter explores the coming revolutions in legal AI and beyond, examining not only what will be possible technically, but also how these capabilities will reshape the practice of law itself. More importantly, we provide actionable guidance on how forward-thinking legal organizations can prepare for and thrive in this radically different future.

## THE EXPONENTIAL FUTURE OF LEGAL AI

### Law's Kurzweilian Moment

The legal profession stands at the threshold of its "Kurzweilian moment"—a period where technological advancement will occur at a pace and scale that defies conventional planning. Just as few in 1995 could have predicted how the internet would transform legal practice, today's practitioners can barely glimpse the transformative potential of next-generation AI systems that will emerge over the next several years.

Andrew Ng, AI pioneer and founder of LandingAI, noted in 2017 that "AI is the new electricity.... Just as electricity transformed almost everything 100 years ago, today I actually have a hard time thinking of an industry that I don't think AI will transform in the next several years."[2] How right he was. For legal practice, this means preparing not just for better tools but also for a fundamentally different professional landscape.

The exponential improvement in AI capabilities isn't theoretical. It's already demonstrable. According to Stanford University's 2025 AI Index Report, adoption of AI has accelerated at an unprecedented rate, especially in 2024.[3] The report indicates explosive global growth in AI investment, particularly by governments investing in AI infrastructure in the hundreds of billions of dollars. It also notes

---

[1] Ray Kurzweil, *The Law of Accelerating Returns*, KurzweilAI.net (Mar. 7, 2001), https://www.writingsbyraykurzweil.com/the-law-of-accelerating-returns.

[2] Shana Lynch, *Andrew Ng: Why AI Is the New Electricity*, Insights by Stanford Business (Mar. 11, 2017), https://www.gsb.stanford.edu/insights/andrew-ng-why-ai-new-electricity.

[3] Stanford University Human-Centered Artificial Intelligence, The 2025 AI Index Report (2025), https://hai.stanford.edu/ai-index/2025-ai-index-report.

equally dramatic global growth in attention to the need for AI-related regulations, with ninefold expansion of mentions of AI in legislative proceedings since 2016. The report also notes that computer and AI science education is expanding world-wide at the K–12 level, and AI projects are earning major scientific awards, including Nobel Prizes.

This trajectory suggests that by 2030, legal AI systems will possess capabilities that make today's most advanced systems appear primitive by comparison. As the report so eloquently states, "AI is no longer just a story of what's possible—it's a story of what's happening now and how we are collectively shaping the future of humanity."[4]

### Breaking Current AI Limitations

Today's legal AI systems face significant limitations: They struggle with complex reasoning, lack a true understanding of legal contexts, and require extensive human oversight. These limitations have led some in the legal profession to view AI as merely an incremental improvement tool rather than a transformative force. We are here to tell you that this view fundamentally misunderstands the exponential trajectory of AI development.

The next generation of AI systems will move beyond statistical pattern matching to develop genuine causal reasoning capabilities. For legal applications, this means systems that won't just find relevant precedents; they will actually understand the underlying legal principles and apply them creatively to novel situations. These systems will analyze complex regulatory structures, identify hidden risks and opportunities, and develop sophisticated legal strategies that consider multiple contingencies and outcomes.

## NEXT-GENERATION LEGAL AI CAPABILITIES

### Advanced Reasoning and Legal Intelligence

The next generation of legal AI will represent a quantitative and qualitative leap in capabilities. At the time of this writing, multiple experts predict that by 2030, legal AI systems will move beyond information retrieval to sophisticated legal reasoning comparable to that of senior associates.

These systems will understand what the law says and what it means in context. They'll grasp the normative reasoning behind legal rules, understand

---

[4] *Id.*

complex interrelationships between different areas of law, and apply this understanding to novel situations. In legal contexts, this means systems that understand the societal purposes and policy goals behind legal doctrines, not just their formal expressions.

The implications for legal practice are profound. Consider complex regulatory compliance, where organizations struggle to navigate conflicting requirements across multiple jurisdictions. Next-generation AI will not only identify relevant regulations but also understand their underlying purposes, resolve apparent conflicts through sophisticated legal reasoning, and develop comprehensive compliance approaches that satisfy technical requirements and policy objectives.

## Radical Personalization and Prediction

Future legal AI will offer unprecedented capability to personalize legal services and predict outcomes with extraordinary precision. Legal prediction systems will likely achieve accuracy rates for litigation outcomes that exceed those of experienced human lawyers.

These systems will analyze vast datasets of case outcomes, judicial decisions, opposing counsel tactics, and client-specific factors to develop highly personalized litigation strategies. They'll identify patterns invisible to human analysis and suggest approaches tailored to specific jurisdictions, judges, and legal contexts. They will support jury selection and attitude analysis during trial, based on deep online searches supported by facial and body language evaluations of prospective and sitting jurors.

Beyond litigation, these personalized prediction capabilities will transform transactional practice. Next-generation contract analysis systems will identify risks and quantify them precisely based on historical outcomes and market conditions. They'll recommend specific contract modifications based on rigorous analysis of thousands of similar transactions and their results. In legal services, this personalization will move from luxury to expectation.

## Autonomous Legal Services

Perhaps most disruptively, future AI systems will increasingly deliver certain legal services autonomously. Richard Susskind, legal futurist and author of "The Future of the Professions," predicted that by 2035, we'll see the emergence of truly autonomous legal services for routine and even complex matters. We could not agree more.

Unlike today's tools that assist lawyers, these systems will independently handle entire categories of legal work, from contract generation and regulatory filings to standard dispute resolution and compliance monitoring. They'll draw on vast legal knowledge, sophisticated reasoning capabilities, and access to real-time data to provide services that match or exceed human lawyer quality for certain tasks. This doesn't mean the end of lawyers, but rather a fundamental shift in how legal expertise is deployed. You will assist the AI tools, rather than the other way around, focusing on novel issues, complex strategic questions, and human-centered aspects of legal representation, while routine matters will increasingly be handled automatically.

## Multimodal and Embodied Legal AI

Tomorrow's legal AI systems won't be confined to text. They'll analyze images, interpret body language, process audio, and integrate information across multiple modalities. Fei-Fei Li, co-director of Stanford's Human-Centered AI Institute and co-founder and CEO of World Labs, has spoken extensively about multimodality as the next major frontier in AI, emphasizing that future systems must understand and reason across different types of information, including images, text, audio, and actions.

For legal practice, multimodal AI will transform evidence analysis, witness preparation, jury selection, forum shopping, courtroom performance, and client interactions. Systems will analyze deposition videos to identify subtle inconsistencies in testimony, evaluate presentation materials for persuasiveness, and help lawyers refine their communication for maximum effectiveness.

More provocatively, we'll see the emergence of embodied AI in legal contexts. Humanoid robots with sophisticated legal AI capabilities will participate in client meetings, attend court proceedings, and provide legal services in physical settings. For litigators, this means preparing for a world where legal AI exists not just in computers but in physical, interactive forms that engage directly with clients and legal systems.

But wait! The use of AI-generated avatars in a courtroom setting isn't something to look for in the future; it is already here. In May 2025, in an Arizona court, a murder victim's sister used an AI-created victim impact statement video featuring the victim himself offering a message to his murderer during the sentencing phase of the case. While the defendant's appeal will include a challenge to the use of the video, we are sure that this won't be the last use of AI avatars in courtroom settings.

## CONVERGENCE WITH OTHER TRANSFORMATIVE TECHNOLOGIES

The revolutionary impact of AI on legal practice will be amplified by its convergence with other rapidly advancing technologies. This technological fusion will create capabilities far beyond what any single technology could achieve alone.

### Quantum Computing and Legal Complexity

Quantum computing represents perhaps the most significant amplifier of AI capabilities on the horizon. For legal AI, quantum computing will allow systems to analyze vastly more complex legal problems than current technologies permit. Consider international tax planning, which involves navigating hundreds of jurisdictions, thousands of regulations, and countless potential structures. Current systems can analyze only a tiny fraction of possible approaches. Quantum-enhanced legal AI could simultaneously evaluate millions of potential structures against all relevant regulations, optimizing for complex, multi-variable objectives in ways currently impossible.

By 2035, if not sooner, quantum computing will routinely solve practical problems that classical computers cannot approach, with complex legal analysis among the applications.

### Blockchain and Computational Law

The convergence of AI with blockchain technology will fundamentally transform how legal agreements function. Smart contracts combined with AI will evolve from simple arrangements to legal systems capable of dealing with more complex terms.

This evolution will create what Harvard Law Professor Lawrence Lessig calls "code as law"—legal arrangements expressed directly in executable code rather than natural language.

These computational legal systems won't just execute predetermined actions; they'll autonomously navigate complex legal environments, adapting to changing conditions while maintaining legal compliance.

By 2030, many commercial arrangements will exist primarily as AI-powered computational systems rather than traditional contracts. These systems will continuously monitor performance, dynamically adjust to changed circumstances, and autonomously resolve routine disputes according to legally binding computational rules. Human lawyers will design and oversee these systems rather than manually implementing the arrangements they embody.

## Augmented Reality and Legal Practice

The intersection of AI with augmented reality (AR) technologies will transform how lawyers interact with legal information and clients. Augmented reality will become common in professional settings, creating persistent information layers over physical environments.

For lawyers, this means practicing in environments where AI-processed legal information is visually overlaid on the physical world. Imagine negotiating a contract while seeing real-time AI analysis of proposed terms floating beside each clause or arguing in court with key precedents and evidence visually highlighted as you speak.

More fundamentally, AR will transform client interactions by bridging geographical distances and enhancing understanding of complex legal concepts. Spatial computing enables the blending of digital content with the physical world to enhance human communication and understanding. Legal services will increasingly be delivered in shared augmented environments where clients and lawyers interact with visualized legal concepts, regardless of physical location.

# SOCIETAL AND PROFESSIONAL TRANSFORMATIONS

The technological revolutions just described will occur alongside—and drive—profound changes in how society views legal services and how the profession operates. Understanding these broader transformations is essential as you plan for the future.

## Client Expectation Revolution

Client expectations regarding legal services are already evolving rapidly, but we stand at the cusp of much more dramatic changes. Corporate clients will increasingly expect their legal service providers to leverage advanced AI for most routine legal work, with human lawyers focusing primarily on strategic guidance and relationship management. Beyond efficiency expectations, clients will increasingly demand personalized, data-driven legal services.

This expectation shift will accelerate as clients experience AI-enhanced services in other professional domains. As clients interact with increasingly sophisticated AI systems in medicine, finance, and other fields, they'll expect similar capabilities from their legal service providers. Organizations that fail to meet these evolving expectations will find themselves at a severe competitive disadvantage.

## Legal Education Transformation

The exponential advancement of legal AI will necessitate fundamental changes in legal education. Leading law schools will reimagine their curricula around the assumption that routine legal work will be largely automated.

Rather than focusing primarily on legal doctrine and analysis, future legal education will emphasize skills that complement advanced AI: complex problem solving, creative strategy development, interdisciplinary thinking, emotional intelligence, and technological fluency. The traditional model of legal education as the accumulation of doctrinal knowledge will give way to education focused on uniquely human capabilities, supplemented with training on the use of AI systems.

This shift will be controversial but inevitable. As Sebastian Thrun, founder of Udacity and Google X, observes about education generally, the half-life of knowledge is decreasing, and education has to shift to developing learning capabilities instead of gaining static knowledge. For legal education, this means developing lawyers who can continuously adapt to new technological environments rather than mastering methods for researching within a body of knowledge.

## Regulatory Revolution

Legal regulation will undergo profound changes to accommodate AI-enabled practice models. Current regulatory structures will soon become incompatible with technological and business model innovations expected to expand access to legal services.

Expect the emergence of regulatory frameworks designed specifically for AI-enabled legal services. These frameworks will focus less on who provides legal services (the traditional focus on licensed attorneys) and more on quality, transparency, and consumer protection regardless of the human–AI mix delivering the service.

This regulatory evolution will be contentious but necessary. Maintaining regulations designed for an analog world of human-only legal services will increasingly harm both the profession and the public by restricting innovations that could improve legal service delivery. Forward-thinking legal organizations will participate in shaping these new regulatory approaches rather than simply reacting to them.

## Cognitive and Organizational Adaptation

Perhaps most profoundly, legal professionals must prepare for unprecedented cognitive and organizational adaptation as AI capabilities accelerate. Futurist

Alvin Toffler foresaw this challenge decades ago, warning that "the illiterate of tomorrow will not be the man who can't read; he will be the man who has not learned how to learn." He argued that education—and by extension, professional competence—must rest on our ability to *learn, unlearn, and relearn* in an age of accelerating change.[5]

For legal professionals, this means developing what Cal Newport, author of "Deep Work," calls "meta-learning" capabilities—the ability to rapidly master new cognitive domains and technological environments. As AI capabilities evolve exponentially, legal professionals must continuously reimagine their roles and develop new skills at an unprecedented pace.

This adaptation extends beyond individual lawyers to organization-level evolution. Law firms and legal departments will need to develop what organizational theorist Peter Senge calls "learning organization" capabilities—the ability to continuously transform in response to changing environments. Traditional law firm structures, with their emphasis on precedent and stability, may prove particularly vulnerable to disruption without conscious efforts to develop adaptive capacity.

## PREPARING FOR THE UNIMAGINABLE

How can legal organizations prepare for a future that may be fundamentally different from the present? The challenge resembles what former U.S. Secretary of Defense Donald Rumsfeld famously called "unknown unknowns"—developments we cannot yet anticipate. Several approaches can help organizations navigate this uncertain future.

### Scenario Planning and Future Sensing

Traditional strategic planning assumes a relatively predictable future. In times of exponential change, organizations need different approaches. Peter Schwartz, futurist and founder of Global Business Network, even back in 1996, advocated scenario planning—developing multiple detailed visions of possible futures to build organizational adaptability.[6] This need still holds true today.

---

[5] Alvin Toffler, Future Shock 414 (1970). Toffler cites psychologist Herbert Gerjuoy in Chapter 18, "Education in the Future Tense," expanding on the need to "learn, unlearn, and relearn." The oft-quoted modern variation referring to the "illiterate of the 21st century" paraphrases this passage.

[6] Peter Schwartz, The Art of the Long View: Planning for the Future in an Uncertain World (1996).

For legal organizations, this means regularly convening diverse groups to imagine different ways AI might transform practice, developing detailed narratives about these possible futures, and identifying strategic options that make sense across multiple scenarios. The goal isn't to predict the future precisely but to expand the organization's ability to recognize and respond to emerging developments.

Beyond formal scenario planning, organizations should develop what futurist Amy Webb calls "future sensing capabilities," which are systematic approaches to identifying weak signals of significant change before they become obvious. These might include dedicated teams tracking emerging technologies, regular engagement with technologists outside the legal sphere, and systematic assessment of early-stage legal technology startups.

## Experimentation Culture and Portfolios

In rapidly changing environments, experimentation becomes more valuable than planning. Legal organizations should develop systematic approaches to low-cost experimentation with emerging technologies. This means creating what innovation expert Stefan Thomke calls "experimentation portfolios," which are collections of small-scale tests designed to generate learning about emerging possibilities. Rather than making large bets on particular technologies, organizations should conduct numerous small experiments, rapidly incorporating learning into subsequent efforts.

The most successful organizations will develop a culture of experimentation and test new approaches without excessive concern about failure. This represents a challenge for legal organizations where perfectionism and precedent often dominate cultural values.

## Capability Building Over Technology Acquisition

In preparing for exponential change, building adaptable capabilities matters more than acquiring specific technologies. Organizations should prioritize developing the capacity to continuously integrate new technologies over investing heavily in current solutions. This capability-focused approach requires significant investment in people and processes. Organizations should create systematic approaches for continuous reskilling, establish technology integration teams with dedicated resources, and develop governance frameworks that can accommodate rapidly evolving technological capabilities.

Organizations that invest in human capital development alongside AI implementation achieve more productivity gains than those focused solely on technology acquisition. The critical importance of human capability development alongside technological advancement cannot be overstated.

### Exponential Ethics and Responsible Innovation

As AI capabilities advance exponentially, ethical considerations become increasingly important. Legal organizations must develop sophisticated approaches to identifying and addressing the ethical implications of advanced AI. This means creating systematic approaches to identifying potential ethical issues before they emerge in practice. Organizations should establish AI ethics committees with diverse membership, develop clear principles for responsible AI use, and create processes for evaluating novel ethical questions as they arise.

Beyond organizational approaches, the legal profession must participate in broader societal discussions about AI governance. The legal profession, with its traditional focus on justice and rights, has a particular responsibility to help develop governance approaches that ensure advanced AI serves human flourishing.

## REVOLUTIONARY IMPACT ON SPECIFIC PRACTICE AREAS

While AI will transform all aspects of legal practice, its impact will manifest differently across practice areas. In Chapter 3, we discussed how different practice areas could leverage AI while addressing their unique challenges and requirements. Here we discuss future considerations and implications of continued AI developments.

### Litigation Transformation

Litigation will undergo perhaps the most visible transformation from exponential AI advancement. By 2030, AI systems will analyze vast case datasets to develop highly personalized litigation strategies, predict judicial decisions with unprecedented accuracy, and generate compelling legal arguments autonomously.

The courtroom itself will change dramatically. In the future, AI will participate in court proceedings, analyzing arguments in real time and suggesting responses to counsel. This will fundamentally change advocacy skills, placing greater emphasis on strategic direction and human connection rather than information recall and basic analytical tasks.

Discovery processes will be completely automated, with advanced AI systems handling document review, deposition analysis, and evidence organization without human involvement except at the strategic level. The question may soon be not whether AI can handle discovery better than humans, but how and where human review adds value.

## Transactional Practice Revolution

Transactional practice will evolve from document creation to relationship architecture. As smart contracts and computational law become dominant, lawyers will increasingly design legal systems rather than drafting documents. Some observers say that by 2035, commercial agreements will exist primarily as code rather than natural language text.

Due diligence will be transformed by AI systems that autonomously analyze vast document collections, identify material issues, and quantify risks with precision far exceeding human capabilities. AI will not only identify issues in due diligence but also be able to assign probabilities and financial impacts to specific risks.

Perhaps most significantly, the line between legal and business advisory work will blur significantly. As routine transactional tasks become automated, lawyers will focus increasingly on strategic business guidance. In AI-enabled law firms, the most successful transactional lawyers will function more like business strategists with legal expertise.

## Regulatory and Compliance Revolution

Regulatory practice will shift from reactive interpretation to proactive, automated compliance. This represents what some are calling "compliance by design"—building legal requirements directly into operational systems rather than checking compliance after the fact. As Lawrence Lessig predicted decades ago, "The code is the law"—technical architecture itself will increasingly embody legal requirements.[7]

For regulatory lawyers, this means a shift from interpretation to system design. The most valuable regulatory practitioners will be those who can translate legal requirements into computational systems and help clients design operations that achieve business objectives within automated compliance frameworks.

---

[7] Lawrence Lessig, Code and Other Laws of Cyberspace (1999).

## THE HUMAN ELEMENT IN AN AI-DOMINATED FUTURE

Despite the exponential advancement of AI capabilities, certain aspects of legal practice will remain fundamentally human. Understanding these enduring human elements helps organizations prepare for a future where lawyers and AI systems work as complementary partners rather than competitors.

### Judgment, Wisdom, and Contextual Understanding

While AI will increasingly match or exceed human capabilities in information processing and pattern recognition, human judgment and wisdom will remain essential. For legal practice, this means human lawyers will continue to provide crucial judgment in unprecedented situations, complex ethical dilemmas, and cases requiring balancing of competing societal values.

### Complex Social Interaction and Empathy

Legal practice fundamentally involves understanding and navigating human relationships, an area where AI will continue to have significant limitations. For lawyers, this means human capabilities in client counseling, negotiation, and courtroom persuasion will remain valuable even as AI handles more analytical tasks. The ability to understand unstated client concerns, navigate complex interpersonal dynamics, and connect authentically with juries and judges will become increasingly central to the lawyer's role.

### Creative Strategy and Interdisciplinary Thinking

While AI will become increasingly capable in routine analysis, human lawyers will retain advantages in creative strategy development and interdisciplinary thinking. Machines are good at identifying patterns in data, but humans are good at making creative connections across domains.

For legal practice, this means lawyers who can integrate insights from multiple fields, develop novel legal theories, and create innovative solutions to unprecedented problems will remain highly valuable. As technology handles more routine work, these creative capabilities will become increasingly central to the lawyer's value proposition.

# CONCLUSION

The coming decades will bring unprecedented changes to legal practice through the exponential advancement of AI and its convergence with other transformative technologies. Organizations that understand and prepare for these changes will not merely survive but thrive in this new environment.

Success requires moving beyond incremental adaptation to embrace substantial innovation, fundamentally rethinking how legal services are conceived, created, and delivered. Organizations must develop not just new technologies but also new business models, skill sets, and organizational structures designed for a radically different future.

Most importantly, legal organizations must maintain their fundamental commitment to justice and client service while embracing technological transformation. For legal organizations, this means developing the capacity for continuous adaptation while preserving the core values that define the profession.

Those who succeed will create what management theorist Jim Collins calls "the genius of the AND," embracing both technological advancement AND human wisdom, both efficiency AND judgment, both innovation AND ethical responsibility. The future belongs not to those who simply adopt new technologies but to those who reimagine what legal service means in an age of exponential change. Be one of those people.

CHAPTER 16

# Building a Future-Ready Organization

## INTRODUCTION

*Success will come not from predicting the future accurately but from building organizations that can thrive under conditions of radical uncertainty.*

Consider this scenario: Your organization has successfully implemented AI across multiple practice areas, developed strong governance frameworks, and trained your people effectively. Yet something still feels missing. Despite all these advances, you face a sobering reality: What constitutes cutting-edge today will be standard practice tomorrow and outdated the day after.

This challenge faces every legal organization today. According to a number of surveys conducted in 2023–2024, a minority report confidence in their overall organizational readiness for future changes. This confidence gap isn't just concerning—it's potentially existential. Organizations that merely adopt today's technologies without building the capacity for continuous transformation risk finding themselves irrelevant.

The pace of AI advancement is not merely accelerating, it's exponential. The legal AI systems that seem impressive today will appear rudimentary within three years. Practice areas we currently consider immune to automation will face profound disruption. Client expectations will evolve faster than traditional service models can adapt.

Building a truly future-ready organization requires going beyond technology adoption to develop what organizational theorists call "dynamic capabilities";

that is, the institutional capacity to sense opportunities, reconfigure resources, and continuously evolve. This chapter explores how legal organizations can develop these capabilities while maintaining the professional standards and service quality that define successful practice.

## BEYOND TRADITIONAL STRATEGIC PLANNING

Traditional strategic planning in legal organizations has become dangerously insufficient. The five-year plans that once provided adequate guidance can become obsolete within months as technological capabilities, client expectations, and competitive dynamics evolve at unprecedented rates.

Future-ready legal organizations are replacing traditional planning approaches with frameworks that provide direction amidst constant change while enabling rapid course correction as conditions evolve. Unlike traditional strategic plans that often sit on shelves between annual reviews, these navigation systems function as living frameworks that inform daily decision-making.

These systems focus on developing three core organizational capabilities:

### Environmental Sensing

Organizations need sophisticated mechanisms for detecting weak signals of change before they become obvious. This goes beyond traditional competitive intelligence to include systematic monitoring of emerging technologies, evolving client needs, regulatory shifts, and cross-industry innovations. Leading organizations create dedicated "future sensing" teams with explicit responsibility for identifying emerging opportunities and threats.

The most sophisticated future-sensing capabilities will emerge from organizations that implement enterprise knowledge models with ontological relationship mapping. Rather than monitoring discrete signals in isolation, these semantic frameworks enable organizations to understand how emerging technologies, regulatory changes, and market shifts interconnect and amplify each other. Future-ready organizations will deploy intelligent data agents that continuously scan the environment, automatically identifying relevant patterns and relationships that human analysts might miss, while preserving institutional learning through tokenized knowledge assets that compound in value over time.

## Adaptive Response

Rather than committing to fixed initiatives, organizations need portfolios of strategic options they can rapidly scale or abandon as conditions change. This includes having some approaches that treat strategic initiatives as experiments designed to generate learning, rather than merely executing predetermined plans.

## Dynamic Resource Allocation

Perhaps most importantly, organizations need mechanisms for continuously reallocating resources toward emerging opportunities. Traditional annual budgeting processes are too slow and rigid for an exponential environment. Leading organizations implement what venture capitalist John Doerr calls OKRs (objectives and key results)—frameworks that align resources with strategic priorities while enabling rapid adjustment as conditions change.

## The Knowledge Evolution Infrastructure

Future-ready legal organizations will require fundamentally different approaches to knowledge architecture that transcend traditional document management toward dynamic, intelligent knowledge systems. This transformation centers on three revolutionary capabilities:

### *Ontological Knowledge Networks*

Rather than storing information in isolated silos, organizations will implement semantic knowledge graphs that understand and preserve the complex relationships between legal concepts, precedents, client patterns, and market dynamics. These ontological frameworks enable AI systems to reason about legal knowledge in ways that traditional databases cannot support, creating compound learning effects where each new matter enhances the organization's collective intelligence.

### *Autonomous Knowledge Agents*

Specialized AI agents will continuously monitor, organize, and enhance organizational knowledge without human intervention. These agents will identify knowledge gaps, automatically extract insights from new matters, maintain currency of precedents and regulations, and proactively suggest knowledge applications to practicing attorneys. Unlike traditional automation that simply processes data, these agents will exhibit emergent intelligence that grows more sophisticated as they interact with the organization's knowledge ecosystem.

### *Tokenized Knowledge Assets*

Organizations will transform their accumulated expertise into standardized, reusable "knowledge tokens" that preserve not just information but also the contextual relationships and decision-making frameworks that make that information valuable. This tokenization enables rapid knowledge deployment across practice areas, seamless integration with AI systems, and preservation of institutional wisdom that traditionally disappeared when experienced attorneys departed.

Together, these capabilities create what we call "living knowledge infrastructures" that evolve continuously, learn from every interaction, and become more valuable over time rather than degrading through use.

The competitive advantage in this environment comes not from having the perfect strategy but from having the most effective strategic adaptation system. Organizations that excel at sensing change, generating options, and reallocating resources will consistently outperform those with more detailed but less adaptable plans.

## ENGINEERING AN INNOVATION ECOSYSTEM

Innovation in legal organizations can no longer be relegated to committees or special initiatives. In an era of exponential change, innovation must become as fundamental to legal practice as research and analysis.

Future-ready organizations deliberately engineer what innovation theorists call "innovation ecosystems"—environments where innovation emerges naturally from daily operations rather than requiring special effort. These ecosystems have several critical elements:

### Psychological Safety

The most innovative legal organizations will create environments where people feel safe to challenge orthodoxy, experiment with new approaches, and learn from failure. This requires leadership that explicitly values learning over perfection, curiosity over certainty, and growth over status. As Harvard's Amy Edmondson has demonstrated, *psychological safety*—the shared belief that a team is safe for interpersonal risk-taking—correlates directly with innovation capacity; yet many organizations unintentionally suppress it through rigid hierarchies and zero-defect expectations.[1]

## Diverse Cognitive Friction

Innovation thrives on the constructive collision of different perspectives, disciplines, and thinking styles. Forward-thinking legal organizations deliberately create what Harvard's Dorothy Leonard calls "creative abrasion"—structured interaction between diverse thinkers that generates novel insights.[2] This means building teams that include not just legal experts but professionals with backgrounds in technology, design, data science, and other disciplines.

## Experimental Infrastructure

Rather than treating innovation as random inspiration, leading organizations build systematic approaches to experimentation. They create what author Eric Ries calls "innovation accounting"—frameworks for testing hypotheses, measuring learning, and making evidence-based decisions about which innovations to scale and which to abandon.[3] This experimental approach is particularly crucial in legal organizations where professional standards require rigorous validation.

## Scaling Mechanisms

Perhaps most importantly, innovative organizations create systems for rapidly scaling successful innovations across the enterprise. Many legal innovations remain trapped in individual practice groups or offices. Future-ready organizations implement processes that identify, validate, and scale innovations wherever they emerge in the organization.

Organizations that systematically engineer these elements don't just produce more innovations—they develop fundamentally different innovation trajectories.

---

[1] AMY C. EDMONDSON, THE FEARLESS ORGANIZATION: CREATING PSYCHOLOGICAL SAFETY IN THE WORKPLACE FOR LEARNING, INNOVATION, AND GROWTH 17–22 (2019); *see also* Amy C. Edmondson, *Psychological Safety and Learning Behavior in Work Teams*, 44(2) ADMIN. SCI. Q. 350–83 (1999).

[2] DOROTHY LEONARD-BARTON, WELLSPRINGS OF KNOWLEDGE: BUILDING AND SUSTAINING THE SOURCES OF INNOVATION 124–28 (1995).

[3] ERIC RIES, THE LEAN STARTUP: HOW TODAY'S ENTREPRENEURS USE CONTINUOUS INNOVATION TO CREATE RADICALLY SUCCESSFUL BUSINESSES 114–22 (2011); *see also* ERIC RIES, THE STARTUP WAY: HOW MODERN COMPANIES USE ENTREPRENEURIAL MANAGEMENT TO TRANSFORM CULTURE AND DRIVE LONG-TERM GROWTH 83–87 (2017).

While traditional legal innovation tends to focus on incremental improvements to existing services, robust innovation ecosystems generate the transformative innovations that redefine what legal service can be.

The most transformative innovation ecosystems will be powered by ontological data architectures that enable pattern recognition and insight generation impossible with traditional information systems. These semantic frameworks allow organizations to identify unexpected connections between seemingly unrelated matters, automatically surface successful strategies from past engagements, and generate novel approaches by recombining proven elements in new configurations. Innovation becomes systemic rather than serendipitous when organizations can harness the full intelligence embedded in their accumulated experience through properly structured knowledge graphs and autonomous reasoning agents.

## REDRAWING COMPETITIVE BOUNDARIES

The traditional boundaries of legal competition are dissolving. Law firms increasingly compete not just with other firms but with alternative legal service providers, technology companies, the Big Four accounting firms, and even their own clients' expanding legal operations departments. Moreover, the very nature of competitive advantage in legal services is fundamentally changing.

This evolving landscape requires a radical reimagining of competitive positioning. Future-ready organizations are developing what Columbia Business School professor Rita Gunther McGrath calls "transient advantage"—the ability to rapidly identify, seize, and exploit short-lived opportunities rather than building positions of sustained competitive advantage that rarely endure in rapidly changing environments.[4]

This approach focuses on several key elements:

### Value Innovation

Rather than competing within existing service categories, forward-thinking organizations are creating what INSEAD Business School professors W. Chan Kim and Renée Mauborgne call "blue oceans"—new market spaces where competition is

[4] Rita Gunther McGrath, *Transient Advantage*, 91(6) Harv. Bus. Rev. 62–70 (June 2013); *see also* Rita Gunther McGrath, The End of Competitive Advantage: How to Keep Your Strategy Moving as Fast as Your Business (2013).

irrelevant because the rules haven't been written yet.[5] This means reimagining what legal service can be, not just how it's delivered. The next generation of legal value innovation will emerge from organizations that can instantly access and recombine their entire knowledge corpus through intelligent data agents and semantic reasoning systems. Imagine legal services where every matter benefits from the accumulated wisdom of thousands of previous engagements, where AI agents automatically identify relevant precedents and strategies, and where client solutions emerge from the dynamic recombination of tokenized expertise. This represents a fundamental shift from labor-intensive service delivery to knowledge-intensive value creation.

## Ecosystem Orchestration

Competitive advantage increasingly comes from orchestrating networks of specialized providers rather than building comprehensive in-house capabilities. Leading organizations are developing what authors Marco Iansiti and Roy Levien call "keystone advantage"—the ability to create and capture value by coordinating specialized providers into client-specific solutions.[6] This requires sophisticated capabilities in partner selection, integration management, and value attribution.

## Client Co-Creation

Perhaps most importantly, future-ready organizations are reimagining the client relationship itself. Rather than delivering predetermined services, they're creating collaborative processes where solutions emerge through deep client engagement. This shifts the competitive focus from service delivery to client collaboration capability.

Organizations that fail to develop these new competitive capabilities risk finding themselves competing primarily on price for increasingly commoditized work.

---

[5] Blue Ocean Strategy, https://www.blueoceanstrategy.com/what-is-blue-ocean-strategy/ (last visited Oct. 2, 2025).

[6] Marco Iansiti & Roy Levien, The Keystone Advantage: What the New Dynamics of Business Ecosystems Mean for Strategy, Innovation, and Sustainability (2004).

## SUSTAINABILITY AND SCALABILITY

Building a future-ready organization requires careful attention to both sustainability and scalability. Consider what this means in practice. Successful organizations develop what we might call "scalable excellence"—the ability to grow while maintaining high standards of professional service. This requires sophisticated approaches to several key areas that together support sustainable growth.

**Process design** becomes increasingly crucial as organizations grow. Traditional law firm approaches, often based on individual attorney autonomy, may not scale effectively. Organizations need to create processes that provide consistency and efficiency while maintaining necessary professional judgment. This might mean developing standard approaches to common tasks while preserving flexibility for complex or novel situations.

**Technology infrastructure** needs to support both current operations and future growth. This goes beyond simply having systems that can handle larger volumes. Organizations need what we might call "adaptive infrastructure"—systems that can evolve as needs change while maintaining performance and security. This might include cloud-based systems that scale automatically, knowledge management systems that grow more valuable with use, and collaboration tools that support expanding teams effectively.

The most adaptive infrastructure will be built on ontological data foundations that understand meaning and relationships rather than simply storing and retrieving information. Organizations implementing enterprise knowledge models with intelligent data agents create infrastructure that becomes more capable over time, automatically identifying optimization opportunities, predicting resource needs, and adapting to changing requirements. This semantic intelligence enables infrastructure that not only scales with growth but actually improves performance through increased utilization.

**Knowledge management** becomes particularly crucial for sustainable growth, but future-ready organizations will transcend traditional approaches toward dynamic, intelligent knowledge systems. Rather than passive repositories, these organizations will implement enterprise knowledge models that capture not just documents but also the semantic relationships, decision contexts, and reasoning patterns that make information valuable. Autonomous knowledge agents will continuously organize, enhance, and deploy this accumulated wisdom, while tokenized knowledge assets ensure that institutional expertise remains accessible and actionable regardless of organizational changes. This approach transforms knowledge from a static resource into a living, evolving capability that compounds in value over time.

**People development** perhaps matters most for sustainable growth. Organizations need effective approaches to developing their people that scale beyond traditional mentorship models. This might mean creating structured development programs, implementing technology-enhanced training systems, and developing clear career paths that support organizational growth while maintaining professional standards.

## TRANSCENDING THE HUMAN–AI DIVIDE

Perhaps the most fundamental transformation facing legal organizations is the evolution beyond viewing AI as tools toward seeing them as teammates. This requires transcending the conceptual separation between human and technological capabilities.

Future-ready legal organizations are developing what cognitive scientists call "extended mind" capabilities—the ability to think, decide, and create through integrated human–AI cognition. This goes far beyond current approaches where humans "use" AI tools to approaches where human and artificial intelligence form integrated cognitive systems.

This transformation will require several new organizational capabilities:

### Cognitive Integration

Organizations need frameworks for effectively combining human and artificial intelligence rather than merely dividing tasks between them. This means developing the ability to identify how human and artificial intelligence can enhance each other rather than merely substitute for each other. For legal practice, this might mean AI systems that enhance human creativity and judgment rather than simply automating routine tasks.

True cognitive integration will require knowledge infrastructures that enable AI systems to understand not just data but also the contextual relationships and professional reasoning that make legal knowledge meaningful. Organizations implementing ontological knowledge models create the foundation for AI systems that can engage in sophisticated legal reasoning, drawing on accumulated institutional wisdom while preserving the nuanced understanding that experienced attorneys develop. This integration becomes possible when knowledge exists in ontologically structured formats that both humans and AI systems can navigate intuitively.

## Trust Calibration

Effective human–AI teaming requires appropriate trust—neither overreliance on AI capabilities nor underutilizing them due to skepticism. Future-ready organizations will develop new approaches for calibrating trust, including structured validation protocols, transparent AI decision processes, and continuous performance monitoring.

## Augmented Communication

As AI systems become more sophisticated, organizations need new approaches to human–AI communication. This includes explainable AI systems that can effectively communicate their reasoning processes to human teammates—and natural interaction interfaces that enable intuitive collaboration between human and artificial intelligence.

## Hybrid Learning Systems

Perhaps most importantly, organizations need approaches where human and artificial intelligence learn continuously from each other. This means creating what organizational theorists called "double-loop learning" for decades—systems that not only improve performance but also question and revise underlying assumptions and approaches.

The organizations that excel at these capabilities won't merely use AI tools more effectively, they'll develop fundamentally different forms of legal cognition, combining human judgment, creativity, and empathy with AI's analytical power, pattern recognition, and tireless processing.

## The Knowledge Compound Effect

Future-ready organizations will harness what we call the "knowledge compounding effect"—the exponential value creation that occurs when properly structured knowledge systems enable learning to accelerate learning. This phenomenon emerges from three reinforcing dynamics:

- **Semantic amplification:** Each new matter processed through ontological knowledge frameworks enhances the system's understanding of legal patterns and relationships, making future analysis more sophisticated and valuable.

- **Agent intelligence evolution:** Autonomous knowledge agents become more capable over time, developing emergent expertise in pattern recognition, insight generation, and strategic recommendation that exceeds their original programming.
- **Tokenized wisdom accumulation:** Organizations systematically convert experiential knowledge into reusable assets that compound in value, creating institutional intelligence that persists and grows regardless of individual practitioner changes.

Organizations that successfully implement these knowledge evolution capabilities will experience nonlinear improvements in service quality, efficiency, and competitive differentiation. The knowledge infrastructure becomes a strategic asset that creates expanding competitive moats over time.

## MEASURING SUCCESS AND ROI

Traditional measures of law firm success—metrics like utilization rates and profit per partner—don't fully capture organizational readiness for future changes. Consider what this means in practice. Successful organizations will develop new dimensions to measure organizational performance. These metrics will go beyond traditional financial measures to capture crucial indicators of long-term sustainability and adaptability.

- **Operational excellence** remains important but needs broader measurement. Beyond traditional efficiency metrics, organizations need to measure what we might call "adaptive efficiency"—the ability to maintain high performance and adhere to professional standards while evolving operations. This might include metrics for process improvement, technology adoption effectiveness, and service delivery innovation.
- **Innovation capability** requires its own measurement framework. Organizations need ways to assess not just how many innovations they implement but how effectively they identify and capture innovation opportunities. This might include metrics for idea generation, implementation success rates, and value creation from innovation initiatives.
- **Client value measurement** needs sophistication beyond satisfaction surveys. Organizations need to understand not just current client satisfaction but their ability to meet evolving client needs. This might mean measuring things like proactive solution development, technology alignment with client needs, and effectiveness in helping clients address emerging challenges.

- **Organizational health measurement** becomes increasingly crucial. Organizations need ways to assess their fundamental capabilities for ongoing adaptation and success. This might include measuring knowledge retention and deployment, skill development effectiveness, and cultural alignment with strategic goals.

## FUTURE CONSIDERATIONS

The pace of change in legal practice shows no signs of slowing and there are crucial trends that organizations need to prepare for. These include:

- **Cognitive augmentation:** The lines between human and machine cognition will blur as legal professionals adopt increasingly sophisticated cognitive enhancement technologies. Organizations must develop ethical frameworks and practical approaches for integrating these capabilities while maintaining professional standards.
- **Market evolution:** The traditional law firm model faces increasing pressure from new competition and changing client expectations. Organizations need to prepare for what we might call "market convergence"—the growing overlap between traditional legal services, technology solutions, and business advisory services.
- **Professional evolution:** The nature of legal practice continues to change. Organizations need to prepare for what we might call "hybrid professionalism"—combining traditional legal expertise with new capabilities in technology, process design, and business advisory services.
- **Workforce evolution:** New generations of legal professionals bring different expectations and capabilities. Organizations need to create what we might call "adaptive cultures" that can evolve while maintaining professional standards and service quality.
- **Technology evolution:** Beyond specific tools, organizations need to prepare for fundamental changes in how technology enables and constrains legal practice. This means developing what we might call "technology flexibility"—the ability to adapt as capabilities and requirements evolve.
- **Knowledge architecture evolution:** The fundamental structure of how legal knowledge is organized, accessed, and deployed will transform from document-centric to relationship-centric models. Organizations must prepare for semantic knowledge systems where meaning and context are preserved alongside information, where AI agents autonomously maintain and

enhance knowledge assets, and where tokenized expertise enables instant access to accumulated institutional wisdom. This shift requires rethinking knowledge management from storage and retrieval toward dynamic intelligence systems.

Two additional trends to consider are:

- **AI judicial systems:** While complete judicial automation remains distant, AI will increasingly adjudicate routine disputes, especially in online contexts and specialized domains. Organizations must prepare for a world where understanding AI decision-making becomes as important as understanding human judicial tendencies.
- **Reality augmentation:** Court proceedings, client meetings, and document review will increasingly occur in augmented reality environments where AI-generated information overlays physical spaces. Organizations must develop capabilities for creating and navigating these hybrid environments effectively.

Success requires building organizations capable of adapting to these changes while maintaining high professional standards. This means creating what we might call "dynamic stability"—the ability to evolve continuously while maintaining core professional values and service quality.

## CONCLUSION

The concept of "future ready" implies a destination—a state where an organization has adequately prepared for what's coming. But in an era of exponential change, readiness is not a state but a process of continuously becoming. The most successful legal organizations will be those that develop what strategic management theorists call "dynamic capabilities"—the ability to sense emerging opportunities, seize them through rapid reconfiguration, and sustain advantage through continuous adaptation.

This requires a fundamental mindset shift from viewing the organization as a stable entity periodically responding to external change to seeing it as a dynamic system in continuous evolution. Success will come not from predicting the future accurately but from building organizations that can thrive under conditions of radical uncertainty.

The legal profession stands at a genuine inflection point. The next decade will bring technological advancement that transforms not just how legal work is done but what legal work is. Organizations that approach this transformation defensively—seeking to preserve traditional models with minimal adaptation—will find themselves increasingly marginalized. Those that embrace it proactively—reimagining what legal service can be in a world of exponential technological capability—will define the future of the profession.

The greatest risk facing legal organizations today is not disruption but inertia—the natural tendency to interpret revolutionary change through the lens of existing models rather than recognizing genuinely new possibilities. The greatest opportunity is not merely adopting new technologies but fundamentally reimagining legal practice for an era when human and artificial intelligence work in seamless partnership.

The future belongs to organizations that don't just adapt to change but metabolize it—converting continuous disruption into continuous innovation. These will be the organizations that maintain an unwavering commitment to core professional values while demonstrating unparalleled flexibility in how those values are expressed in practice. They will be organizations that understand that in a world of exponential change, the most dangerous decision is to continue operating according to the assumptions of yesterday.

## ACTION ITEMS

1. **Establish Strategic Navigation and Adaptation Systems**
    - Create environmental sensing mechanisms for detecting emerging opportunities and threats
    - Develop adaptive response frameworks with strategic options portfolios
    - Implement dynamic resource allocation processes that rapidly adjust to changing conditions
2. **Engineer Innovation Ecosystems**
    - Build psychological safety frameworks that encourage experimentation and learning from failure
    - Create diverse cognitive friction through cross-disciplinary collaboration
    - Establish experimental infrastructure with systematic approaches to testing and scaling innovations
3. **Redefine Competitive Positioning**
    - Develop value innovation strategies that create new market spaces beyond traditional competition

- Build ecosystem orchestration capabilities coordinating specialized providers
- Create client co-creation processes for collaborative solution development

4. **Build Sustainability and Scalability Frameworks**
   - Design scalable processes that maintain quality while supporting growth
   - Create adaptive technology infrastructure that evolves with changing needs
   - Establish knowledge management systems that preserve and deploy expertise effectively
5. **Transcend Human–AI Integration**
   - Develop extended mind capabilities combining human and artificial intelligence
   - Create trust calibration frameworks for appropriate human–AI collaboration
   - Establish augmented communication and hybrid learning systems
6. **Implement Future-Oriented Measurement and Success Metrics**
   - Design balanced scorecards measuring operational excellence, innovation capability, and organizational health
   - Create adaptive measurement systems that evolve with organizational maturity
   - Establish forward-looking metrics predicting future readiness and capability

# Appendix A

# Ten Essential Recommendations for Law Firms Preparing for the AI Era

## 1. DEVELOP AN AI COMPETENCY FRAMEWORK

Create a structured approach to developing AI literacy across your firm. This should include tiered competency levels from basic awareness to advanced implementation skills. Rather than viewing AI as solely an IT function, establish it as a core competency that spans legal practice areas, operations, and business development.

## 2. IMPLEMENT "AI ETHICS BY DESIGN" PROTOCOLS

Establish formal protocols for evaluating AI tools against ethical standards before deployment. This should include assessments for bias, transparency, accountability, and alignment with your firm's values. The goal is to prevent ethical issues rather than addressing them after implementation.

## 3. CREATE CLIENT-FACING AI VALUE PROPOSITIONS

Develop specific service offerings that leverage AI capabilities to deliver unique value to clients. This goes beyond internal efficiency to position your firm as an innovative partner that can help clients navigate their own AI challenges through legal expertise combined with technological capability.

## 4. INSTITUTE A "RESOURCE REALLOCATION STRATEGY"

As AI takes over routine tasks, proactively plan how to redeploy human capital toward higher-value activities. This isn't simply about reducing headcount but strategically shifting resources toward more complex advisory roles, relationship management, and creative problem solving that AI cannot replicate.

## 5. BUILD CROSS-DISCIPLINARY AI GOVERNANCE TEAMS

Form dedicated teams that bring together legal, technical, and business perspectives to govern AI use within the firm. These teams should establish policies, evaluate tools, monitor compliance, and guide implementation across practice groups to ensure coordinated adoption.

## 6. ESTABLISH "AI-AUGMENTED" PRACTICE AREAS

Rather than viewing AI as separate from legal practice, integrate it directly into specific practice areas. For example, create an "AI-Augmented M&A" service that leverages specific AI capabilities for due diligence, document analysis, and risk assessment to deliver superior client outcomes.

## 7. IMPLEMENT DATA QUALITY MANAGEMENT SYSTEMS

Recognize that AI systems are only as good as their underlying data. Establish formal processes to ensure the quality, accuracy, and proper categorization of all firm data that might be used to train or operate AI systems. This includes historical case information, client communications, and work product.

## 8. CREATE CLIENT AI EDUCATION PROGRAMS

Position your firm as a thought leader by developing educational resources for clients on legal issues related to AI. This might include workshops, white papers, and advisory services that help clients understand regulatory compliance, liability risks, and strategic opportunities related to AI in their industries.

## 9. REDESIGN PERFORMANCE METRICS FOR THE AI ERA

Develop new ways to measure lawyer performance that account for the effective use of AI. Traditional metrics like billable hours may become less relevant as AI increases efficiency. Consider metrics around strategic value added, client outcomes achieved, and effective human–AI collaboration.

## 10. IMPLEMENT "AI IMPACT ASSESSMENTS" FOR LEGAL MATTERS

For significant legal matters, conduct formal assessments of how AI could impact the case strategy, resource requirements, and potential outcomes. This ensures a systematic approach to leveraging AI capabilities rather than ad hoc adoption and helps identify where human expertise remains essential.

# Appendix B

# Ten Essential Recommendations for In-House Counsel Preparing for the AI Era

## 1. DEVELOP CROSS-FUNCTIONAL AI GOVERNANCE FRAMEWORKS

Rather than focusing exclusively on AI competency within the legal team, create governance frameworks that connect legal expertise with IT, compliance, risk management, and business units. This enables in-house counsel to be an important participant for AI governance across the entire organization, ensuring both legal compliance and business alignment. This must include establishment of strong data quality and categorization processes for all data that might be used to train or operate AI systems.

## 2. BUILD AI CONTRACT MANAGEMENT SYSTEMS

Develop specialized systems for managing AI vendor contracts, data processing agreements, and intellectual property rights. This should include standardized terms for AI implementations, clear liability provisions, and comprehensive data usage rights that protect your organization's interests while enabling innovation.

## 3. CREATE AI RISK ASSESSMENT PROTOCOLS

Establish structured methodologies for evaluating AI-related legal and compliance risks specific to your industry. These should include regulatory compliance checks, liability assessments, and integration with existing enterprise risk management systems to ensure AI initiatives align with organizational risk tolerance.

## 4. IMPLEMENT "LEGAL-BY-DESIGN" AI DEVELOPMENT PROCESSES

Work with product and technology teams to integrate legal requirements directly into AI development workflows. This shifts legal from a gatekeeper role to a collaborative partner in the creation process, ensuring compliance is built into AI systems from conception rather than added as an afterthought.

## 5. DEVELOP INDUSTRY-SPECIFIC AI COMPLIANCE PLAYBOOKS

Create tailored guidance for how your specific industry's regulations apply to AI implementation. These playbooks should translate complex regulatory requirements into practical guidelines that business and technology teams can follow when developing or deploying AI solutions.

## 6. ESTABLISH AI INCIDENT RESPONSE PROTOCOLS

Develop comprehensive plans for addressing potential AI failures, bias incidents, or algorithmic errors. These protocols should define clear responsibilities, communication strategies, and remediation approaches to minimize legal exposure and maintain stakeholder trust when issues arise.

## 7. CREATE LEGAL DEPARTMENT AI TRANSFORMATION ROAD MAPS

Develop a strategic plan for transforming your own legal department through AI adoption. This should include identifying high-value automation opportunities, necessary skill development, integration with existing legal operations, and metrics to measure success beyond cost reduction.

## 8. BUILD BOARD-LEVEL AI REPORTING FRAMEWORKS

Develop structured approaches for communicating AI risks, opportunities, and governance to executive leadership and boards of directors. This positions legal as a strategic advisor on AI rather than merely a compliance function, and ensures leadership has appropriate visibility into AI-related legal considerations.

## 9. IMPLEMENT AI TRAINING PROGRAMS FOR BUSINESS UNITS

Create tailored education on AI legal and ethical issues for different organizational functions. This empowers business units to identify potential legal issues early in the AI development process and builds a culture of compliance that reduces the need for legal intervention later.

## 10. DEVELOP "AI LEGAL TECH EVALUATION CRITERIA"

Establish clear standards for evaluating legal-specific AI tools being considered for the legal department. These criteria should address not only functionality but also unique considerations for attorney work product, privilege protection, and alignment with ethical obligations that external vendors may overlook, requiring in-house counsel to define and enforce standards for confidentiality, accuracy, and ethical compliance.

# Appendix C

# Twenty-Five Discussion Questions About AI Strategy and Implementation

## STRATEGY

1. Do we know which business units, departments, or functions already use AI, in what ways, and for what purposes?
2. How does AI fit into our strategies and plans for the next few years?
3. How will we monitor the performance of our AI models and evaluate their impacts, and what methods and metrics will we use to measure success and identify areas for improve?
4. What principles guide (or should guide) the development, deployment, and use of AI in our organization?
5. Do we have defined and documented governance processes for developing, deploying, and using AI?
6. Do we have an enterprise-wide system of record for where and how AI is used in our operations or decision-making?
7. How do or will we ensure that our development, deployment, and use of AI is well-governed, transparent, explainable, secure, and accountable?

## RISK MANAGEMENT

8. Do we have a rigorous methodology for evaluating gaps, overlaps, and risks in our use of AI?

9. Do we identify and manage the reputational, relational, regulatory, and operational risks associated with our use of AI and do so with sufficient agility to keep up with the velocity of change?
10. How are we identifying potential bias or discrimination issues that may arise from the use of AI, and what are we doing to ensure that our use of AI is not perpetuating or exacerbating past biases or inequities?
11. How are we preparing for potential disruptions or failures in our AI systems, and what contingency plans do we have in place to minimize the impact of these events on the organization?

## COMPLIANCE

12. How are we incorporating compliance considerations into our AI development and deployment processes, and what controls do we have to ensure compliance risks are analyzed and addressed at each stage of the process?
13. What processes do we have in place to stay up to date with any changes to relevant laws, rules, regulations, and industry standards regarding the use of AI?
14. What policies and procedures have been implemented to ensure that AI is being used responsibly and ethically, is risk-informed, and is compliant?

## TRAINING AND EDUCATION

15. How are employees being trained to work effectively and safely with AI, and what measures are in place to ensure their ongoing education and development?
16. How are we training employees and other stakeholders on compliance risks and considerations related to AI, and what resources are available to help them understand these risks and their responsibilities in mitigating them?

## DATA USE AND SECURITY

17. What data is being used to train the AI systems, and how is this data being collected, stored, prepared, and protected?
18. What controls are in place to prevent data quality issues from impacting the reliability, accuracy, trustworthiness, and relevance of our AI models?

19. How are we incorporating cybersecurity and data privacy considerations into our AI systems?

## MODEL ASSURANCE

20. How do we ensure that the algorithms and models developed in our AI systems are explainable, reliable, and trustworthy?
21. How are we assuring that our design, deployment, and use of AI models comply with all relevant laws, regulations, industry standards, and internal policies, and what processes and systems are we implementing to monitor, report on, and ensure compliance over time?
22. How are we monitoring and evaluating the effectiveness of our AI compliance program, and what metrics are we using to measure success and identify areas for improvement?

## STAKEHOLDER MANAGEMENT

23. How can we build and maintain trust with our customers, partners, and other stakeholders when using AI in our business operations?
24. How are we monitoring and evaluating the impact of our use of AI on our stakeholders, including employees, customers, and the wider community?
25. How can we ensure consistent AI compliance and risk management practices across our entire extended enterprise, including suppliers, subcontractors, and third-party AI providers?

**Note:** For a detailed discussion of these questions and answers you should seek, look at the OCEG publication, "The Essential Guide to AI Governance."[1] You can use the Guide in several ways, including:

- As a reference manual for addressing specific AI-related challenges.
- As a tool for assessing and benchmarking current AI governance practices.
- As a resource for developing internal training programs on AI GRC.
- As a starting point for cross-functional AI strategy and risk management discussions.

Keep in mind that not all of these questions will be relevant to your organization and their use may vary depending on the stage of development you are in.

[1] OCEG, https://www.oceg.org/essential-guide-to-ai-governance/ (last visited Oct. 2, 2025).

# Index